THE
RESEARCH
FUNDING
GUIDEBOOK

THE RESEARCH FUNDING GUIDEBOOK

Getting It,
Managing It,
& Renewing It

Joanne B. Ries
Carl G. Leukefeld

SAGE Publications
International Educational and Professional Publisher
Thousand Oaks London New Delhi

For information:

 SAGE Publications, Inc.
2455 Teller Road
Thousand Oaks, California 91320
E-mail: order@sagepub.com

SAGE Publications Ltd
1 Oliver's Yard
55 City Road
London EC1Y 1SP

SAGE Publications India Pvt Ltd
B-42, Panchsheel Enclave
Post Box 4109
New Delhi 110 017

Printed in the United States of America

Library of Congress Cataloging-in-Publication Data

Ries, Joanne B.
    The research funding guidebook: Getting it, managing it, and renewing it /
by Joanne B. Ries and Carl G. Leukefeld.
      p. cm.
    Includes bibliographical references and index.
    ISBN 0-7619-0230-9 (cloth: acid-free paper).—ISBN 0-7619-0231-7
(pbk.: acid-free paper)
    1. Research grants. 2. Proposal writing for grants.
I. Leukefeld, Carl G. II. Title.
    HG177.R533 1997
    658.15′224—dc21   97-4829

99 00 01 02 03 10 9 8 7 6 5 4 3 2

Acquiring Editor:	Jim Nageotte
Editorial Assistant:	Kathleen Derby
Production Editor:	Michele Lingre
Production Assistant:	Denise Santoyo
Typesetter/Designer:	Marion Warren
Cover Designer:	Candice Harman
Print Buyer:	Anna Chin

Contents

Part I. Resubmitting a Not-Funded Application: Issues and Decisions

1. Not Funded? Identify the Reasons 3

Part III. Funded! Welcome to the Small Business World

Part VI. Other Considerations

Preface

Although external funding parameters continually change, one of the most consistent features over the past several years is that researchers are expected to get and maintain external funding from grants and contracts early in their careers. The major thrust of this book is that getting and maintaining external funding involves considerable thought, ongoing planning, sound management, and clear decisions. It also requires the ability to work with a variety of people with a variety of skills and education. Preparing a competitive application or managing a funded project is closely related, but can also be independent of the scientific aspects of creatively transforming an idea, which is the heart of science, into a successful application or project. In other words, the core of the scientific enterprise is ideas, thinking, and curiosity. However, the application process (the forms, the formatting, and the presentation) can be as important for a competitive application as can the administrative aspects of managing a funded project be to its successful completion.

This book was prepared to provide information about coping with alternatives: the discouragement attendant on receiving notice that an application was not funded, the exhilaration and anxiety associated with receiving funding, and the dilemmas associated with attempts to design a competitive project to maintain an established research program. The National Institutes of Health (NIH) application and review model are used in this volume as they were in our book *Applying for Research Funding: Getting Started and Getting*

Funded, published by Sage in 1995. We address the career stages and material associated with each career stage so that the entire book does not have to be read if a reader is only interested in a particular career stage. The one exception is the material on what to include in an application and how to write it. This material, abstracted from our previous book, is relevant to any application preparation endeavor. In *Applying for Research Funding: Getting Started and Getting Funded,* we discussed briefly the different career stages, but in this volume we present the imperatives for each stage in detail. Coaching, by definition, is repetitive and addresses the basic tasks that lead to success. Overall, the focus of this volume is on coaching within each of the career stages.

The underlying theme of this volume is that new or experienced investigators must keep thinking and planning scientifically as well as procedurally. In the following pages, we present principles and processes that have been useful in submitting and resubmitting applications, managing funded projects, and maintaining external funding. Of course, there is no single way to obtain or maintain funding. However, we present suggestions that we have found useful in obtaining and maintaining external funding and that can serve as points for discussion.

On a personal note, we would like to thank the many unnamed investigators and others with whom we have talked about the application process and who helped shape our thoughts. We would also like to thank our families for their continuous support and ongoing nurturing.

Introduction: Getting It, Managing It, and Renewing It

Three critical events require strategic decisions by investigators who are applying for external funding. These important events are notification that a project is not funded, notification that a project is funded, and completing the next to last project year accompanied by continuation planning. Each of these events is accompanied by unique emotional and intellectual reactions and requires that investigators invest time in reflecting and planning. Investigators should base their decisions on informed consideration of their current circumstance and their scientific interests whether they need to design plans for effectively resubmitting a not-funded application, develop an organizational plan for managing a funded project, or determine the best focus and best funding source for the continuation project. A variety of factors interact for the final plan. However, a factor that is easily overlooked is time. Time influences the project's success because of changes associated with time passage such as availability of project materials, participants or subjects, and environmental support.

We draw many of our examples from projects in the behavioral and health sciences where both of us have had most of our direct experience. However, colleagues in other fields have indicated that they find our insights about handling application rejection, learning about project management, and determining the next project's focus relevant to their work. This book is divided into six parts.

Part I addresses issues and the kinds of decisions surrounding the resubmission of a not-funded application. It examines the funding climate to help investigators understand their position for external funding. In addition, application scores and the general characteristics of not-funded applications are briefly discussed. It provides tips for withstanding the emotional blast of negative reviews and concludes with information about modifying the application for resubmission to the same funding source or as a new application.

Part II and Part III focus on issues related to managing an award and discuss the kinds of people, activities, organizational configuration, and other factors that principal investigators (PIs) most frequently encounter when they manage funded projects. Part IV targets the prospects of obtaining funding to continuing work begun with an award.

In Part V and Part VI, we consider overarching issues. Part V focuses on application style, content, and various strategies that can enhance an application's competitiveness. This material is an abstracted version of what we presented in our previous book *Applying for Research Funding: Getting Started and Getting Funded.* It outlines application requirements and suggests some tools for presubmission reviews. In Part VI, we review selected issues that are currently in the forefront (women and minority issues), as well as issues that have ongoing concern to scientists (ethics), and we briefly discusses the foundation of an investigator's efforts: thinking.

The Research Funding Guidebook: Getting It, Managing It, and Renewing It is a guide and reference for investigators in different developmental stages of the project funding process. It is designed so each part can be used with only minimal reference to other parts. We have used the National Institutes of Health (NIH) and the National Science Foundation as models for applications and funding source procedures because of their inclusiveness and the extensive information available. In this way, we believe we have provided a base from which investigators can generalize to other funding sources. Action strategies, presented at the end of each chapter, describe activities, related to that chapter's topic, that investigators can implement to move their project forward.

I. Resubmitting a Not-Funded Application: Issues and Decisions

Chapter 1, "Not Funded? Identify the Reasons," discusses project funding. With diminishing financial resources and an increasing number of applications, it is more common to receive notification that an application is not funded. For example, new applications to the NIH increased from 13,006 in 1985 to 15,115 in 1994 (NIH, Division of Research Grants, 1995). We present selected characteristics of not-funded applications so an investigator can more easily focus on those areas of his or her application that need attention. We conclude this chapter with a brief discussion of alternatives to resubmitting an application to the same funding source.

"Contending With Reviewers' Comments" (Chapter 2) targets emotions that investigators experience when confronted with reviewers' comments. These emotions are sometimes referred to as the "pink sheet syndrome," because NIH reviewer comments were printed on pink paper. This chapter provides guidance on how to handle the sometimes intense emotional response that can accompany reading review comments. We provide suggestions on how to get the most mileage from both negative and positive review comments. Funding options for a revised application are also discussed.

Chapter 3, "Modifying the Application," provides guidance on how to resubmit an application as a revised application to the same funding source by calling attention to various research features, which can change with time. In addition, a brief discussion focuses on ways in which the appearance of the application is important to reviewers' overall perception about the application. Options for seeking funding for an application that has been significantly altered, and therefore cannot be submitted as a revised application, are reviewed.

II. Funded! Practical Issues

"Taking Advantage of the Award's Rights and Responsibilities" (Chapter 4) presents differences and similarities among several kinds of funding agreements. Once a funding agreement has been entered, it cannot easily be modified, and the rights and responsibilities are different under different agreements for both the PI and the organization. The kinds of funding agreements discussed are grants, contracts, subcontracts, and gifts.

In Chapter 5, "Build Effective Organizational Relationships," we describe in some detail the people and organizational positions with which a funded PI interacts. These descriptions are intended to help a PI locate his or her organizational representatives, who are integral to the successful completion of the funded project. These individuals are located in the PI's immediate organization (e.g., department); outside this unit but inside the PI's larger organization (e.g., university), such as the public relations office or the sponsored projects office; and in the community, such as newspapers and TV stations, which might be used by the PI for study-participant recruitment or which might find the project newsworthy.

III. Funded! Welcome to the Small Business World

We consider several structural elements in Chapter 6, "Designing an Organization for the Project," that come into play if a research project is to be successful. Many PIs have carried out research that required limited financial support and no other personnel except a graduate student. However, because funded projects are larger, they require more organizational structure. The PI's plan should include defining the project team's objectives; outlining what is expected of each team member; and identifying the kinds of schedules that need to be developed, such as individual work schedules and schedules for group meetings and conferences.

A project's outcome may depend on successfully balancing the available financial resources with the science. Chapter 7, "Establishing Financial Procedures," delves into the critical topic of finances, including the manner in which the project budget is handled. The budget items that may be the responsibility of the PI include salaries, supplies, equipment, and services. However, other organizational components also control some items, such as indirect cost rate and return, salary savings, and program income. Although most organizations have accountants to assist a PI in managing the project budgets, the PI is ultimately responsible for the successful management of both the budget and the science. Some of the important fiscal issues that require attention are allowable costs, the disposition of unexpended funds, and regulations related to encumbering funds for future expenses.

Chapter 8, "Selecting Project Personnel," presents a close look at staffing issues including developing job descriptions, advertising, recruiting, and interviewing prospective personnel. PIs must follow employment policies of their organization. Understanding and following these regulations are important for project success.

In Chapter 9, "Communicating With Organizations and With the Scientific Community," we provide a bird's-eye view of the kinds of reports that can be required of a funded PI. Some of these reports are statistical, some are scientific, and some are public relations narratives. Making plans to develop these reports and narratives before their due dates will facilitate the production of high-quality materials that meet planned and unplanned requests. Most funding sources require at least annual progress reports; however, depending on the type of funding agreement more frequent reports might also be required. Communicating project results to the scientific community in journal articles is important and necessary and is often a criterion for continued project funding.

IV. Continuing a Project by Submitting a Competitive Application

In Chapter 10, "Strategies to Identify a Continuation Project," we discuss how a PI might select the content for the next research project. Although it seems as if this would be a simple matter, many times it turns out to be complicated. We present a process for systematically sorting through possibilities. Part IV concludes with Chapter 11, "Selecting a Funding Mechanism for a Continuation Project," in which we review the kinds of applications that might be considered and used to continue research begun with external funding.

V. Application Preparation

"What to Include in a Project Application" (Chapter 12) presents a description of the kinds of material required in a competitive application. PIs using identical application materials can submit applications that include different kinds of approaches as well as highlighting different information and different science. This chapter emphasizes the importance of making the extra effort to submit an application using available instructions. We discuss each part of the application research plan: title, abstract, objectives, literature review, preliminary studies or pilot work, experimental design and methods, research timeline, and human or animal subject protection issues.

Chapter 13, "Writing to Be Competitive," presents material on writing style and the overall appearance of a competitive application. To be competitive, it is imperative, in our opinion, that an application be persuasive. The ingredients that result in a persuasive application are discussed. We also discuss how a project plan's structure can be used to an investigator's advantage; the importance of the language used in a proposal; and the power of efficient, precise, and effective communication with the reviewers.

"Seeing It Through the Reviewers' Eyes" (Chapter 14) provides guidelines that can be used to determine how well an application will meet the review committee's expectations. In our opinion, an application must please the reviewers' eyes as well as their intellects. The relationship of the reviewers to the funding source as well as the review structure provides a filter through which each reviewer reads the application. The process governing the reviewers' actions, their everyday lives, and their professional experiences produces biases that are not overcome during the application review process.

VI. Other Considerations

Chapter 15, "Related Research Issues," is focused on scientific ethics and scientific misconduct. These issues have received, and are expected to receive, more attention during the coming years as science comes under more public scrutiny. Finally, in Chapter 16, "Thinking as the Heart of Science," we discuss the importance of spending time with ideas and developing projects that have roots in previous work and theory. Although there is no magic formula for developing project ideas, there are situations and contacts that can be established to help a PI ease this process and make it exciting.

PART I

Resubmitting a Not-Funded Application: Issues and Decisions

chapter 1

Not Funded? Identify the Reasons

For some investigators, receiving notice that an application has not been funded is one of the more difficult events encountered in their professional lives. This notice can be particularly distressing for new investigators because they may have little experience with which to interpret the application score and reviewer comments. Even experienced investigators can be confused by comments from funding sources when the procedures or norms governing application review change. Many changes implemented in the 1990s reflect a funding climate that includes increased application volume, static or reduced resources, and implementation of new procedures to improve the review process. This chapter discusses the impact of the funding climate on the investigators' choice of a funding mechanism, describes the kinds of application deficits usually associated with application scores, and provides guidelines for interpreting selected reviewers' comments.

Examine the Funding Climate

In the current funding climate, the number of not-funded applications is far greater than the number of funded applications (Mandel, 1995). There are a number of contributing factors: the federal government's static pool of funds for new project funding; the advent of tying extramural funding to promotion and tenure in many academic departments, which can encourage if not "force" investigators to submit applications earlier in their careers than previously; the planned depletion of some foundation funds (Sankaran, 1995); and the national scope of most funding competitions. For these reasons, investigators who do get an application funded are most likely to have submitted a revised application at least once, and maybe twice, before being funded. National Institutes of Health (NIH) data suggest that there is no common investigator variable correlated with funded or not-funded applications. Placement into the funded or not-funded group appears to be governed primarily by the reviewers' perception of an application's excellence and the probability of producing results within programmatic and theoretical expectations.

The information on NIH funding (NIH, Division of Research Grants, 1995) suggests that experience alone is not a key element for success, because experienced as well as new investigators do not get funded. However, it appears that experience gained early in a career is influential, because age is not a helpful predictor after age 25 but a higher percentage of investigators under age 25 than over age 25 do not get funded. Whether an applicant is an M.D. or a Ph.D. does not seem to play a large role, although a larger number of Ph.D.s than M.D.s submit applications. It appears that reviewers rank high exceptionally well-prepared applications that are submitted by investigators with adequate credentials to implement and complete the project. Because a project's science must be comprehensible, we agree with the opinion that well-presented moderate-quality science can win over poorly presented high-quality science.

New investigators who have had their first application returned from NIH are members of a fairly large club, which includes both new and experienced investigators. Approximately 88% of all (new or experienced investigator) unamended submissions are not funded, and two out of three investigators are also unable to obtain funding to continue their research (Mandel, 1995). Investigators who do not have their resubmitted applications funded are another large group. In 1993, for example, the overall funding rate for NIH was about 15% for all (amended and new) investigator-initiated research projects (R01s) (Mandel, 1995). Rates of funding new and revised applications vary across NIH institutes. For example, during FY 1994 the success rates for new investigator-initiated research grants across institutes ranged from 7.1% to 29.0% (Mandel, 1995).

Some of the not-funded projects are judged to fall into the category of risky research. Despite efforts to fund risky research, the scientific community's consensus is "that proposals for risky, innovative research stand very little chance of being funded by federal granting agencies" (Goodman, 1995, p. 1). The projects in this group are not only those that include unconventional ideas but also those that have a short or disputed track record (Goodman, 1995). The efforts by NIH to identify high-risk/high-impact proposals, that is, proposals that are innovative, potentially risky, but with a likely high payoff, could lead to more of this type of research being funded, but reviewers are hesitant to use the designation (Goodman, 1995). For some disciplines, other resources are available. For example, in 1995 the Procter & Gamble Company invited proposals for exploratory research in the chemical, biological, and engineering sciences considered too speculative for funding through the regular funding mechanisms, even though the projects have a high potential for being successful. Awards were for a maximum of $50,000 per year for up to 3 years through the University of Exploratory Research Program. The Pew Charitable Trusts of Philadelphia also offers awards intended to encourage investigators to be adventurous during the early years of their careers. These 4-year, $200,000 awards are available to junior faculty members ("A Pew Good Scholars," 1995). The September 1996 program announcement of the National Institute on Deafness and Other Communication Disorders, "Exploratory/Developmental Grants for High Risk/High Impact Research," is another example of specific efforts being made to fund "groundbreaking" and "paradigm shifting" research (NIH, 1996d).

Although three fourths of proposals received by NIH are research project grants (R01s), other kinds of awards are available. The rates of investigators succeeding in getting funding with these are different from the R01 rates. In FY 1994, 9% of competing research project grants awarded were First Independent Research Support and Transition Awards (R29s); a success rate of about 26.4%. The Small Grant Program of NIH had a similar success rate in FY 1994 (24.3%). Experienced investigators who submitted research program project grants (P01s) experienced a success rate of 42.0% (Rhein, 1996a). Other funding sources, for example, the National Science Foundation and the Robert Wood Johnson Foundation, also use some of these alternatives to the regular research project mechanism.

The Notice

The notice of not being funded might be a letter stating the decision and discussing the application or it might be a terse computer-generated notice. The basis for the decision, the reviewer comments, may or may not be provided. We recommend that investigators call the funding source to determine the procedure for getting the reviewer comments if they are not received and the application packet does not indicate the funding source's procedures. In our opinion, it is more frustrating for an investigator not to have any comments than to read negative comments about the application. Whether or not the funding source provides comments, we suggest that before doing anything else, a principal investigator (PI) should reassess the application's scientific merits, its presentation quality, and its conformity to the funding source's guidelines.

Reassess the Application

The two-step process described here parallels the NIH process and that of many funding sources. For a fair review, applications need to adhere to the instructions of the funding source. Funding sources vary in their willingness to accept applications that do not strictly adhere to their format instructions. Applications to the NIH that exceed the prescribed page limits, use an incorrect type size, or misuse the appendix are returned to investigators and do not enter the review process. Applications that clear administrative barriers have their scientific value assessed to determine if they warrant full consideration by the review panel. Key factors are the project's scientific integrity and the potential for its successful completion. Applications considered to be poor prospects for contributing to scientific knowledge are eliminated early in the review process. At the NIH, applications judged to fall below the 50th percentile of the reviewed applications are returned to investigators without benefit of full consideration (triage). However, the NIH provides complete reviewer comments to the investigator when an application is triaged.

Funding sources vary on the scientific latitude given to applications. Investigators might be pleasantly surprised when their application is accepted in spite of it being marginally within the funding source's mission, or disappointed, when the funding source does not share the investigator's view of the project's relevance to the forward movement of its mission.

Administrative Review

Start the administrative reassessment of your application with a review of the funding source's list of preferred topic areas and verify that the project is within these interests. Confirm that the application budget and time frame are within the recommended guidelines. Review each restriction to determine if any apply, for example, being outside a geographical region targeted for funding. Review the entire project plan for comprehensivness and realism. Challenge the methods and procedures to be certain that the time frames are realistic and that the activities can be completed using the proposed systems in the PI's environment. Carefully review the discussion of women and minority issues in the project plan; a brief statement saying that they are being considered is not adequate. Reread all the material provided by the funding source and examine the application carefully to determine if any of the administrative requirements were missed.

Scientific Review

Get a good review of the science. Ask one or two knowledgeable colleagues and coinvestigators to review the project plan and provide a rigorous critique. Be sure that the ability of the investigators to successfully implement the project is strongly substantiated.

After completing the scientific review and discussing the results, investigators need to decide the application's fate. This can be done by assigning a score using a scale from 1 to 5, with 1 being outstanding. If the funding source did not assign a score, this information will be valuable in considering the modifications required to make the application competitive, with scores between 3 and 5 reflecting a weak application that will require significant rewriting. If the funding source used a scale of 1 to 5 to score the application, a comparison of the ranks will give the investigators information about how their opinions of the project and those of the review panel coincide.

Interpreting the Application's Score

Not all funding sources provide a numerical score to investigators, but many do provide some indication of how the application compared with others reviewed during the same cycle. Beginning with the reviews for the October 1996 Councils, NIH peer review groups are being asked to recalibrate their scoring by spreading their scores over a wider range of the priority score scale (Rhein, 1996b). As a model, we will use the NIH scoring system previously used. We are using this model because we would like to provide readers with historical information about the relationship between application scores and reviewers' opinions and also provide guidelines for investigators to assess their own applications when scores are not provided by the funding source. Until 1996, this system included six scores: triage and 1 through 5 (or 100 through 500).

Triage (Streamlined Review Process)

The streamlined review process was implemented for investigator-initiated research projects (R01s) and First Independent Research Support and Transition Awards (R29s) by the NIH in February 1995.

> In the streamlined review process, peer reviewers are asked to prepare written critiques of each and to identify, before the study section meeting, the applications (approximately half) that represent the better applications reviewed by that study section. The other applications are not discussed and are not given numerical scores. However, if even one member of the study section wishes to discuss an application, that application is discussed and if, after discussion it is judged to be among the better applications reviewed by the group, it is scored. (NIH, 1995a)

Applications that are returned after the triage process, by definition, either are found to lack significant and substantial scientific and technical merit or the reviewers have significant concerns about the protection of participants. These are the issues investigators must grapple with when they choose to revise and resubmit the application. Because the style and manner of presenting ideas has a great deal to do with the fidelity of idea communication, having an application returned without further review does not mean that the project should be abandoned.

Applications that fall below the 50th percentile might be the result of a very abbreviated preparation time culminating in a poorly presented rationale or an incomplete Research Design and Methods section. A poorly developed and presented Background and Significance section makes it difficult for reviewers to determine the importance of the project or its place in the current body of scientific knowledge. It can also lead reviewers to question an investigator's ability to integrate past, proposed, and future research findings in a cohesive system based on either supporting current theory or developing new theory. Applications with fatal flaws are also found in this group. A fatal flaw is not one that is irremediable; it is a flaw that is viewed as fatal to the project as proposed. This type of flaw can result from an oversight on the part of an investigator and therefore be easily remedied, or it may be a serious flaw in the conceptualization and/or logic, which when taken into account prohibits continuation of the particular line of development.

Another group of applications that might fall into the triage category are those that use a methodology perceived as novel and therefore risky with respect to data integrity and completeness. Computer technology provides opportunities for developing customized data collection methods and for intermingling theory and data entry by project participants. The qualitative paradigm is increasingly being recognized as a means to expand the kinds of information available about variables when used in conjunction with quantitative methods. This has prompted inclusion of qualitative research methods and designs in proposals using primarily quantitative methods. Quantitative methodology and statistical techniques also continue to develop in response to information demands. With the variety of quantitative and qualitative methodologies and techniques available for data analysis, it is difficult for individuals to be fully aware of the potential, as well as pitfalls, associated with each of them. In view of this situation, it is important to describe methodologies and statistical techniques in sufficient detail to assure reviewers that the investigators have a thorough understanding of them, that they are correct for the proposed work, and that they are appropriate for effectively and efficiently collecting and analyzing the data. Without such information, reviewers might decide that the project is not likely to produce useful information, is methodologically weak, or uses an incorrect design or statistical analyses. In summary, a good review is most likely to be obtained when relevant material is presented in a usable format and a coherent manner.

Scores Between 400 and 500

Applications with scores in this range often are not salvageable without major effort. The decision to revise and resubmit should be made only after careful thought and consultation with colleagues and scrutiny of the review comments to determine whether the review group discourages resubmission. Generally, the reviewers like these application topics and believe that the information gathered would be valuable. However, they find shortcomings, which in their estimation can impede the project's successful conclusion. Common shortcomings are (a) focus (either too broad, too narrow, or uncertain); (b) methodology (with participant selection being particularly scrutinized); (c) data analysis strategies (appropriateness and relationship to hypotheses); (d) scope (too ambitious for the talent or time of the investigator, or for the project duration); and (e) investigator credentials (including investigators who do not have sufficient background or experience in the project area). The last point is one that can occur when the PI has expertise in one area but is proposing a project that requires a collaborator with expertise in another area. Investigators must collaborate with individuals with strong track records in the project area even if this means searching beyond their immediate colleagues and forming new relationships.

The negative comments on an application with a score between 400 and 500 are not necessarily numerous, but those offered are serious in the eyes of the review group. Revisions in response to these comments can result in a project that is very different from the original. In this instance, the PI may decide to resubmit it, with a changed title when the project plan is significantly changed, or submit it as a new application to the same or a different funding source.

Scores Between 300 and 399

Applications with scores in this range generally have a number of problem areas identified. This does not mean that the basic idea is faulty, or not fundable, unless the reviewers so indicate. Often reviews begin with comments that are complimentary about the topic and about the potential contribution of the data to science. Investigators should not allow these comments to divert them from carefully examining the critical remarks, but if there is no indication of the value of the topic or the overall scientific contribution it is possible that the review group has little interest in the project. Usually, investigators resubmit applications with scores in this range if not explicitly discouraged by the review panel. The project design and analysis often require major rewriting, as does the Background and Significance section. A project with Background and Significance, Design, and Analysis sections that all require extensive modification might also require new specific aims. In most cases, resubmitted projects retain the original title. However, if changes to a project make the title inaccurate, it can be changed, and the project will be accepted as a resubmission by most funding sources.

Although many applications with scores in this range are easily modified, some, such as those scored 400-500, need to be carefully reviewed to determine if the project plan is too flawed to be revised for resubmission. Depending on the focus of the criticisms, the modified project can seriously deviate from the investigator's intentions, and possibly the funding source's interests. An alternative to resubmitting the proposal is to design a new project using the reviewers' comments.

Scores Between 149 and 299

Reviewer comments on applications scored within this range can be numerous including almost every section of the application, or a few that are critical to effective project completion. An application within this range is a candidate for resubmission. If possible, it should be submitted for the very next review cycle, so it will benefit from being reviewed by many of the reviewers who participated in its first review. Although reviewers do not necessarily receive copies of initial applications during the review of resubmissions, they often remember projects that they discussed at a review group meeting, and they are very likely to remember an application on which they were the primary reviewer. Because of the investment of reviewers' time and thought, conscientious rephrasing and effective remedies for the deficiencies initially noted help place a resubmitted application in an improved competitive position.

Scores Between 100 and 150

Applications with scores in this range generally require very few modifications, and those at the lower end of the range are funded. Other than specific changes suggested by reviewers and with which investigators agree, making changes is difficult because of the risk of getting a less favorable score. This is a real risk for at least two reasons. First, review group membership does not always remain the same from one funding cycle to the next. A project plan modification responsive to a suggestion from one review group might not be perceived as an improvement by a subsequent reviewer or review group. Second, it is possible that changes might uncover previously unnoticed minor project deficiencies, which cumulatively can influence the score. We have found that investigators with a score in this range do different things. They might leave the application in the system with the hope that the score will be within funding range at the next funding cycle. When this is not an option, it is our recommendation that only changes in response to the review group comments be made with great vigilance about their appropriateness.

Some funding sources recognize the dilemma faced by investigators with scores near the payline and expedite re-review of regular research project applications. The NIH has pilot procedures that are being used by some institutes. In the NIH process, the eligible applications would be identified

> with predetermined criteria developed in concert with their advisory councils or boards. For example, the ICs (Institutes and Centers) may consider only applications within a specific scoring range or vary the payline for different areas of science, e.g., basic science versus patient-oriented research. For these applications, an abbreviated revision in the form of a 3- to 5-page letter responding to the reviewers' could be sent to the IC and reviewed internally by staff or with or without external advice. (NIH, 1996c)

Get Familiar With the Characteristics of Not-Funded Applications

Scientific Issues

Anyone, experienced or inexperienced, can write an application that gets rejected. Some of the common reviewer criticisms are outlined below.

Unoriginal research plan. One of the necessary characteristics of a funded application is that it propose significant and original science. Most investigators believe that their proposal describes significant science as well as appropriate data collection and analytic techniques. Whether the science is or can be original is a difficult issue, because originality like beauty may well be in the eye of the beholder. An entire research program might fall under the heading original, but that does not necessarily mean that each step in the process can meet this criterion. Therefore, the next step in a particular research program might not meet the criteria of being original. If this step cannot be taken without external funding, then the investigator must conceptualize and present the research in a manner that captures the attention of the reviewers. This is discussed further in Chapter 11, "Selecting a Funding Mechanism for a Continuation Project."

Unfocused research plan. An unfocused research plan is often more easily recognized by someone other than the PI. One of the challenges of writing a project plan is limiting the material only to that which is relevant to the topic under investigation. An unfocused appearance can be produced by including ideas and information that may underlie some of the major constructs but is basic to the entire area being investigated and does not, therefore, directly influence the current project. The unfocused appearance might also arise from including, in the Background and Significance section, material that is not relevant to the logic of the investigation. An example might be including an extensive, detailed section on test construction in conjunction with the literature on the results of using a particular instrument on groups similar to those proposed. In this case, the focus might incorrectly appear to be test construction. Another way to give the impression of an unfocused project is to use a concept, or variable, without providing sufficient groundwork. A project plan that has been judged unfocused needs to be scrutinized to determine if it is truly unfocused, or if the presentation is faulty.

Unacceptable scientific rationale. Criticisms of the scientific rationale often arise from insufficient information. For example, it could occur when seemingly extraneous variables must be accepted as part of the scientific background. If convincing evidence is not presented for the required relationship among the variables, the scientific rationale appears weak. This criticism could also occur when a program of investigation relies heavily on a particular method. If the investigator does not effectively communicate that the project's theoretical contribution is as important as the method, it can appear that the method is being used again and again "just to see what happens" with no interest in specifically challenging current theory. Investigators, therefore, need to distinguish between using a method to access data not otherwise available and testing the reliability of the method.

Insufficient experimental detail. Investigators can forget that not everyone knows their procedures as well as they do and consequently describe them in global rather than specific terms. It is important to include enough detail so a reviewer can get a general picture of the process. Naming the process, or a series of processes, is not sufficient. Whether the methodology is quantitative or qualitative, a thorough description of the data collection stream is required. Sufficient detail about all groups needs to be provided so their distinctiveness is apparent. Data collection sources such as questionnaires, forms, computer programs, laboratory material, and other technology must be described in detail. The description of the procedures also needs to be sufficiently complete so that their major components and activity sequence are apparent.

Unrealistic approach. This criticism arises when investigators do not present enough information to persuade reviewers that they not only can describe how they want to implement the process but also actually have experience in doing the work. Investigators omit pertinent information when they do not recognize that their process is open to this criticism. Having colleagues review applications is one way to flag the potential for an approach being labeled unrealistic. This might be the case, for example, when high-tech data collection procedures are used or when success of participant recruitment is an issue. In these instances, and others of this nature, it is important that investigators discuss their experiences with the particular situation and address directly the questions raised about the procedures and their outcome. Although it may seem a simple thing to respond directly to the reviewers' questions, it is not always clear-cut. Sometimes investigators respond by explaining or defending what they have presented, rather than rewriting what was presented in a more concise or clear manner. Other times, they will change the technique, method, or procedure but, again, not really answer the reviewer's question. In general, we believe it is best to respond directly to the reviewers' comments and not attempt to sidestep them.

Overly ambitious. This criticism is usually based on the size of the project proposed although it might also arise when the investigator already has a heavy workload. Reviewers are usually investigators with a variety of experiences and, therefore, have firsthand information on the complexity and time commitment required by specific procedures. Investigators need to present pilot work of critical procedures that are complicated and/or time consuming so that they can deflect criticisms about the project time requirements. The scope of the project is another factor that might trigger this comment. In most instances, we suggest that proposals address a single issue. If the project has multiple studies, each study must be limited and not be the equivalent of a major project. That is, each of the studies must clearly provide the means for testing hypotheses associated with the project's specific aims. Multisite projects can also be viewed as overly ambitious for new investigators or investigators without the kind of scientific administrative experience required for a multisite project. Reviewers look for evidence within the application of the PI's ability to coordinate and complete large or multisite projects.

Not aware of relevant work. Investigators need to do everything possible to learn about the methodological and scientific work of others in their field. Usually, it is not sufficient to consider only published works, because of publication lag. Works in progress and personal communications with investigators should be included whenever possible. It is in this area, maybe more than any other, that the professional activity of the PI is apparent. Often it is only through attending professional meetings and remaining in contact with colleagues that investigators know what is currently happening and, perhaps more important, what is about to happen.

Not experienced in essential methodology. Reviewers need to consider the possibility that the proposed project cannot be completed by the investigator. If the primary data collection requires methodology with which the PI has little or no experience, reviewers cannot assume the project will be completed. If there are project modules that require a methodology in which the PI is inexperienced, and coinvestigators are not included for these modules, the reviewers will also be concerned.

Uncertainty about future directions. Funding sources would like to support projects that will have an influence in the future. If there is no indication that there is a theoretical benefit or a practical benefit that extends beyond the project, reviewers will not feel confident that the PI is able to use the project to continue work in the particular area of interest.

Project Presentation Issues

Another set of issues relates to the project presentation. Although there is no question that scientific quality should take precedence in funding decisions, the way a project is presented can facilitate or impede appreciation of the science. It is advisable that investigators take advantage of all opportunities provided by the application process to impress the review panel with their multifaceted competence.

Reviewers expect an application to have the order and appearance requested in the application instructions. All funding source instructions must be followed including those concerned with type size, total number of pages or number of pages for particular sections, mailing instructions (such as mailing address and number of copies), appendixes restrictions, and receipt deadlines. It is common for PIs to be immersed in developing the project plan and neglect the other application parts. The seriousness of this neglect depends on the funding source's policies. As indicated above, some funding sources return applications without review for infractions of their format instructions and administrative requirements. Although it may seem that these matters are trivial, they often provide opportunities for the investigators to demonstrate competence and experience in matters of detail.

Chapter 13 of this book outlines additional presentation issues. Some presentation problems are serious enough for an application to be returned without review. Others, although seemingly minor, can have a negative influence on a reviewer's attitude about the application. Unfortunately, these issues are rarely addressed in reviewer comments, so an investigator does not know if a portion of the negative response was influenced by presentation problems.

Consider Alternative Submission Strategies

Funding sources are not alike in the way they handle resubmitted applications. Funding sources might treat each submission as a new submission whether or not it was previously reviewed, or might not permit resubmission because of their funding cycle or the timeline of preferred project topics. Certain kinds of applications might be eligible for resubmission and others not, for example, the NIH requests for application (RFA) and requests for proposals (RFP) usually have a one-time submission date.

For applications that can be resubmitted, the decision investigators make about what to do should be related to the application's score, the perception of the extent to which the criticisms arose from miscommunication, the viability of the project in the future, and the work that has been completed since the project was submitted. Although each application is unique, the alternative chosen most often is to resubmit to the same funding source, whenever that is acceptable to the source.

Whether a funding source accepts resubmissions is only one side of the resubmission issue. The other side is whether the PI and coinvestigators believe that a resubmission is fundable. Most applications are resubmitted once, many of them twice, and investigators generally accept this as a likely scenario. However, in today's scientific environment, we recommend that investigators submit an application no more than three times, including the initial submission. After this, it should be rewritten for submission as a new application to the same or a new funding source, depending on the results of a careful comparison of the project's objectives with those of the funding source.

Investigators who are in fast-moving research areas certainly need to consider the consequences of a second resubmission. By the time a second resubmission is mailed to the NIH, the project has been on the drawing board for almost 2 years. During this time, the field and the investigators may have moved beyond the proposal topic. Rather than a second resubmission to the original funding source, a first submission to a funding source that has 6 months or less turnaround—and a specific interest in the proposal topic— might be a good alternative. Another option is to consider a different funding mechanism.

Action Strategies

Delay Making Decisions

We suggest reading the next chapter in this volume before taking any action that will be difficult to reverse. Comments to coinvestigators or colleagues that arise from frustration and disappointment about the application's score can be viewed as unprofessional behavior and might leave a lasting impression that influences future collaborations. It is important that investigators stay focused on the larger picture of their careers and strive to maintain a balanced perspective that enables ultimate achievement of their long-term goals.

Discuss the Application Score With Others

Discussing an application's score and reviewer comments with others who have applied for funding helps the investigators place themselves in the current funding context. Scientific knowledge, methodologies, and priorities generally fluctuate over time. In addition, each funding source must be responsive to the priorities of statutes, supporters, and/or governing boards. All of these factors influence an application's score as well as the kinds of issues that reviewers highlight. In discussions with colleagues, investigators may discover that the areas in which the application was found deficient are areas that applications of colleagues have also been found deficient.

Consider Another Type of Grant

If a regular grant has been resubmitted several times and has not been funded, investigators might consider submitting it as a small grant, or developing a program project grant. Whether these are viable options depends on the nature of the criticisms as well as the associated eligibility criteria.

Intramural Funding Application Ranks

If the application was submitted for intramural funding, it is critical that the investigator review the comments and the application with individuals who have been in the system long enough to know the system's customs. Some intramural review groups have definite preferences that become apparent only when comments on a nonpreferred topic are received. There may also be preferences for designs or language customs that would not be apparent to a newcomer, and comments arising from these preferences might seem inexplicable. Investigators who do not receive intramural funding need to assess carefully the probability of a successful application, or the professional or collegial gains that might be made from a resubmission. An intramural funding source like an extramural funding source has preferences. Although investigators might disagree with the preferences, their only option is to identify sources with interests similar to theirs to which to submit their application. If investigators wish to express their disagreement with a funding source's policies and preferences, they should determine the proper channels for this type of interchange and not try to do it within the application submission arena.

TABLE 1.1
Funding Source Search Resources

Directory of Financial Aids for Minorities, 1995-1997. Gail Ann Schlachter, R. David Weber, Reference Service Press, San Carlos, CA, 1995

Directory of Financial Aids for Women, 1995-1997. Gail Ann Schlachter, Reference Service Press, San Carlos, CA, 1995

Foundation Reporter, 1996. 27th ed. James DeAngelis (Ed.), The Taft Group, Rockville, MD, 1995

Directory of Biomedical and Health Care Grants, 1995. 9th ed. Oryx Press, Phoenix, AZ, 1994

The Foundation Directory, 1995 Edition. The Foundation Center, New York, 1995

The Foundation Directory, Part 2. (entries for foundations with less than $2 million in assets with annual grant programs from $50,000 to $200,000)

Research Funding and Resource Manual: Mental Health and Addictive Disorders. Harold Alan Pincus, M.D. (Ed.), American Psychiatric Association, Washington, DC, 1995

University of Exploratory Research Program, Procter & Gamble Co., Miami Valley Laboratories, P.O. Box 538707, Cincinnati, OH 45253-8707

Worldwide Web sites with program and funding information

Federal Information Exchange (FEDIX), including the Departments of Agriculture, Energy, and Air Force, plus FAA, NASA, NIEHS, NIAID, and ONR
http://www.fie.com/

Department of Commerce, including NIST, etc.
http://www.doc.gov/resources/doc.agencies.html

Department of Education
http://www.ed.gov/

Department of Health and Human Services, including NIH, CDC, etc.
http://www.os.dhhs.gov/

Department of Transportation
http://www.dot.gov/

Environmental Protection Agency
http://www.epa.gov/

National Endowment for the Humanities
http://www.neh.fed.us/

National Science Foundation
http://www.nsf.gov/

Smithsonian Institution
http://www.si.edu/youandsi/ofgfel.htm

U.S. Information Agency
http://www.usia.gov/

Review Credentials

PIs of funded projects are expected to have at least minimal experience in several areas related to being a successful scientist. The following are the experience guidelines suggested by Ries and Leukefeld (1995). The main categories are research experience, which includes publications, research review function, collaboration/consultation, research methods of previous work, formal courses, research hypotheses consideration, pilot data, and mentoring; positioning, which includes knowledge of the PI's organizational research infrastructure; and personal style, which includes activities falling generally in the category of management skills.

Be Realistic About Options

Before deciding to submit a not-funded application to another funding source, assess the availability of a more appropriate source. Listed in Table 1.1 are some of the resources for this search. Unless the funding source has clearly indicated disinterest in the project, we suggest caution in changing funding sources. The reviewers and the organization have invested in the application and unless otherwise indicated probably have interest. Also keep in mind that the original choice of a funding source was based not on whim but on careful investigation and deliberation of the pros and cons for the PI and the funding potential of the specific project.

chapter 2

Contending With Reviewers' Comments

Investigators' reactions to comments about their application may be unique in their ebb, flow, and intensity, but their substance is similar. When an application is funded, the mood is one of elation moderated by reaction to the negative comments, which inevitably are included. When an application is not funded, the mood is disappointment, frustration, and sometimes discouragement and resignation. This chapter is about investigators' behavioral and emotional responses to not being funded and suggests strategies that might help keep their research program on course.

Reestablish Control

It is our recommendation that before responding to the reviewers' comments an investigator recall the events that led to the application's submission. This reminiscing can clarify the role the application was perceived to play in their career plans and can rekindle motivation. These memories can provide a platform from which to evaluate their past decisions and inform the decision about continuing the application process.

Reviewers' comments usually hold surprises for investigators. Sometimes when investigators learn that they have not been funded, they quickly conclude that it was a specific factor that reviewers did not like. When an investigator can identify a weakness, a sense of control can be maintained, and the investigator's coping systems remain in good order. The review

19

comments, however, might be very different from those anticipated, and the investigator is left to deal with criticism for which he or she is unprepared.

An expected characteristic of review comments is the unrelenting demand for scientific rigor, theoretical relevance, and important societal implications. Whether the competition is in-house, regional, or national, reviewers generally demand a high level of scientific rigor. Sometimes investigators believe that the demands of some reviewers for detail in the project design, analysis section, and comprehensives in the literature review are excessive—even bordering on being picky. Minor criticisms can evoke a variety of emotional responses, and suggestions of inadequate scientific rigor in the project plan or that the project has little theoretical importance strike at the heart of an investigator's self-image as a scientist.

Professional careers seem to be fraught with opportunities to receive criticism. Consequently, it is important that investigators develop coping mechanisms for dealing with criticism, and often strategies for doing so are actively sought. The effectiveness of these strategies frequently depends on the source of the criticism, the personal relevance of what is criticized, and whether the criticism appears in a public forum. With experience as the target for criticism comes the ability to ignore criticism that is unfair or unjustified and to search diligently for the value in criticism from an informed source. Reviewers' comments are particularly difficult for investigators to deal with because they have a strong belief in the importance of their project and they might perceive reviewers to be important sources of information. This already difficult situation is made more difficult because the usual coping mechanisms developed for dealing with criticism in professional life are often different from what is required if an investigator wishes to revise and resubmit an application. Reviewer comments, therefore, have the potential to push investigators beyond their usual coping systems. However, if investigators wish to resubmit an application, they cannot retreat from or ignore the comments. The only choice they have is to respond to each of the criticisms whether it is perceived as being unfair, unjustified, or arising out of misinformation.

Develop an Adaptive Behavioral Response

Receiving news that a project has not been funded can influence multiple aspects of investigators' professional lives whether they are clinicians, basic scientists, community practitioners/scientists, or administrators. In some cases, it may not matter how close the project's score was to the funding payline because project complications can arise from delays incurred with a resubmission. For example, those who had arranged to free up time for the project may now have to reschedule that time as well as free up future time if the project is to be resubmitted. For investigators who were relying on the funding to keep their program going, the delay of another funding cycle might place their program in jeopardy. For others, being close to the funding payline can be significant. If, for example, the not-funded application was a second or third resubmission and was given a poor score, an investigator may have to face a decision about continuing the particular line of investigation or seeking an alternative funding source. Whereas if the score is excellent or outstanding, the time and effort of resubmitting could be well spent.

A project application eventually involves a spectrum of people (e.g., administrators, collaborators at other sites, colleagues, administrative staff such as department heads/chairs, deans). Many of these people often meet with the principal investigator (PI), attend the same professional meetings, and possibly are collaborators on other projects. In view of this small but influential community that evolves from a project application, it is critical that investigators, whatever their internal state, maintain a public appearance as stable, rational individuals who learn from their experiences.

We have known investigators who, on receiving news that their application was not funded, essentially stopped their research careers. Sometimes this was their intention. They were not able to maintain their coping mechanisms or could not find answers to questions posed by the reviewers and eventually decided that having externally funded projects was not desirable. Others may, by their behavior, give the impression that they have resigned. Their colleagues perceive them as not being intellectually responsive, as using their time for other pursuits, and as no longer being reliable consultants and collaborators. To prevent such an impression, it is imperative that investigators continue to interact with their colleagues and, if anything, make their ongoing projects more visible, however serious the disruption is from not being funded. It is important to remember that many careers require external funding to sustain advancement and that most applications require collaborators. Until investigators definitely decide to segue out of the external funding stream, it is imperative that they continue to behave as competent and reliable investigators who are able to complete projects and overcome barriers. It is only in this way that investigators can successfully negotiate with colleagues for their valuable time and in turn continue to be considered a valuable asset on their projects.

Develop an Adaptive Psychological Response

Investigators have different strategies for developing an adaptive psychological stance to deal with reviewer comments. One common strategy is to read the comments, get the gist of them, and then put them out of sight for a few weeks. This is not to be viewed as an act of procrastination. Investigators faced with reviewer comments are on the threshold of making important decisions. Putting the comments aside can give them time to come to terms with being criticized and to get better acquainted not only with the nature of the criticisms but also with the reviewers' perceptions of the application's strengths. This strategy helps to ensure that the decisions made about the project are based on its value, not on the intensity of fluctuating emotions.

Fuller wrote about the course through which an investigator's emotions might flow after reading the reviewers' comments for the first time. She called this course the "pink sheet syndrome" (Fuller, 1982) after the color of the paper on which the reviewer comments were then printed. It seems that emotional detachment is difficult to maintain when an investigator's favorite ideas and professional abilities are being criticized. Even when a proposal receives a fundable score, it is difficult to read the reviewer's negative comments with equanimity. When, however, the score places the proposal in the not-funded group, emotional detachment is not only difficult but usually impossible to achieve. This reaction is understandable considering the amount of intellectual and administrative work embodied in a completed application. Usually, investigators have battled with competing theories, designs, analyses, and data sources before arriving at the product that was reviewed. Investigators become intellectually attached to the final project, are convinced of its significance, and are hopeful that they have communicated their vision and their enthusiasm. In addition to investing creativity, the investigator has endured the mundane labor of producing the application forms and presenting the project plan according to funding source instructions—an activity rarely done under conditions of calm confidence. For some investigators, the mere thought of repeating this activity is onerous. In spite of this, the review comments must be read and evaluated, and ultimately responded to with emotional neutrality.

The negative comments make the biggest impression the first time the reviewer's comments are read. Fuller (1982) calls this Stage I: the onset of anxiety and panic. During this stage, the investigator places exaggerated importance on comments that seem directed at the viability of the project. Sometimes serious thought is given to abandoning the line of investigation and "moving on to something less demanding." The counterpoints that investigators find during this stage are the positive comments often provided. Although these comments seldom are sufficient to quickly restore an investigator's emotional equilibrium, they do provide encouragement and inhibit precipitous abandonment of the project.

Stage II, according to Fuller, can take the form of depression, shame, or anger. Investigators are besieged by doubts of their ability to think and to achieve success, shame about what others will say when they learn that the project has not been funded, and anger at the funding source for failing to understand the value of the proposed project. During this period, because it is fraught with emotional uncertainty, we suggest that investigators resist making public statements about reviewers (investigators do not know who knows whom), calling members of the review panel (usually against the rules), or calling program officers (unless a prepared script is used and emotional equilibrium restored). Cultivating a demeanor that makes a good impression on colleagues and the funding source representatives is as important during this phase as it was when the initial contacts were made.

The key to career longevity for many investigators is to develop a psychological stance that enables them to revise the application and to benefit from the experience. A good way to maintain a positive attitude is to remember how the project was thought about during its early stages of development. Recognize that the predominant theme during that time, whether it was stated or not, was risk taking. Science requires intellectual risks such as public discussions of new ideas and submitting new ideas for competition. Investigators recognize that not taking risks can lead to intellectual stagnation. Expanding a knowledge base requires investigators to take risks knowing that inherent in this pursuit is the potential for failure, and occasional failure should not be surprising. Failures, when put to work, can be the foundation for future successes. Investigators, to take advantage of these opportunities for future success, need to be teachable and be open to all learning opportunities.

A unique educational opportunity is offered in the review comments. They could be considered to be courses designed by national experts as a guide to future work. If investigators ask themselves, "Would I have sent this application to an eminent scientist in my field for review?" most would answer no. (If the answer is yes, it is hoped that it was sent before submission and that comments were incorporated in the application.) In fact, that is exactly what investigators do when they submit an application for funding. From that perspective, the most rational action for investigators is to make the best possible use of the opportunity for career development by using the reviewer comments in the revised application.

The emotional response to the second reading of the comments is usually less intense and is often quickly followed by asking colleagues for opinions about the comments. To reap the greatest advantage from reviewers' comments, investigators need to get help from someone who has already been through the process, responded to comments, and is alert for information gleaned from "reading between the lines." Sometimes reviewer comments have been compiled by staff from the original reviewer statements and may have been edited to keep the tone from being harsh. Other times an investigator receives the comments exactly as written by the reviewer. The second method provides a better opportunity to understand how each reviewer saw the project, and it enables following their line of thought. In many instances, it also provides the investigator with better insight into where the communication between the reviewers and the investigator went astray.

Sometimes the overall project will be discussed in positive terms and perhaps specifically, for example, its value or the value of the unique data to be collected. These comments are to be interpreted within the context of the other positive and negative comments that follow. The introductory comments should be evaluated in terms of what they say and do not say. Although the absence of comments about the value of the project, the data collected, or the scientific endeavor need not spawn discouragement, it does need to be taken seriously. Investigators need to determine if there has been an oversight or if the reviewers are actually discouraging further project development. One way to get a better understanding of how to use these opening comments is to read comments received by a colleague. The objectivity inherent in this situation allows an examination of the pattern of reviewer comments, an understanding of the way negative and positive comments are developed, and how these might have been weighted during the decision-making process.

The weight given negative and positive comments is usually reflected in the application's score. It is this score that needs improving. This is best done by realistically assessing the positive comments and making plans to respond to the negative comments. Sometimes, however, there are very few or very minor criticisms with not many positive comments and a poor score. This kind of review usually represents a situation in which, for some reason, the reviewers reacted negatively to the application and were unable to state their objections. In this situation, an investigator needs to contact the program official by telephone to try to determine how the disparity between the score and the comments arose.

Continue to Be the Project Leader

Maintaining leadership requires that PIs continue to be actively involved with the application development group and rigorously reassess the project science as presented in the application.

Interacting With the Application Development Group

PIs need to stay in touch with all coinvestigators and others who have a vested interest in the fate of the application. The coinvestigators were chosen because they have characteristics and expertise critical to the project. These are the characteristics, however, that lead to their time being in demand and to their being either PIs or routinely in the midst of application preparation. It is important, therefore, that PIs behave as competent, mature, and organized investigators by actively maintaining open communication channels with others on the project and doing nothing to erode confidence in the project's prospects. They need to set aside personal reactions to not being funded long enough to touch base with coinvestigators and consultants to let them know the plans for the project. PIs must avoid conveying to coinvestigators that they are taken for granted, that the project is a low-priority item, or that they are relieved of their commitment to the project.

The first information a PI has about the project's funding status, often sketchy because it is received in a telephone call, should be quickly passed along to coinvestigators and consultants. When the complete review comments are received, the PI should send a copy to all project investigators. Information on funding status should also be sent to administrative personnel and to those involved in scheduling arrangements that may need alteration. It is a good idea for the PI to have a plan about what he or she will say to colleagues when they call after reading the comments—and they will call! Even though the PI may have put the comments out of sight and wishes everyone else did the same, it is important that the PI hear the initial reactions of coinvestigators and consultants because they are most likely to be uncensored and can be enlightening about the project's deficits. They might also provide alternative interpretations of the comments that can help shape the PI's reactions and final responses. During these conversations, the PI can schedule a meeting for more thorough discussion of the comments.

Scientific Reassessment

The PI and the coinvestigators must maintain control over the project's science. PIs should not consider blindly following each suggestion. Revisions done in this fashion rarely result in an integrated proposal; they appear to be what they are, projects developed by a committee. Responses to many of the comments will require a change in the project, but the form the change takes must be determined by the project and the investigators' vision, not the perception or misperception of a reviewer. Distinguish between the comments based in *what* was written and those that arise out of *how* it was written. Identify comments fostered by miscommunication, and modify the presentation to improve communication fidelity. Through this process, PIs, coinvestigators, and reviewers become collaborators to produce a fundable proposal.

After PIs have read the reviewer comments at least once, they should put them aside and return to the project to check the science. The PI is, after all, one of the most knowledgeable individuals about the area under investigation.

The science should be reviewed from the current knowledge base—remember, the project was crafted nearly a year before! Although some people are resistant to following the approach presented here, we offer it as a strategy for an objective project review. The PI needs to verify that the proposal communicated the project as intended and to reevaluate the importance and strength of the project as envisioned. We suggest that the PI start at the beginning with the broad, long-term objectives and proceed methodically through the entire project plan. This review is probably easiest as a three-step process. First, identify all the parts that need clarification; second, make notes on required editing, rewriting, and redesigning; and third, determine if the project has moved in a new direction as a function of the changes. A checklist is provided in Form 2.1 that can be used to organize this review.

Broad, Long-Term Objectives

Are the project's broad, long-term objectives precisely stated and appropriately restricted? Are the project goals clearly stated and the relationship between them and the broad, long-term objectives obvious?

Specific Aims

Are the project aims stated as objectives rather than methods? Are the research hypotheses or questions relevant to each of the aims clearly expressed? Do the aims and the hypotheses or questions foretell the data that will be collected and give some definite clues to the project design?

Background and Significance
(Literature Review)

This section's purpose is to develop the rationale for the project. The material and its presentation should lead the reviewer to conclude that the proposed project is a natural continuation of previous work. If this section is written in the same style used for journal articles, it probably needs editing if a persuasive case is to be made for the project. One way of doing this is to present the previous work that forms the basis for the current project in an integrated manner that highlights the PI's argument, rather than a list that requires reviewers to synthesize the material. It is important to keep in mind that the literature review is not a backdrop for the procedures and analysis, but an argument for the conduct of the proposed project. A writing style that engages the reviewer in the various aspects of the argument is most effective. Be alert for instances where additional material might be needed, or where developing a new perspective would lend strength to the stated specific aims and choice of project design.

Methods

This is the statement of how the project will be conducted and must be presented in sufficient detail that another investigator could replicate the plan. It must also fulfill the promises of the specific aims and be based in the material presented in the Background and Significance section. The following are examples of details that might need consideration.

Participants/subjects. It is important to identify participants as completely as possible for project results to contribute to the scientific database. Without appropriate identification, the findings cannot be generalized, and comparisons, for example, across groups, cannot be made.

Complete information is required on sample size, including recruitment procedures, inclusion criteria, exclusion criteria, assignment to group procedures, participant reimbursement, other agreements (debriefing, transportation, or time commitment), and demographic characteristics.

Apparatus, questionnaires, instrumentation. Describe the data-gathering devices in as complete detail as possible. Apparatus and instrumentation that is standard can be identified by name and manufacturer or catalog number. Reliability data should be provided whenever possible. Paper-and-pencil questionnaires should be described fully, and reliability and validity information should also be provided when available. If the instrument is not standardized, developed specifically for the project, or a modification of a standardized instrument, sample items should be included in the Research Design and Methods section and a complete copy of the instrument, or the addenda, included in an appendix. The latter also applies when instruments are translated into another language, and in addition, the method of translation should also be included.

Setting. Project settings can influence data. If the area of investigation is one where settings are considered to be influential, they should be described in detail so that the work can be replicated, and reviewers are assured that the PI is aware of the reactivity of the setting. This is an instance where even if the reviewers know, PIs need to demonstrate that they also know about the reactivity potential.

Procedure. The Procedure section is a summary of the participants' project experiences. The instructions to each participant should be paraphrased with direct quotes of any instructions that are unusual or include experimental manipulation. In addition, the timeline for the participant activities should be presented, so that the order of variable influence is clear. If participants have different languages as their first language, describe how this will be handled. Debriefing procedures should also be included when relevant.

Topic	Page Number	Needs Editing	Needs Rewriting	Needs Rethinking
Specific aims				
Rationale				
Broad, long-term objective				
Project purpose				
First specific aim				
Hypothesis 1:				
Hypothesis 2:				
Second specific aim				
Hypothesis 1:				
Hypothesis 2:				
Third specific aim				
Hypothesis 1:				
Hypothesis 2:				
Page length—one page recommended				
Background and significance				
Background leading to present project				
Evaluation of existing knowledge				
Identification of gaps				
Importance of project				
Relationship to funding source mission				
Relation of specific aims to broad, long-term objectives				
Page length—three pages recommended				
Preliminary studies				
PI's previous relevant work				
Relevant work of coinvestigators				
Integrated summary directed at current project				

Form 2.1. Project Reassessment Checklist

Topic	Page Number	Needs Editing	Needs Rewriting	Needs Rethinking
References submitted/accepted				
Design and methods				
Design				
Procedures				
Data collection procedures				
Data analysis procedures				
New methodology?				
Potential difficulties				
Alternatives to difficulties				
Project timetable				
Gender and minority issues				
Human participant issues				
Participant characteristics				
Sources of research material				
Recruitment plans				
Potential risks				
Procedures for protecting against risks				
Explain why risks are reasonable				
Vertebrate animals				
Description of use				
Justify use of animals				
Information on veterinary care				
Safety and comfort procedures				
Euthanasia method				
Literature cited				
Match against text				
Complete				

Form 2.1. Continued

The Procedure section is also a description of the framework within which the data are collected. Procedures for assigning participants to groups should be described in detail, including randomizing, counterbalancing, or using a convenience group. Design features, for example, controls, should be described, particularly if the design might be viewed as complex.

Data management. Present a clear statement of how the collected data will be managed whether they are data bases, tissue samples, videotapes, sound recordings, or photographs. Describe how the data will be entered, what reliability techniques will be used, where and how data will be stored, and back-up procedures and other strategies for maintaining the data's integrity.

Statistical analysis. Outline the plans for descriptive statistics and preliminary data manipulation. Discuss any foreseen needs for transforming data. Describe the analyses planned, and associate them whenever possible with the hypotheses, for example, indicate specifically whether the analysis planned is ANOVA, MANOVA, regression analysis, or structural equation modeling. Do not merely state that multivariate analyses will be carried out. Indicate whether content analysis or ethnographic data analysis will be carried out. Do not merely state that qualitative data analysis techniques will be used.

Expected results and interpretation. If possible, discuss the results expected and how they will be interpreted. It is usually possible to do this with quantitative studies. Sometimes it is not possible with qualitative studies to discuss in advance the exact outcomes, but some statement needs to be made about the kinds of conclusions the investigators might draw based on the study objectives.

Statistical significance, effect size, and power analysis. State the level of significance at which results will be accepted. If a level other than .05 or less is chosen, discuss the reasons underlying the choice. Discuss the effect size selected. For some types of research only small differences are important, and for other research large differences are important. Include estimates of the power of the statistical tests to be used. Do not estimate power for one analysis and assume that it will apply to all others unless this assumption can be defended. Investigators who use statistical programs to calculate power need to be sure that the design information entered corresponds to the proposed design.

Coordination of multiple experiments. If multiple experiments or a multisite investigation is being proposed, it is critical that reviewers are assured that the investigators can handle the level of scientific and administrative complexity inherent in such an endeavor. State in as much detail as possible the communication strategies planned, anticipated data transmission methods, and quality assurance techniques.

Assessing the Viability of the Project

After collecting the results of the above review, the PI can use them, in conjunction with the reviewers' comments, to formulate an opinion about the viability of the project, given the planned improvements, with a start date 9 to 12 months in the future. The first consideration for investigators is their expected career status and scientific interests at the future funding date. In rapidly progressing areas of science, this can be of paramount importance even with the first resubmission, but in most areas of investigation it becomes an issue with the second resubmission. If the area of investigation will have moved beyond the proposed project plans by the time funding would be received, or if the investigators' interests are developing along a new line, then perhaps the project should not be resubmitted.

The future start date also influences the project conduct, the participants, and coinvestigators and consultants. The following are some examples of the kinds of situations that might confront an investigator with a changed start date. With the new start date, ability to recruit participants, use space, and share resources may no longer be possible or may be seriously impaired. Individuals who have given permission for any aspect of the project may not be amenable to providing that permission for the new time period. The project might require modification if particular patient, client, or student groups are not going to be available during the new time period. Delayed start dates can be a problem for projects with longitudinal designs. In particular, projects that coordinate the start date with a cohort of participants, in a particular phase of life, may not be feasible with the new start date, or may have to be delayed 1 full year. Projects that require high-tech instrumentation might also be at risk if the instrumentation's availability cannot be confirmed or if upgrading is required for data to be considered accurate during the new time period.

Finally, and of significant importance, are the application's score and the reviewer comments. Resubmission is possibly not a good option if the comments indicated that the funding source was not interested in funding the kind of project proposed, or if the comments suggested, or stated, that the project was viewed as not being viable, of little scientific interest, or too ambitious for the PI's experience. If the PI chooses to continue the line of investigation developed in the project, it is our opinion that it is best done as a new application.

Making the Resubmission Decision

The first consideration when making a resubmission decision is the regulations of the funding source with respect to the number of times an investigator is permitted to resubmit an application. Some funding sources limit the number of resubmissions and others do not. Currently, the National Institutes of Health's (1996c) policy is to accept no more than two resubmissions, and to accept no resubmission if it has been more than 2 years since the original submission.

There are advantages to resubmitting an application if the funding source has special procedures for resubmissions. If submissions are all treated as new submissions, whether they are in fact resubmissions, there are only chance advantages. One chance advantage is that the same reviewers might get the application, and if their suggestions have been followed, they usually are more positive about it. When funding sources have revised application procedures, many of the current reviewers might have reviewed the application previously and are in a better position to understand it and to appreciate the modifications made in response to their review.

The following are some general decision guidelines. If reevaluation of the project produced major changes in the specific aims, and these changes place it in a different overall area of investigation, it might be best to submit it as a new project. If, however, the specific aims have changed, with the associated changes in the project plan, but the overall area of investigation remains the same, it can be resubmitted as a revised application. In this case, the title undoubtedly will need to be changed to mirror the new project direction. If reevaluation has resulted in clarification and editing but has not resulted in major modifications to the project plan or area of investigation, resubmitting as a revised application, under the same title, is probably the best alternative to choose. To determine the alternatives available to them, PIs should consult their funding source contact or their application instructions.

Internal Competition

If the initial submission was to an internal competition, the first date for resubmitting might be as soon as 4 weeks or as distant as 12 months. Most investigators prefer to move their application forward as quickly as possible. With this in mind, a decision to resubmit might be made if applications are accepted fairly often. If, however, the earliest resubmission would be in 12 months, an alternative choice is to submit the revised project as a small grant to a foundation or to the federal government. Using the reviewers' comments and rewriting sections that lack high-fidelity communication, the project can be shaped into a competitive submission fairly quickly. The important relevant feature of small grants is that they are usually for smaller amounts of money with limitations on the project length (i.e., perhaps $25,000 for 1 year or $50,000 per year for 2 years). Some small grants also do not cover investigator salaries. For investigators who want to submit a small project, either a resubmission to the original source or to an external source that funds small projects are viable options.

Regional Competition

If the project plan was designed for a particular geographical region, and it remains viable, consideration should be given to revising it and resubmitting to the same funding source. If resubmissions are not accepted, or only one submission a year is accepted from the same PI, an investigator might consider submitting to a large foundation with regional interests. The federal government is also a potential source if a case can be made for generalizing the results beyond the particular region, or a need for other regions to have comparative information.

National Competition

In most instances, investigators who submit their applications for national competition plan to resubmit. Although this decision is often made without much thought, we recommend that it be a decision made after careful consideration of the requirements and consequences for the investigators and the scientific endeavor. The further away the application's score is from the funding line, the more important it is to resist implementing the automatic decision to resubmit. To get an application that has been ranked fair or good into competitive funding range requires a lot of thought and effort and is not usually done with one resubmission. Sometimes it is easier to resubmit as a new application because the need to respond to all of the reviewer comments is less urgent.

Action Strategies

Review Information on Vulnerable Populations' Availability

Recently, there have been efforts to provide protection for vulnerable populations that can have far-reaching effects on research. For example, a New York state judge issued a restraining order that brings to a standstill psychiatric research involving patients considered to be unable to make judgments that are in their best interests in state-run facilities (K.H., 1996). Children are another group for which more protection is being sought. The availability of children as research participants is not the only concern, however. Even when it is possible to recruit and obtain informed consent from participants, the cost to secure participants will undoubtedly increase ("Bill Threatens," 1995).

Seek Advice From the Funding Source

A PI's funding source contact can be a valuable adviser with respect to interpreting the reviewers' comments. Sometimes they can be directive about which issues were of greatest concern during the review meeting. At the very least, contact persons can read the comments and tell PIs their opinions and help PIs with reading between the lines. When a PI seeks this type of advice, it is preferable for the contact person to be given a forewarning so that he or she can review the material from the project beforehand. This might be done by making a telephone call and requesting that the discussion about the project be held during another telephone call at an arranged time.

chapter 3

Modifying the Application

Funding sources attempt to keep their review and administrative policies congruent with the status of scientific knowledge, societal needs for information, and overall availability of resources to investigators. The National Institutes of Health (NIH), and other funding sources, routinely evaluate their review process and implement modifications that reflect the funding environment. Principal investigators (PIs) sometimes believe that a different review system would have produced a more favorable outcome for their application. Whatever they might believe, PIs choosing to revise and resubmit their application must adhere to their funding source's current conventions. In this chapter, we discuss the process of modifying an application.

Evaluating Reviewer Comments

Evaluating the reviewers' comments is an important exercise that is most often done several times and is usually associated with a wide range of reactions as discussed in the previous chapter. Eventually, however, PIs are able to objectively evaluate the comments and modify the application. Sometimes the reviewers' perspective is quite obvious, and well-articulated responses quickly come to mind. Other times, developing responses is a frustrating process, particularly when the application has received a poor score in spite of favorable presubmission critiques from one or more scientists. When this occurs, PIs need to focus on the comments from the review panel and their responses and not be distracted by dwelling on possible reasons for the conflicting comments.

In our experience, apparently conflicting opinions of presubmission reviewers and the funding source reviewers arise primarily from internal and external reviewers following different guidelines. Internal reviewers may have thought they were being asked to respond to the reasonableness of the idea from their point of view. In this case, the proposal might have received cursory attention, with no attempt made to evaluate the presentation, design, or analysis. The internal reviewer may have known the project area so well that missing information was unconsciously provided and faulty arguments were not expected and therefore overlooked. Familiarity with an area of science is often accompanied by the colleague assuming that the PI knows the project area very well. Thus, comments are withheld about conceptualization and design. Finally, the internal reviewer may just not have had enough time to complete a detailed review, and opted for summary comments such as "I think this is a great idea." Funding source reviewers follow specific guidelines, which usually require comment on all aspects of the application concerning the scientific value of the application as well as the PI's credentials. Funding source reviewers will not, therefore, overlook indications that a project's time frame cannot accommodate its complexity, or accept a PI implicitly suggesting, "Trust me, I am an expert," or overlook project features that possibly place it in the realm of "risky."

Appealing the Decision

If a PI concludes that the review was not proper, an appeal process (rebuttal) can be considered, but not all funding sources offer an appeal option. Although the process might be similar across funding sources offering the option, it is best to assume that each organization has procedures and criteria tailored to meet its needs. Some funding sources might provide only general guidelines for the appeal, whereas others might provide detailed instructions as do the NIH (1996b) and the National Science Foundation (NSF, 1995). Be forewarned, however, that making an argument that the application did not receive an appropriate "peer" review, a common criterion, is difficult.

If the funding source accepts rebuttal letters, investigators can choose this route to request their application be re-reviewed. With submissions to the NIH, this request should be made only when investigators believe a serious error in the assignment of the application occurred, or if the process or substance of the review is believed to be seriously flawed. The NSF labels its process "reconsideration." It provides the following instructions for investigators dissatisfied with the program officer's explanation for a project not being funded:

He/she may request that the cognizant NSF Assistant Director reconsider the action to determine whether the proposal received review that was fair and reasonable, both substantively and procedurally. The request for reconsideration must be in writing and must be received within 90 days of the date of the declination letter. (NSF, 1995, p. 15)

In our opinion, PIs should write rebuttal letters only after extensive consultation with colleagues and collaborators. If an investigator chooses this option for an NIH application, the appropriate recipient of the appeal must be identified. Usually, it is addressed to the program staff rather than to the reviewers. The Grants Information Office, Division of Research Grants, Office of Extramural Outreach & Information Resources, NIH, 6701 Rockledge Drive, MSC 7910, Bethesda, MD 20892-7910 can provide information about NIH procedures. Suggestions about the content of this letter are provided by Reif-Lehrer (1995), who encourages investigators to use a constructive and positive tone: "Intrusion of sarcasm, righteous indignation, and 'sour grapes' statements in a letter of rebuttal helps no one, least of all you! Under no circumstances should you attempt to contact individual Study Group members" (p. 117). Whether an application was submitted to a federal or foundation funding source, letters of rebuttal must be polite, and their content focused on the perceived review errors rather than on the investigator's emotional response to them.

Letters of rebuttal may or may not secure a second review of the application, and even if a second review is achieved, the outcome being an improved score or an award is not at all assured. The process of developing a rebuttal letter is time-consuming and can distract an investigator for a considerable time from advancing his or her career through scientific pursuits. Because the outcome of rebuttal letters is uncertain, we believe that the time and energy required to write the letter can be better used to revise the application or to prepare it for submission as a new application to the same or to another funding source. On the other hand, we have also witnessed that composing a rebuttal can have a calming effect for PIs. Often the process stimulates new insights, and the frustration with the review panel is turned into creative energy, the rebuttal abandoned, and the ideas incorporated into a revised application.

Revise and Resubmit

When PIs decide to revise and resubmit an application, the funding source's policy on resubmissions should be reviewed. Funding sources change their application procedures as needed with application format, submission dates, or required documentation being just a few items that could change from one review cycle to the next.

Develop an Application Revision Timeline

Unfortunately, an investigator often gets the complete set of reviewer comments a month or so before the next application deadline. Although resubmissions are not as difficult to write as the original application because much of the text is already in place, and much of the logic often remains the same, there is usually still a great deal of work to be done. A timeline for a 6-week revision period can be found under Action Strategies in this chapter. A quick glance at it brings home the reality of the time crunch facing an investigator planning to resubmit within this time frame.

For applications with a score close to the funding payline, a great deal of time is consumed in thinking and talking with colleagues and coinvestigators about the best strategy so that a resubmission does not receive a less favorable score. For applications with scores further from the funding payline, not only is new thinking usually required, but often rewriting can be difficult because it must fit into the initial application and be responsive to reviewer comments. Another feature of resubmissions that requires time is the possible need for additional data to support the viability of the hypotheses or questions.

Although it is often advisable to resubmit an application for the next review cycle, this should be done only if high-quality work can be achieved within the time allowed. If a first resubmission is being planned, it is better to risk having several new reviewers on the panel than to submit an application that includes responses to the previous reviewers but does not present an improved application overall. Investigators attempting to develop a resubmission under great time pressure are particularly vulnerable to acquiescing in the assumption that most elements of the application will not need modification. It is particularly dangerous to assume that all coinvestigators will be interested in remaining with the project. Projects with time or seasonal restrictions also usually require extensive changes throughout the proposal. To ignore these and other possibilities can result in an application that appears to be hurriedly prepared and may contain inaccuracies.

Update All Application Components

Most application components are affected either by changes in the project plan made in response to the reviewer comments or by the passage of time since the original submission. Therefore, investigators need to review and update many application components.

Personnel documentation. Biographical sketches and other research support information for the PI, coinvestigators, and consultants should be updated. This information must also be included for investigators or consultants not included in the initial submission. We recommend that personnel changes be made only when replacements are necessary or when the project design requires additional expertise.

Budget items. Budget items that usually require updating are inflation factors, salary increases related to changes in fringe benefits or other employee-related expenses, consulting fee modifications, and equipment costs, particularly when high-tech instrumentation is required. Modified designs and data collection procedures might require changes in related disposable supplies and other items, and participant reimbursement when the subject volume is changed.

Whenever possible, we believe it is advisable not to change the personnel effort from the previous submission; however, if reviewers request reduction in effort for particular personnel, it is best to do so when it is appropriate. Review the comment sheets for other budget items that have been deleted by reviewers, and exclude them from the budget if appropriate. If one part of the proposed project has been completed since the submission, delete the budget items related to that part of the project and substitute those for a replacement project, if one is proposed. It is important that the budget match the proposed project's requirements. If a project's duration is revised downward, be sure that the summary budget reflects the change. Some budget items are not within the control of the investigator and are, therefore, difficult to modify in response to reviewers' requests. The PI, in this case, must either find other resources to support the item or write a detailed explanation of the factors contributing to the item costs.

We do not believe that adding unfunded expert coinvestigators is necessarily a strength. Such investigators are generally experts in a particular area of knowledge and known to be productive and busy people. Their inclusion might weaken the project if reviewers assume they are unlikely to be actively involved in the project. If unfunded expert coinvestigators are included, a detailed description in the budget justification of the expectations for these investigators is appreciated by reviewers.

Project resources. Project resources fluctuate with time. These could include, for example, high-tech equipment proven too costly to maintain, no longer available, or planned upgrades not completed possibly rendering it inadequate for the purposes of the proposed research. On the other hand, new resources may be available to the project and should be presented in appropriate detail.

Abstract. The abstract must be rewritten to reflect all project plan modifications. Although the abstract is a very important application component, investigators often give it cursory attention. A special effort must be made to review the abstract carefully so that it clearly outlines the revised project. Keep in mind that some reviewers only look at the abstract. Do not risk having the revised project appear to these reviewers to be the same as the previous project.

Administrative unit. Changes in this unit might include a revised indirect cost (overhead) rate or indirect cost liability, availability of clerical staff or equipment, and perhaps provision of disposable supply support, changed circumstances, or new administrator (new supervisor or department head) budget policies.

Human and animal subject protection. If human or animal subjects are involved, review the current Institutional Review Board (IRB) or the Institutional Animal Care and Use Committee (IACUC) regulations. It is imperative to resubmit the forms for project approval and update the consent forms when applicable. Even if no changes are made in the project plan, the funding source will want a current approval date from the IRB or IACUC. The 7th edition of the *Guide for the Care and Use of Laboratory Animals,* published by the National Research Council's Institute of Laboratory Animal Resources (ILAR), was made available in 1996. In this revision, greater reliance is placed on scientific judgment in the housing and care of research animals than in the previous edition. The ILAR guide's requirements are binding on all research supported by Public Health Service agencies (Finn, 1996).

Responding to Reviewer Comments

Depending on the funding source, instructions may or may not be given on how to indicate changes to the application in response to reviewer comments. When no instructions are available, investigators need to use their judgment and organize a presentation that achieves their goal of presenting an improved document that includes responses to reviewers' comments. They might use instructions from other funding sources as a model. When instructions are provided, PIs should follow them closely.

In some cases, the funding source requires only a response to the reviewers' comments without submitting a new application. This might be the case when reviewers are uncertain about specific aspects of a proposal and desire to have full information for the review group meeting. A request such as this is also made when a funding source is interested in making a decision during the current funding cycle and reviewers require additional information to make the decision. When answers to specific questions are requested before review, it is critical that a direct answer be given to each question. Sometimes investigators defend what they wrote in the proposal rather than responding to the question. This can result in new issues being introduced and additional material for the reviewer to integrate into the proposal. A response of this type is not recommended unless it is specifically requested. One way for an investigator to test the directness of an answer is to respond to the question with a yes or no followed by the supporting material.

When a funding source is interested in making an award after receiving clarification on some aspects of the proposal, the investigator should completely address all questions. The responses should be worded to express complete thoughts and potentially communicate sufficient meaning without reference to the complete application. Organize the responses so their place within the application is apparent. This can be done with headings or by referring to the application section or subsection by name. Misperceptions or problems arising from the organization of the original proposal need to be handled comprehensively. In our opinion, it is best to suggest a reorganization and then to state how the reorganization influences the line of thought.

Some funding sources give very specific instructions about their preferred format for responding to reviewer comments and how to indicate application modifications within the document. In this situation, we suggest following the instructions! For example, the instructions for the Public Health Service PHS 398 are to use an introduction (limited to three single-spaced pages) and to indicate changes in the research plan by appropriate bracketing, indenting, or changes in typeface, with underlining and shading prohibited. If the changes in the document are quite extensive and include most of the text, these indicators are not to be used. In this case, the PI needs to write a brief statement reflecting that the modifications involve large portions of the text and, therefore, highlighting is not used. If it is possible to highlight material containing critical modifications, this should be done and mentioned in the introductory statement.

There are also funding sources that give no information about how to show changes in the application and that process all applications as new submissions whether or not they have been revised in response to reviewer comments. In this situation, we suggest including a cover letter that recognizes the reviewers' efforts and that indicates careful consideration has been given to their comments in developing the current application. If the comments have been extensive or directed specifically at the project procedures, rationale, or statistical design, an introductory section outlining the changes made in response to the reviewers' comments is helpful to a new review group. If suggested changes have not been incorporated, PIs should briefly discuss the rationale for the decision. Keep in mind that even though a funding source might not officially have a policy for handling resubmissions, an application might be reviewed by the same scientists because of the project's content. Intellectual exchange and acknowledgment of the source of ideas are as important in the grant review process as they are in all other aspects of scientific pursuit.

Whatever the instructions, PIs should include a cover letter, or an introduction to the application. The introduction generally discusses the responses to the comments and expresses appreciation for the time and effort the reviewers have given to the project. In the midst of the emotions accompanying the return of a not-funded application, it is easy to forget that the reviewers are contributing to the investigator's development. The NIH places a three-page limit on an introduction of this type. The NSF does not provide specific instructions about how revisions are to be handled. If the funding source does not provide specific instructions, it is probably best to remain within a three-page limit and present text modifications in a clear but nonintrusive manner.

Introductory Comments

PIs choose to write the introductory comments at different points in the revision process. Some PIs write these comments first and use them as a guide for making the modifications within the application; others write them last, using the application modifications as a guide for the introductory comments; and others write them concurrently, editing each as required by the developing thoughts and project strategies.

We suggest that these comments begin with a brief statement recognizing the reviewers' contributions and expressing appreciation. Follow this statement with a paragraph or two that presents a summary of any major changes in the project plan that are a result of the review comments. This will help orient reviewers who are seeing the application for a second time to the new directions or strategies being added. It also helps new reviewers to understand the thrust of the project and, it is hoped, deflects requests for revisions that would return the project to its original form. Although these are general introductory statements, they should be ordered according to the application format to facilitate the reviewers' comprehension of how the application has changed since the previous submission. For example, statements such as the following might be included: "In response to reviewer comments Specific Aim #2 has been modified, and #3 dropped"; "The Background and Significance section has been rewritten to highlight . . . "; "The Research and Design section has been clarified by inclusion of . . . "; "In addition, results of studies by . . . and . . . have been added to strengthen our argument about . . . ."

Often reviewer comments include a summary statement. It contains what are believed to be the most significant problems deterring funding.

Responding to these issues might require explaining the project's theoretical position, the rationale for the chosen design, or an explanation of instrumentation choice. In our opinion, it is best to respond in a comprehensive and detailed way to these statements in the order they are presented. Indicate if the application text has changed as a result of the responses to reviewer comments and how these changes are highlighted, for example, by a change in typeface.

Following these general statements, address each reviewer's comments as they appear in the comment sheets. This approach produces an orderly presentation that facilitates the new review group's understanding of the changes made, of decisions to forgo changes, and the rationale for those actions. This procedure simplifies reference to previous reviewers' comments when opinions are similar or in disagreement. A statement such as "This issue was responded to under responses to reviewer #1" when an issue appears a second or third time, or a statement such as "Reviewers #2 and #3 also raised this issue" can be used the first time you respond to a particular issue. Keep in mind that the comments in the introduction are detailed with respect to theory and methodological justification, but are not detailed with respect to changed wording and document organization. In our opinion, PIs should handle changes in wording and organization within the document and highlight them for the reviewers' convenience.

Content of Responses

Reviewers necessarily approach the procedures and rationale of each application from their perspective, within their time frame, and within their intellectual style. A common perspective of reviewers is "educate me!" The reviewers' education about the project is dependent on how lucid the investigator is about the application's intent, the specificity of the design, and the clarity of the expressed relationship among aims, objectives, hypotheses, statistical procedures, and results. Because it is difficult to obtain absolute clarity in writing a project plan, sometimes actions suggested by reviewer comments cannot be incorporated.

Although it is the investigator's responsibility to communicate the project's intent and all aspects of the project plan in a manner readily comprehensible, this is sometimes difficult to achieve. Whenever a reviewer's comments are clearly the consequence of miscommunication, and therefore, the action suggested is not appropriate, indicate how the particular section might have been initially presented to achieve improved fidelity. Also, discuss the rationale for the original plan as well as the rationale for retaining it, in light of the reviewers' comments. The response tone when adjusting perceptions due to miscommunication must be polite and reasonable without a hint of disparagement. Often minor text changes can adjust the flow of thought;

however, rewriting or reorganizing the section might be needed to clarify the intention and to underscore the correctness of the original plan.

Sometimes the reviewers' comments address issues with which the PI has struggled and finally included what he or she thought to be the best compromise, because the ideal is not realistically achievable. In this situation, an effective approach, in our opinion, is to state the reasons for the course selected, agreeing with the reviewer on what the ideal course is, although it is unattainable. If the reviewer offers an alternative that had not been considered, or that had been considered and discarded in favor of what was presented, discuss the alternatives. If the reviewer's alternative is not workable, discuss the reasons it is not feasible and outline clearly the reasons for retaining the original or an alternative plan. On the other hand, if the reviewer's alternative is one that can be adopted, and is an improved option, attempt to incorporate it, making note of the associated changes in procedure and cost that will arise. If these can be withstood within the project's scope and budgetary restrictions, then it is clearly in the best interest of science to adopt the suggested plan. Again, whatever the decision, be watchful that the tone of the discussion remains friendly and reflects an interest in presenting and conducting science that is as good as possible given the situation and constraints dictated by the subject matter and fiscal resources.

Reviewers' comments about design, statistical analyses, and hypotheses need to be taken very seriously, in our opinion. These sections form the heart of the project, and flaws can compromise the entire endeavor. Reviewers have been known to express high praise for the proposal organization and writing but find it not fundable because of perceived flaws in one or more of these sections. Comments can range from questions about how data will be recorded or protected to statements that the proposed design will not enable the proposed hypotheses to be tested or proposed questions to be answered. An investigator needs to invest time and patience in reviewing comments focused on these sections and solicit advice from colleagues, coinvestigators, and technical experts. The possible complications that can arise in multidisciplinary projects together with the feasibility of analyzing very complex data create a situation in which people are expert in only a few areas of design and analysis. Even though the PI presumably is one of the experts in the application's scientific area, reliance is also placed on coinvestigators and consultants.

The style of collaboration among project team members influences the final application. Although in an ideal world every critical piece has been checked and rechecked, in the real world that does not always happen and application sections can appear to be merely strung together. The kinds of errors or misjudgments spawned by this process are those that reviewers find and question. These kinds of problems, because they arise from discontinuity across proposal sections, are usually easily corrected with a change to the procedures or budget sections. If they are substantive, however, the investigators need to discuss the consequences of the changes for the entire project, with the reverberation of the final plan being incorporated in all application components.

An interesting comment, in our opinion, is one that notes the varying levels of expertise reflected in different sections of an application. For example, a comment might include a remark that the level of interest and expertise shown in the Data Analysis section did not seem to be present in the Literature Review section or that the data analyses were definitely planned to test hypotheses, but those hypotheses were poorly stated or not stated at all in the earlier sections of the project plan. These comments can arise from a PI having varying levels of expertise or limited confidence in his or her mastery of the material required in the application sections or from different people having written each section and then the sections being joined and not subsequently reviewed by the investigators. There is little that one can do with this comment except to try to upgrade the parts that need upgrading and truly collaborate with coinvestigators so that the final project is seamless.

Examples of Reviewer Comments

Modifications in the project plan must be made in response to reviewer comments, or an explanation for not making changes presented in the introductory paragraph. The most common reviewer comments fall into four major categories:

1. Conceptualization, which includes the subcategories of area of investigation, project design, and literature review
2. Implementation, which includes the subcategories of doability, analyzability, interpretability, and qualifications of personnel
3. Data issues
4. Allocation of fiscal resources

We cannot suggest specific responses to reviewer comments because they are unique to each application. However, the following sections, which paraphrase reviewer comments, present examples of the kinds of shortcomings reviewers target and alert PIs to the variety of reviewer comments possible. PIs should recognize that whatever comments they receive, other investigators have struggled with similar issues and dilemmas. The following list is presented to motivate PIs to scrutinize their final application carefully to assure themselves that they have not only responded to the specific review panel comments, but they have also deflected other criticisms that they or their coinvestigators, collaborators, and consultants can identify.

Conceptualization

A well-conceptualized project fits clearly within the overall long-term objectives. The relationship between the project objectives and prior research and theory is visible, strong, and defensible. The hypotheses or questions are exquisitely crafted and are testable or answerable. The project design is well suited to the material and to the hypotheses or questions. The data collection procedures are developed in light of the specific aims, hypotheses, or questions and the prior research and theory. Strategies for data analyses are chosen to reveal the results sought through the project implementation. Table 3.1 presents a sample of reviewer comments on project conceptualization.

Implementation

Successful project implementation comprises a number of areas, all of which are important to the funding source. They are important because without a satisfactory resolution to problems in this category, the project cannot meet the goal of supporting a significant contribution to a particular knowledge base or area of investigation. Table 3.2 presents a sample of reviewer comments in these areas.

Data and Allocation of Fiscal Resources Issues

Reviewers are particularly interested in the methods and procedures associated with data collection, storage, analysis, and appropriateness, and also with the fiscal resources to successfully conclude the project. In an environment of fiscal resource scarcity, it is no surprise that reviewers are interested in making awards for projects that are perceived to be cost-effective. Note that this does not mean that legitimate costs are to be neglected, but that reasonable costs are desired. Table 3.3 presents samples of review comments related to these data and fiscal resources.

Action Strategies

Restrain Yourself From Making Suggestions About the Shortcomings of the Review System

Because the project funding arena is dynamic, whatever the current review system, investigators find fault and offer suggestions for improvement (Rosenberg, 1995). Ideas and opinions about system improvement are important. However, in our opinion, it is best that these suggestions are not intermingled with the application submission process. During the application

TABLE 3.1
Reviewer Comments Related to Project Conceptualization

Area of investigation

Unfortunately, the study design neither permits a good test of this hypothesis nor does it permit other issues described to be appropriately addressed.

The central focus of this proposal is not well addressed in the data analysis.

The problem is of insufficient importance or is unlikely to produce any new or useful information.

The problem is more complex than the investigator appears to realize.

The problem is scientifically premature and warrants, at most, a pilot study.

The research as proposed is overly involved with too many elements under simultaneous investigation.

Project design

Justification for measurement of . . . should be presented.

The proposal is not sufficiently specific with respect to some aspects of the procedure.

The analysis plan does not indicate that the study will examine what the proposal promises.

Variables seem to be added to regression equations with little systematic modeling being evident.

This project uses a very complex design. The difficulties of recruiting subjects all at one time are prohibitive.

Literature review

It was somewhat surprising to the reviewers that the investigator did not discuss . . . , which was published in the *Journal of* . . . .

The literature review is little more than a summary of recent studies—little effort is made by the applicant to integrate these studies.

The theoretical framework was said to be . . . , but no attention was subsequently paid to this theory.

The theoretical conceptualization remains weak.

The application provides no statements about future directions.

---

submission process, investigators must be responsive to the current review and administrative systems and use them, whenever possible, to positively influence the final funding decision on their application.

Use the 6-Week Timeline in Table 3.4 as a Guide for Pacing Project Revisions

Include a Cover Letter

Cover letters provide another opportunity to help funding source staff refer applications to the most appropriate reviewers. Funding sources reserve

TABLE 3.2
Reviewer Comments Related to Project Implementation

Subjects and sample size

Recruitment of subjects is addressed at length, yet doubt remains. No previous experience of this group of researchers suggests likely success in this area.

Given the presumably small pool of interested, willing persons of the right type in the area at any given time, it is difficult to see how the research could be successfully carried out.

A rationale for the choice of subjects is never provided.

The amount of data collection work required of each participant is not clear and appears to be excessive.

There is no explicit accounting for the sample size selected. There is no information given that would allow for judgment that the sample sizes selected were either too large, too small, or just right.

Project size and resource requirements

The proposed project uses an unrealistic approach.

The proposed project is overly ambitious.

The availability of appropriate resources is not clearly presented.

It is not clear if sufficient time has been allotted for . . . .

Other responsibilities appear to prevent devotion of sufficient time and attention to the research.

The institutional setting, as described, is unfavorable.

Project personnel

The investigator's expertise is not adequately presented.

The PI's skill and organization of the research needs to be better justified. More detail is needed concerning some aspects of the work itself.

The investigator does not have adequate training or experience for the proposed study.

The investigator appears to be unfamiliar with pertinent literature . . . or methods . . . or both.

The investigator's previously published work in this area does not inspire confidence.

The investigator needs more liaison with colleagues in this field or with collateral fields.

---

the right to make the decision about who reviews applications, but they do consider recommendations offered by PIs. Funding sources seek ways to keep review section membership flexible, both to ease the burden for reviewers and to provide appropriate reviews. For example, the NIH has revised its policy on reviewer rating and scoring. This makes it possible for any "fully participating reviewer" to vote and assign a score (NIH, 1996c). In this review climate, it is, therefore, more important than in previous years for PIs to include a cover letter to assist the funding source in directing their application. This letter should include at least the application identification (e.g., title and

TABLE 3.3

Reviewer Comments Related to Data and Allocation of Fiscal
Resources Issues

Data issues

Several questions remain as to how the data will be used . . . data not used are very expensive
data . . . .

It was noted that there is little indication of the arrangements that have been made with the outside
laboratory to conduct the proposed tests.

It seems doubtful that a single assessment will provide an adequate measure of . . . .

The method used for the . . . assay is not discussed. This is not a simple procedure, and it is not
clear that the necessary expertise will be available.

There is limited discussion of how longitudinal data will be handled.

Fiscal resources issues

This is a very time-consuming protocol for the amount of information it will yield.

$_____ is requested for . . . but no justification for this amount is provided.

The budget does not appear to be sufficient for the proposed project.

---

funding source number if it has been assigned), a statement about the specific
area of inquiry, and the aspects of the investigation that require particular
expertise for proper evaluation.

It is often suggested that PIs make a review group recommendation. The
best choice for a resubmitted application is the previous review group if it was
appropriate. However, if the previous review group did not seem to be
appropriate, indicate that and suggest it be reviewed by another group or
suggest ad hoc reviewers that are specialists in the area that might be able to
address the unique characteristics of the application. Do not neglect to also
indicate if there are individuals who might not be appropriate for conflict of
interest or other reasons. It is not always possible for a PI to know which
review group to request. If that is the case, then a request should not be
included. The difficulty with knowing the appropriate group is that the groups'
titles alone do not provide sufficient information about what the group
reviews, and its particular expertise. PIs can seek information about review
groups and membership. However, rather than to specifically request an
inappropriate group, in our opinion, it would be better to rely on the project
description and the cover letter content to assist funding source staff to
appropriately direct the application. Of course, in this matter, as with the entire
letter, use a tone of courtesy and respect. For NIH applications, specifying,
on the first page of the application, the announcement to which the application
is a response will help assist appropriate review group assignment.

TABLE 3.4
6-Week Application Preparation Timeline

November 1, 1997 Receipt Date		
The dates shown are completion dates, unless otherwise specified.		

September 1	Monday	Review comments and develop an outline of comments, by application section. Categorize the comments according to the level of effort required to respond to them; e.g., rewrite to clarify; minimal additions or deletions; major rewriting, conceptualization, or literature search needed.
September 1	Monday	Contact coinvestigators and arrange a meeting.
September 5	Friday	Meet with coinvestigators.
September 5	Friday	Preliminary Studies: Outline of material to be added in view of reviewer comments, and new work completed since submission.
September 9	Tuesday	Specific Aims: Comprehensive draft completed, modified to meet concerns of reviewers. (Aims clearly formed with accompanying hypotheses or questions. Editing for clarity still required.)
September 12	Friday	Background and Significance: First draft—clarified to meet reviewer comments and material added if appropriate.
September 19	Friday	Research Design and Methods: First draft—clarified and revised to meet reviewer comments, with particular attention to procedures and sample size so that the budget can be modified if required.
September 19	Friday	Resources: Complete with special attention to those resource features directly relevant to your research. Be sure to add resources that come into play as a function of revisions in light of reviewer comments.
September 19	Friday	Request updated Other Support information and biographical sketches from coinvestigators. Set a deadline, e.g., September 22. (Request that the bio sketches reflect work relevant to the revised research project.)
September 19	Friday	Request letters of agreement from consultants; letters of cooperation or permissions from agencies or individuals with whom you will be working. Set a deadline, e.g., September 22.
September 19	Friday	Alert consortium/contractual organizations that it is required that they give you a separate detailed budget for the initial budget period and for the entire proposed project periods. Request that this budget include additional items and costs incurred as a result of modifying the proposal to meet reviewer concerns. Set a deadline, e.g., September 18.
September 24	Wednesday	First draft of Specific Aims, Background and Significance, and Preliminary Studies in single document.
September 24	Wednesday	First draft of Introduction, which responds to reviewer comments.

TABLE 3.4
Continued

September 24 Wednesday	Review your list of budget categories and modify as appropriate with respect to changed Specific Aims and Research Design and Methods sections. Reestimate item quantities and cost, and add new items as required by your response to reviewer concerns in the following areas:

a. Personnel

b. Consultants

c. Equipment—unit acquisition cost of $500 or more

d. Supplies, e.g., glassware, chemicals, animals, data collection supplies

e. Travel

f. Patient care costs

g. Alterations and renovations

h. Other expenses, e.g., patient travel, lodging, volunteer fees; publication costs; computer charges; rentals and leases; equipment maintenance

i. Consortium/contractual costs

September 24 Wednesday	Make an appointment with your fiscal representative to meet on Monday, September 29, to discuss the budget items.
September 26 Friday	Research Design and Methods: Comprehensive draft modified to meet reviewer concerns. (Precise descriptions of the design, procedures, subjects, statistical analysis, and other relevant Items.)
September 29 Monday	Meet with fiscal representative and finalize budget.
September 29 Monday	Review budget justification and modify where required in light of changes made in response to reviewer comments.
September 29 Monday	Complete final draft of Preliminary Studies.
September 30 Tuesday	Follow up requests for Other Support and bio sketches from coinvestigators. Set a deadline, e.g., Tuesday, October 7.
September 30 Tuesday	Follow up requests for letters of agreement from consultants; letters of collaboration or permissions from agencies or individuals with whom you will be working. Set a deadline, e.g., Tuesday, October 7.
September 30 Tuesday	Complete final draft of Specific Aims and Research Design and Methods sections.
October 3 Friday	Complete final draft of Background and Significance. Match your list of changes required against this draft and modify as appropriate.

(*continued*)

TABLE 3.4
Continued

October 6	Monday	Final draft of entire research plan. Edited for consistency across sections, clarity, readability, spelling, and word accuracy, with responses to reviewer comments highlighted.
October 6	Monday	Final draft of the Introduction. Match against reviewer comments and against the outline you developed earlier.
October 6	Monday	Request review from colleague. Set a deadline, e.g., Friday, October 17.
October 6	Monday	Revise Literature Cited. Scrutinize carefully for citations that need to be added and those that need to be deleted. Be sure to follow funding source guidelines.
October 8	Wednesday	Request outstanding letters, bio sketches, and Other Support information be faxed. Set a deadline, e.g., October 24.
October 8	Wednesday	Rewrite abstract. For NIH applications, note that the revised PHS 398 form's space allowance is smaller. Also, remember that this description is entered into the NIH database (CRISP) and becomes public information if the application is funded.
October 8	Wednesday	Review appendixes and add new material or remove material as appropriate.
October 10	Wednesday	Complete Proposal Routing Sheet and route internally. (This process may require 2 weeks or 2 days; check organizational policy.)
October 17	Friday	Incorporate suggestions of internal reviewer as appropriate.
October 24	Friday	Final copy of complete application, from face page through appendixes.
October 27	Monday	Production and assembly of final original copy.
October 29	Wednesday	Make copies and prepare for mailing.
October 31	Friday	Mail.
November 1	Wednesday	Received by NIH.

Review the Application for Conceptual Clarity and Strength

Ask a colleague with expertise to review the project plan's content and persuasiveness. Reviewing for persuasiveness must be specifically requested because it is often not considered. There are several questions, in our opinion, on which this reviewer must focus when reviewing the project plan. First, is the specific project reasonable in view of the current knowledge base? Second, could the project be viewed as too novel? Even though this is a resubmission, this question needs to be asked, and if the answer is yes a determination should be made about how it can be reframed so that it will be viewed as a nonrisky attempt to advance knowledge. Third, does the project engender excitement? Fourth, is the Background and Significance section designed to bring the reviewers to the same conclusions as those of the PI? It is particularly important with projects that are challenging current paradigms that the Background and Significance section be structured to focus and direct the reviewers' attention, rather than a simple statement about the research to date. If the literature is not integrated to present a strong case for the proposed approach, the reviewer can arrive at a scientific conclusion that is different from the PIs, or be unable to reach a conclusions and decide that the available data is inconclusive and does not warrant the proposed project.

Review the Application for Completeness and Continuity

Ask a colleague to review the application, page by page, starting with the face page or cover page to be certain that the reverberations of changes are correctly represented throughout the application. We have noticed that PIs are most satisfied with collegial reviews when they have taken time to discuss the application briefly and be very specific about what is being requested of this reviewer. Of course, help with grammar and typos is always welcome, but the primary task of this individual is to focus on the supporting material and the science. A copy of the checklist presented in Table 3.5 might be included with the request.

Do Not Rely on a Colleague's Previously Submitted Application to Determine an Application's Format, Completeness, or Scientific Requirements

Sometimes it is easier for PIs to organize an application after they have seen a completed one. This is very helpful because it can reassure a PI that the funding source really does expect all the pieces to be included. However, because funding sources modify their requirements periodically, the only reliable information about what to include in a current application is the funding source's most recent instructions and guidelines.

PIs also often look for reassurance, in a colleague's application, about their scientific presentation. If they are having problems with solving the power section, for example, and they review an application that did not include a power section but received a fundable score, they might believe the power section is not necessary. Be aware that the application score is arrived at through a process of balancing positive and negative features of an application. Perhaps the power section did not produce a large score decrement because of other strong overriding features of the application. However,

TABLE 3.5
Application Review Checklist

Item	Content
Face or cover page	Title, project dates, project cost: first year and all years, institutional review board approval date
Abstract	Objectives, hypotheses or questions, participants/subjects
Key personnel	Add names of new investigators, remove names of those no longer participating
Location of project activity	Verify
Table of contents	Check section page numbers against document
Introduction/Changes Summary	Compare this section with the reviewer comments. Each comment should have a response indicated either in the Introduction, cover letter, or the body of the document
Specific Aims	Check the words and phrases for accuracy
Background and Significance	Use the Specific Aims as a guide to determine if this section is complete and that it does not include more than is needed
Preliminary Studies	Verify that all related new work has been added, that previous work included is relevant to the revised application, and that the reason for including the information as preliminary studies is clear
Research Design and Methods	*Participants:* Verify that the number, groups, and inclusion and exclusion criteria are accurate and appropriate for testing the stated hypotheses
	Recruitment: Verify that the methods used are appropriate and completely described
	Procedures: Verify that the procedures are completely described. That is, sufficient detail is provided so that an individual can visualize the process to which each participant will be exposed

difficult as it might be, include everything in the project plan that the funding source requires to make a persuasive presentation of a strong plan. The checklist in Table 3.5 is provided to assist with determining the application's completeness.

Use the Checklist in Table 3.5 for Independent Application Reviews

TABLE 3.5
Continued

Item	Content
	Data analysis: Verify that the analyses presented will test the proposed hypotheses and that discussions of data appropriateness are present if required by the data type or the analyses
	Data management: Review to determine that the procedures are reasonable, doable, and do not compromise the safety of the data
Literature cited	Review for completeness and accuracy
Human or animal subjects	Verify that the information is correct and that it coincides with the proposed Research Design and Methods section
Budget	*Personnel:* Verify that new salaries and fringe benefits are included in the calculations; add new personnel, remove personnel no longer included in the project; match personnel against project needs
	Equipment: Determine that equipment requests and estimated costs are appropriate
	Supplies and other: Match these categories against the Procedure section and determine that updates have been made, such as changing quantities if the number of participants has changed. Apply an inflation factor to each cost
Budget justification	The major items in each budget category must be justified. Particular attention needs to be paid to large expenditures and expenditures that fluctuate from one budget period to the next. The inflation factor used needs to be stated and if other than that recommended by the funding source, explained

PART

Funded! Practical Issues

Taking Advantage of the Award's Rights and Responsibilities

When projects are funded, investigators enjoy moments of basking in the good wishes of their colleagues and the unique excitement shared with coinvestigators. However, they are also likely to experience anxiety as the professional and personal consequences of having the award flash through their minds. "I guess I should read that proposal and find out what I've gotten myself into!" is a comment usually made lightly, but motivated by a serious concern. Another source of concern is the administrative responsibilities associated with being a funded principal investigator (PI). The award seems to be a lot of money for which to be responsible, and yet there is doubt that it will be enough to complete the project. PIs quickly conclude that to manage a successful project they will need to learn all that they can about the rights and responsibilities of their award. This chapter provides some guidelines on the PI's rights and responsibilities after their organization has accepted the award.

Identify the Official Award Recipient

PIs usually are not the official award recipient. In most instances, the application is submitted and the award received on behalf of the PI by their organization. Fellowship awards and awards from some funding sources are exceptions. In these cases, the PI is the payee on a check from the funding source for an agreed on amount. When it is appropriate for a PI to be the payee and make the required payments for expenditures, they must develop procedures for these transactions. These awards are considered to be personal income for the PI and are taxed accordingly. If, however, it is not appropriate for a PI to be the payee, they must follow their organization's regulations for processing the award. This often entails nothing more than endorsing the check and passing it to an organizational official for further handling. PIs are then subject to the policies and procedures of their organization as well as the funding source with respect to all fiscal aspects of the award.

Rights and Responsibilities

Each funding mechanism has some unique rights and responsibilities. For example, there are likely to be important administrative differences among grants, contracts, and gifts and between private and governmental awards. It is important that investigators be aware that their relationship with the funding source is different for each funding mechanism because the award mechanism—grant, contract, or gift—determines award allocation procedures and the extent to which PIs control project procedures and expenditures.

Grants

Grants are financial awards in support of projects with anticipated but not guaranteed outcomes. They permit investigators to design and conduct projects from theoretical positions and with methodologies that they themselves value. In effect, grants support the investigator's pursuit of scientific knowledge with only limited restrictions. Announcements from the various funding sources generally describe their missions and interests and the availability of funds.

Some grant applications, Investigator-Initiated Research Grants, arise from the desire of an investigator and his or her collaborators to pursue an interesting and important line of investigation, or to develop a specific program or intervention. Preferably, the topic under investigation directs the scope of the project and the personnel requirements, which in turn affect the special application chosen. Other types of awards require multiple investigators in which collaborators and consultants might be required. These include career development grants, program project grants, and Investigator-Initiated Interactive Research Project Grants (IRPGs).

All of these grant awards entail rights and responsibilities that must be adhered to by PIs and their organizations. Whichever of the above mechanisms apply, and whether the award amount is that requested in the application, the amount requested reduced by some percentage, or the amount requested less some amount that has been negotiated with the PI, the PI's rights and responsibilities are activated with a notice of award.

Notice of Grant Award

The notice of grant award is the official announcement to the PI from the funding source that a grant application has been funded. This notification is usually written, although we have heard of instances when there was only a telephone call, followed by a check. However the notice of award is handled, to paraphrase one of our colleagues, "Now the fun begins."

The first thing to keep in mind is that most grant awards are *not made to the PI*. The award is made to the PI's institution. The money is not the PI's to spend as he or she chooses, but is subject to rules and regulations of the funding source and the grantee institution. PIs must give both sets of regulations conscientious attention. The project management and implementation limitations placed on PIs by their institution are primarily fiscal. On receipt of the award, the PI's institution agrees to abide by the funding source's expenditure guidelines, but also has its own guidelines. The PI's institution's guidelines probably become most apparent when a PI decides to move to another institution and take the project along. Moving the funded project must be negotiated by the PI, the current institution, and the new institution. Both the PI and the institution that received the award could be losers if an agreement about moving the study is not reached. In fact, in the worst-case scenario, the award could be terminated.

Whatever form the funding source uses for the award statement, all of the information it contains is important. We will discuss all of the information provided on the Public Health Service (PHS) Notice of Grant Award, knowing full well that other agencies and funding sources will have a different format. However, we think it will be useful to examine this format in detail.

The grant number is the identifier used by the funding source to refer to the grant throughout the funding period. We suggest that this number be placed at the top of all grant-related correspondence and other written material. The first digit of the grant number indicates the type of application (e.g., 1 indicates a new application); the next three characters indicate the kind of project (research, training, etc.), for example, R01 is the identifier for a regular investigator-initiated research grant and T32 is the identifier for a training grant); the next set of characters represents the institute (e.g., CA is National Cancer Institute, MH is National Institute of Mental Health); the serial number, a five-digit number, is next; the grant support year is the next two-digit number (01 for the first year, 02 for the second year, etc.); and finally, whether the application has been previously reviewed is indicated (i.e., A2 for the second review, A3 for the third), for example, 1 R01 MH12345-01A2.

The entire project period (usually 3 to 5 years), beginning and ending dates, and dates for the current budget period (first year) are stated. The approved budget indicates, by category, amounts approved for items such as salaries and wages, fringe benefits (employee-related expenses), consultant costs, equipment, supplies, travel, patient care, alterations and renovations, consortium/contractual costs, and, if appropriate, costs related to training for training grants.

The projected funding level for each grant year is specified. This amount is the recommended yearly direct cost amount (which is either the requested amount or less). Indirect costs are computed on the base amount of the grant award for the grant period and are paid to the grantee institution for each yearly period. The total award amount shown for the first year is the sum of the direct costs and the indirect costs. These figures are arrived at through a cost analysis, which is normally performed for every grant application approved for funding by PHS except for awards that do not require detailed budgets such as fellowships. The form and extent of the cost analysis is based on information obtained from the review process, the amount and type of costs being requested, the nature of the project, and past experience with the applicant institution. Any restrictions on how funds can be spent, or options for carrying them over to future years, are indicated. Special terms and conditions are also included that are binding on the award and general terms applicable to the award.

Both the names of the grants management specialist at the funding institute and the National Institutes of Health (NIH) institute's program official are listed on the award. These people are the primary contacts for the PI. The grants management specialist is responsible for all fiscal and budget matters related to the grant. The program official, who is responsible for working with the PI, can act as an advocate for the project and can be used as a sounding board to discuss issues and possible changes that need to be made to the study or the protocol. If the award is from a funding source other than the NIH, the PI will probably find similar information on the notice of award, or can get it on request.

The notice of grant award is signed by the chief of the Grants Management Branch, who is the fiscal officer of the awarding NIH institute. The chief of the Grants Management Branch also has responsibility for fiscal matters and supervises the institutes' grants management specialists. Special terms and conditions may also be attached to the grant award; these statements pinpoint additional issues related to receipt of funding and should receive attention. For example, the salary funds for a research assistant may be restricted to use only during the current budget year. This means that if the funds are not used, they must be returned to the funding source. We recommend that PIs read the entire notice of award carefully, because overlooking award restrictions can have long-range negative consequences on the project.

In summary, a notice of grant award usually includes the dates for the grant period and the approved budget, and it can include specific terms and conditions related to the grant, in addition to specifying the amount of the indirect costs included in the award. This is the official notice sent by the funding source that the award has been made, and in most instances includes the fiscal contacts for the funded grant.

Acceptance

Under all PHS grant awards, a grantee indicates acceptance of the terms of an award by requesting funds from the grant payment system. If the grantee cannot accept the terms it should notify the GMO [grants management officer]. If resolution cannot be reached, the grant will become void. The grantee does not have appeal rights with respect to the terms appearing on the NGA [notice of grant award] or with respect to a denial by the PHS awarding office of a request to change the terms of the award, since the actions and decisions resulting in the issuance of the award document are normally considered to be preaward determinations. (U.S. Department of Health and Human Services, Public Health Service, 1994, p. 5-1)

With a grant from the PHS, acceptance of the terms indicated on the award notice is indicated by a request for funds from the grant payment system. PIs with awards from other sources need to determine how to notify the source of official acceptance and the time frame within which this must occur.

Fund availability. "All PHS discretionary grants are funded either by a single award covering the entire period of support or incrementally by a series of successive awards. . . . When incremental funding is used, projects may be programmatically approved for support in their entirety or in part, but funded in annual increments called budget periods. . . . The initial grant award provides funds for conducting the project during the first budget period" (U.S. Department of Health and Human Services, Public Health Service, 1994, pp. 5-1, 5-2).

The amount of awards for the remaining project years usually depends on such things as the annual noncompeting continuation budget, the project's progress, and fund availability. Funding sources may require that funds not spent during the current year be returned, or they may allow PIs to carry them forward. It is important that PIs know the policies of their funding source so that funds awarded for project use are not placed in jeopardy.

Release of information. The Freedom of Information Act (FOIA) (Public Law 90-23) as amended and associated public information regulations of Health and Human Services (45 CFR Part 5) require the release by PHS of certain grant documents and records requested by members of the public. These policies and regulations apply to information in the possession of PHS and do not require recipients or contractors under grants to permit public access to their records.

The following types of information will generally be released:

Funded applications

Approved and disapproved noncompeting continuation applications

Notices of grant award

Financial status reports

Final reports of any audit . . . that have been transmitted to the grantee organization. (U.S. Department of Health and Human Services, Public Health Service, 1994, pp. 4-11, 4-12)

When material is requested, the organization that submitted the application will be given an opportunity to identify potentially patentable or commercially valuable information that should not be disclosed. The PHS will notify the grantee of the agency's decision as to what documents and to whom the documents will be released. Information that will be held on request includes pending grant applications or unfunded new and competing continuations; salary information; personal information; opinions of government officers, employees, or consultants; trade secrets; and commercial, financial, and otherwise intrinsically valuable information. When documents contain both disclosable and nondisclosable information, the nondisclosable information will be deleted by a designated official.

Changes in Expenditures or Activities

Sometimes the PI may decide to initiate changes, either in the project or in the budget, after an award has been made. Because this is not uncommon, most funding sources have guidelines about the kinds of changes that the PI and grantee organization can make without permission from the funding source. In addition, other changes are also allowed but require prior approval of the funding source. The following material is from the PHS instructions.

Budget changes. The PHS allows the grantee institution to rebudget within and between budget categories in the approved total direct cost budget to meet unanticipated requirements or to implement programmatic changes. When this occurs, grantees must ensure that all costs charged to the award are allowable, allocable, and reasonable. Rebudgeting is considered significant when the cumulative amount of transfers among direct cost categories for the current budget period exceeds 25% of the total amount awarded or $250,000, whichever is less.

The following are examples of some actions that the recipient can implement under special grants administration provisions (i.e., expanded authorities) without prior PHS approval.

Extension without additional funds. The grantee institution may extend the final budget period of a research project one time for a period of 12 months beyond the original expiration date shown on the notice of grant award. An extension of this kind can be made when (a) there are no additional funds due from the awarding office; (b) there will be no change in the project's originally approved scope or objectives; and (c) either additional time is required to assure adequate completion of the project or continuity of PHS grant support is required while a competing continuation application is under review, or the extension is necessary to permit an orderly phase out of a project that will not receive continued support. Having unobligated funds at the expiration date of the grant is not a sufficient reason for an extension without additional funds.

Preaward costs. A grantee organization may, prior to the beginning date of an award and at its own risk, incur obligations and expenditures if the costs incurred are considered necessary for the conduct of the project, the costs are allowable under the potential award, and PHS written prior approval is obtained when required. These costs may be incurred within 90 days prior to the beginning date of the award without PHS prior approval. Preaward costs incurred more than 90 days prior to the beginning date require prior approval by the PHS. Incurring of these costs by a potential grantee institution imposes no obligation on the PHS to make the award (U.S. Department of Health and Human Services, Public Health Service, 1994, p. 8-6).

Carryover of unobligated balance. Unobligated funds at the end of a budget period can be carried over unless they are restricted on a notice of grant award. If these funds are in excess of 25% of the total award or $250,000, whichever is less, the awarding office will review the circumstances to assure that these funds are necessary to complete the project. A notice of grant award will not be issued to reflect the carryover. Unobligated balances not specified for carryover on the financial status report will be available to the PHS awarding office.

Use of program income. With the exception of non-SBIR (small business) for-profit organizations, grantee organizations may use the additional costs alternative of general program income, unless regulations or the notice of grant award specifically specifies another alternative or a combination of alternatives.

Project matters. In general, the PI or project director may make minor changes in methodology, approach, or other aspects of the project objectives. PIs on "research grants may make significant changes in methods or procedures that need only be reported to the awarding office in the progress report for the applicable period" (p. 8-1).

Prior Approval

Limitations are placed on grantees by the PHS for NIH grants, and this can also be the case for other funding organizations. For example, some budget categories might be restricted to expenditures shown within the original application, unless prior approval is received for increasing or decreasing them. This regulation clearly might influence the kinds of modifications a PI might want to make in a project plan to accommodate a smaller than requested award.

Because failure to obtain prior approval could result in cost disallowances, it is important that PIs learn how to work within these restrictions. These limitations pertain to direct costs but have nothing to do with indirect costs because the indirect cost rate is established for the institution.

On an NIH-funded grant, prior approval by the NIH is necessary for some changes requested by the PI. These regulations also apply to all Department of Health and Human Services grants, but they vary by the type of grant award (i.e., research, construction, or training). If there are doubts about the need for approval of changes, we recommend that the assigned grants management officer identified on the NIH award statement be contacted.

The following are examples of areas (U.S. Department of Health and Human Services, Public Health Service, 1994, pp. 8-7, 8-8) that need prior approval before budget changes can be made.

- Change in scope of the project or research objectives. This includes major changes in the aims, objectives, or goals.
- Change in PI.
- Changes of grantee organization.
- Deviations from award terms and conditions.
- Audiovisuals and publications charges that exceed $25,000 for a single audiovisual or for a single printed publication.
- Preaward costs incurred 90 days prior to award.
- Drawings, specifications for alterations, and renovations over $50,000.
- Indemnification against third parties for any indemnification not covered by insurance.
- Capital expenditures for land and buildings.
- Extensions of the budget period other than the extension of the final budget period for up to 1 year beyond the original termination date on the notice of grant award.

In summary, we want to stress that these are examples identified in the NIH guidelines for which prior approval is required. It is important to note that in general, prior approval is needed for any major modifications related to changing the PI, shifts in major budget categories, renovation, printing and publication expenses if either exceeds $25,000, or extensions in length of time of the award. PIs need to familiarize themselves with their funding source's prior approval policies and adhere to the requirements.

Cooperative Agreements

Federally employed scientists who work in collaboration with other scientists from nonfederal organizations carry out *cooperative agreement* research. This funding mechanism is the same as a grant, except that it provides for direct involvement of the funding agency in the project design and also provides research support for portions of the project. Cooperative agreements, therefore, combine aspects of both the grant and the contract mechanisms, with the PI and the federal agency being partners. A multisite research project of the National Institute on Drug Abuse (NIDA), for example, would involve the cooperation of investigators from the Coordinating Center, Collaborative Treatment Sites, and the NIDA Treatment Research Branch, Division of Clinical Research.

Investigators who obtain awards under this mechanism administer their award much as do investigators who have grant awards. The primary difference is the extent of interaction between the PI and the government scientists, which usually commences after the award is made. Because of the need for close cooperation, and sometimes multiple sites, more time is allotted for meetings and travel. It is important that investigators with this type of award have a clear understanding of the project protocol and outcomes for which they are responsible. Under this type of agreement, protocol changes are usually not made at the discretion of the PI but only after review and agreement from the other investigators and the funding source.

Fund availability is like that of a grant. However, PIs need to carefully review their responsibilities to determine if start-up funds from their organization will be required to maintain the agreed on schedule.

Contracts

Overview

Contracts and grants are at opposite ends of the funding continuum. A grant is a mechanism that rewards the investigator for innovation and creativity in thinking through an issue or problem by developing an approach to meet the overall grant aim developed and initiated by the applicant. A contract, on the other hand, is a mechanism used by a funding source to accomplish a specific objective or objectives. It is a mechanism used to secure a product or products according to a funding source's specifications, and there is very little room for creativity or innovation by the organization/persons who receive the contract. A specific example is NIDA's solicitation for proposals to develop analytical methods, carry out quality control tests, prepare dosage forms, and perform stability studies for the compounds and dosage forms to be used in the institute's medications development program. An investigator interested in doing this work requests the detailed specifications outlined in the request for proposal (RFP) package, decides whether he or she can do the prescribed work, and writes a competitive proposal. After a contract is reviewed and accepted by the organization, the agreement is binding. Investigators who believe that they can modify the protocol, timeline, or any other aspect of the project after the award is made are courting problems.

Contract Process

The contract process is relatively straightforward, and whether the organization seeking bids is a for-profit corporation or a government agency, the major aspects of the bidding process and the procedures after a contract is awarded are similar. It begins with a bidder developing a proposal or bid that responds to the contract specifications developed by the contracting organization. This bid is reviewed competitively and independently to determine if the bidder meets contract specifications and if the bid is competitive financially. Bidders in the competitive range participate in contract negotiations. These negotiations focus on balancing the contracting organization's required activities (established by the contractor) with costs and activities (proposed by the bidder) to assure that the best product, and frequently at the lowest cost, is obtained for the services or goods described in the contract scope of work.

Unlike grants where the timeline for developing the grant application is established by the investigators, timelines for contracts are established by the contracting organization and are short—usually 45 to 90 days. Contracts are advertised for bids. Bidders are expected to respond to the specifications described by the contracting organization. The written bid includes a description of how the specifications will be achieved and a cost proposal describing the funds needed to complete them. At the federal level, contract specifications are described in the statement of work (SOW), which is published in the *Commerce Business Daily*, the *Federal Register*, or the *NIH Guide*.

The SOW describes the tasks and activities to be undertaken by the successful bidder (contractor). This can, for example, include the number of participants or subjects, the sampling frame, and the time frame for data collection and other very specific details. The contract review criteria are also included in the SOW.

Contract protocols are developed before the award by the bidder or by the funding source. Bidders use these protocols to assess whether the project is feasible for their expertise and facility resources. Funding sources can help bidders make these determinations by holding bidders' conferences at which both governmental program representatives and the contracting officer provide clarification and answer questions regarding the SOW.

Thus, the written bid responds to the SOW describes the methods and procedures, the type of staff, the time frame, and the costs needed to meet the SOW's specifications and requirements. It incorporates the approach that the offeror (e.g., a university) will use to produce the specific product or services presented in the SOW. The intent of the contract bidding process is generally to get the best product or service at the lowest possible cost within the SOW specifications. Contract proposals are usually composed of a technical (scientific) proposal, which describes the work to be done, and the business proposal, which is a description of the rights and responsibilities of the contracting parties, a detailed budget, and budget justification. Because of the complexity and potential broad organizational impact of the business proposal, organizations usually have contract officers who develop this proposals in cooperation with PIs.

Contract review process. Contract proposals are not accepted if received at the contract office after the deadline. Proposals are reviewed in a closed meeting by external reviewers who have expertise in the area in which the contract will be awarded and who have no established relationships with any of the contract bidders. The business proposal review is usually done parallel with, but independently of, the scientific proposal review.

After the review process, clarifying questions are usually sent to offerors who were found to be within the competitive range. Replies in response to specific technical questions are again reviewed, and the external review group may be asked to rate each contract proposal again taking into account the additional information. After this final scoring, those proposals determined to be acceptable are within the competitive range. After the competitive range is established, the contracting officer, in cooperation with technical staff, makes a final choice to award the contract based on negotiations related to costs and achieving the SOW activities. After a contract award announcement is made, bidders who did not receive the award can appeal the decision. When this occurs, a lengthy process of examining the review procedures and possibly rebidding the contract or even resoliciting the entire bid can ensue.

In addition to the investigators reviewing the requirements and work conditions, their organization's contract and legal departments also should review the pertinent documents. Any requirements, restrictions, or changes in wording required by them need to be brought to the attention of the contracting organization. When human or animal subjects are involved, the investigators must obtain approval from their Institutional Review Board or Animal Care and Use Committee. The contract can only be accepted if the requirements of these groups are met.

Notice of Contract Award

The notice of a contract award may be an award notice, such as that for grants, or there may be no notice other than receipt of the signed contract. As soon as the contract is official, the timeline agreed to by the investigator is effective. The process of bidding for a contract ensures that when an individual announces, "I got the contract!" there is no question about what work was promised, or the timeline. The negotiated budget submitted for review is not a proposed budget, but an exact budget. There is often, however, concern about the negotiated budget and whether the work can be done for the agreed on fee. If the time lapse between preparing the final budget and receiving the notice of award is several months, investigators need to scrutinize the budget and make whatever arrangements are necessary to guarantee completion of the promised work on time. In some instances, investigators receive contract funds only for work completed. This requires that PIs have some way of underwriting the costs incurred during the first phases of the contract.

If there are questions or issues related to budget changes, purchasing, or changing line items, they should be addressed to the contract management specialist. These changes should be discussed initially with both the program project officer and the contract management specialist, and a copy of the request for change should be sent to the program official. Contracts, because they are developed to obtain a specific product or service, are usually more tightly controlled, and billing statements must specify the exact amount of the expenditure for the billing period, usually monthly or quarterly.

Reporting

Contracts require more interaction with the funding source than any other type of funding mechanism. Unlike grants, contracts require regular and detailed progress reports, usually monthly, quarterly, and annually. Face-to-face and written and electronic reporting are all part of the reporting processes. Some funding organizations only require annual reports, but more frequent reporting is generally the rule. The funding source specifies the frequency and contents of these reports, and bidders should include reporting costs in the proposal.

Gifts

Awards are potentially classified as gifts when the source names it a gift and when the source places few restrictions on the use of the award. However, the decision as to whether the award is processed as a gift, a grant, or a contract by the recipient organization depends on agreement about the nature and extent of the funding sources requirements. The primary variables that come into play are the extent of detail included for the purpose of the award and the kinds and frequency of reports required.

A PI who receives an award labeled a gift should contact his or her organization's fiscal affairs office to determine the proper procedures given the source's requirements. It is also important to note that projects supported by gifts are not exempt from other requirements such as human or animal subject approval.

Learn About Indirect Costs

Indirect costs are recovered from the funding source by the applicant organization to support the project. The items covered include expenses such as utilities, building and lab maintenance, clerical support, research support personnel, graduate student support, and upkeep of libraries. The amount of indirect costs received with an award can be negotiated by the funding source and the applicant organization, or the funding source might have a standing policy about indirect costs from which it does not deviate. Universities periodically negotiate an indirect cost rate with the federal government. Many foundations have predetermined rates, which can range from zero to the federal government's negotiated rate. Awards labeled gifts do not have indirect costs attached to them. When bidding on a contract, the addition of the indirect costs to the direct costs can make a difference in the competitiveness of a bid. In such cases, PIs need to try to negotiate an agreement with their organization that will not place the bid out of competitive range. The amount of indirect costs recovery is of interest to PIs not only because it increases the cost of a project, but also because often a portion of these costs can be returned to them for support of further research.

Understand Internal Budget Arrangements

Internal budget arrangements are those of the PI's particular unit and the larger organization. These arrangements come in a wide variety of structures and range from simple to complex depending on the particular organizational requirements. PIs must learn as much about the broader organizational system as required to manage their project. The system that most PIs interact with on a day-to-day basis is that of their unit or department. Each system has its own priorities and objectives and unique methods of achieving them. Although an organization that receives a federal grant is subject to the policies and regulations associated with it, some of these can be modified to meet the individual organizational needs. The units or departments in turn must abide by the policies and regulations of the larger organization, but again, some of these can be modified to meet the unit or department needs. Although colleagues might be relied on for information about the kinds of questions to ask to orchestrate the most efficient use of the award, a PI's best source of information about how his or her award will be administered is the responsible individual in the PI's unit or department. Be forewarned! Purchases and financial commitments should not be made until the system to process the documents is in place and individuals who can authorize expenditures are named.

Action Strategies

Review the Agreement Made With the Funding Source

After the award is made, "the piper must be paid." The realization that what was promised must now be delivered is a sobering thought to many PIs. The first thing PIs and contractors need to do after hearing that they have been funded is to review the proposal. The procedure section of grant proposals is often more general than remembered. Rarely can it be used as a work plan. In addition, some aspects of the plan, science, or technology might be out-of-date because of the time lapse between submission and funding. It is important that the PI begins immediately to consider solutions to personnel, design, procedure, and financial issues. These solutions might entail redesigning the study or drastically reducing personnel costs. Talking with coinvestigators and other PIs can be a source of ideas for achieving the scientific goal within the awarded budget. Although the project must be implemented as quickly as possible, modifications made in haste might be regretted. Remember that the program officer needs to be involved in any significant changes. The overall strategy must be to get the project implemented as quickly as possible, but not at the expense of quality or regulation infraction.

Contractors might not remember all the details of the agreement in spite of the number of times they were reviewed during the preparation of the bid. The PI of a contract that is viewed as inadequate has fewer options than a PI on a similarly viewed grant. Contractors are bound to this agreement and if funds are inadequate the difference must be picked up by the contractor. The contractor must find a method for keeping the agreement and also keeping costs within the agreed on amount. Some agreements do not include start-up funds. When this is the case, contractors must find the resources to support the project until they are paid for product delivery. A review of the contract will provide information about the extent of funds required and the legitimate uses of start-up funds provided.

The PI as a Financial Manager

It is imperative that when a notice of grant or contract award is received, PIs focus on their role of financial manager. Cost overruns usually cannot be tolerated whether the project is supported by a grant or a contract. The PI needs to develop a system for staying in touch with expenditures from the first day of the project. PIs can either do it themselves or delegate all or some of the duties to someone else. Chapter 6 details some of the organizational relationships and positions that come into play and with whom the PI must become acquainted.

Develop an Implementation Timeline

Taking time to develop a timeline for the project activities provides a way for a PI to think through primary issues and potential problems. A top priority is developing a list of project or contract activities that have irrevocable deadlines. Contract agreements generally have several deadlines with expected deliverables. Grant project deadlines are more likely to be related to participants' availability, high-tech equipment, or perhaps time of year.

Because a timeline ties actions and activities with dates, it can serve as an early warning system for deficits, the need to initiate new purchases or personnel, or accumulation of funds that need to be processed before the end of the budget year. Developing this timeline in conjunction with the business manager who will be processing receipts and expenditures is an effective way to avoid surprises that can slow a project's forward movement.

Investigate Obligations and Ask About Autonomy

To learn how obligations and autonomy are going to influence the conduct of their project, PIs must rely on their previous experience and take time to talk with others about the rules of getting funded and how others have dealt with this situation. A fruitful way for funded PIs to spend time is to seek out other PIs in their institution and also in other organizations to discuss project management. Although initially PIs may not grasp the importance of all that is said, these conversations can direct PIs to the organizational resources available to them and also alert them to the most troublesome issues with respect to rights and responsibilities of receiving an award. We recommend that experienced PIs also renew their information about their obligations and autonomy under their current award.

Receiving an award, whether it be a grant or contract, creates legal relationships. When the award is for a grant, the institution that employs the principal investigator is the grantee and is legally responsible for the scientific and financial conduct of the grant. The institution, not the principal investigator, "owns" the grant. The principal investigator is responsible for conducting the science but also may have certain financial responsibilities, such as ensuring that funds from one grant are not used to purchase equipment to be used on another grant. Most cases involving alleged financial improprieties on the part of the principal investigators can be traced to a total lack of understanding of the rules that govern federal grants . . . if you are going to earn your living through a specific type of legal relationship, you should understand that relationship. (Charrow, 1993, p. 78)

Other Areas of Responsibility

In addition to the responsibilities investigators have to administrative units and to the scientific community, responsibilities arise from the nature of the research, an important one being health and safety issues. We advise funded investigators to seek advice from their immediate supervisor and other administrative officials about the kinds of responsibilities incurred with the acceptance of a project award. Some information on health and safety issues is provided here.

Health and Safety for Grantees and Contractors

Organizations receiving federal government grant and contract awards are responsible for protecting their employees from hazardous conditions (NIH, 1995e). The following are classes of hazards posing potential danger: biohazards, for example, human immunodeficiency virus (HIV), other infectious agents, and oncogenic viruses; radioactive materials; and chemical hazards, for example, carcinogens, chemotherapeutic agents, other toxic chemicals, and flammable or explosive materials. Guidelines are available to assist PIs in providing a safe research work environment. Publications can be obtained from the PI's human resources office, or from the National Academy Press, 2102 Constitution Avenue, N.W., Washington, D.C., 20418.

Although special hazards are usually identified during the initial review of grant applications and contract proposals, concerns can be expressed by consultants at any time prior to award, and funding delayed until the situation is resolved to the satisfaction of the funding source. Suspension of work under the grant or contract can also occur if special hazards are identified after an award has been made. Although grantee and contractor organizations are not required to document that specific attention has been directed to the guidelines and standards, they should be able to provide evidence that pertinent health and safety standards have been considered and put into practice as appropriate.

CHAPTER 5

Build Effective Organizational Relationships

Every principal investigator (PI) must interact with individuals in organizational positions who can influence the implementation and completion of a funded project. During the application development process, PIs interact with coinvestigators, representatives of organizational units, and others who may have roles in the project or its administration. The depth of these interactions depends on the level of detail required by the application and project plan as well as the type of funding mechanism. After a project is funded, this group of individuals often expands to include others whose roles are directly related to project activities. Understanding how they view the project and the relationships among their roles can be key to the PI's effective management of relevant intraorganizational relationships.

One way to do this is to review the project plan from the perspective of administrative and operational requirements. Do not make assumptions about which persons in what organizational positions might be involved and when. In addition, do not assume that administrative work and interactions will occur on a familiar schedule and pace. Instead, we recommend making a tasks-timeline list. Compiling this list of tasks and when they might occur will alert the PI to where and how much lead time needs to be included and any possible barriers to successfully completing the project, and it will also provide a basis for developing a system for getting things done. PIs should exchange a vague understanding of the administrative procedures, and a reliance on others "who know how to do it," for a willingness to learn about the system and to let it work at its pace.

Understand Your Immediate Supervisor's Expectations

Because there is usually a considerable time lapse between application submission and award information, a PI should arrange a meeting with his or her
immediate supervisor when it is learned that a project has been funded, rather
than wait for the official award notice. This is the time to review the project
plan and its requirements; reestablish and/or modify any agreements made
before the application was submitted; and define the relationships among the
PI, her or his supervisor, the project, and the unit. In addition, it is also a time
to discuss the influence on the project of administrative changes caused by
increasing economic pressures, for example, specific expectations of faculty
economic performance.

PI's schedule. PIs need to know the extent to which they are responsible
for teaching, clinical, and administrative duties along with their project
responsibilities. A key item is the percentage of the PI's time devoted to the
project. Effort of 20%, 30%, or 50% might have seemed quite reasonable
during the application phase, but now that the award has been received,
arrangements for allowing the PI this time may require considerable resched-
uling. Units/departments may have customs related to information dissemination that involve presentations at seminars or professional meetings. A PI
might also be expected to mentor junior investigators by assisting with project
application development or by developing one of the supplemental applications available to PIs with funded projects.

Space. The project timeline and budget were designed in light of the
project's scope and specific personnel and operational requirements. One of
the key resources discussed before application submission was space for
housing the project. Sometimes the host organization has space that can be
dedicated to a single project and that is suitable for the project. However,
sharing space is more common. Space-sharing arrangements might involve
integrating project needs with the developed space of another project (in
which case there might be a fee), or it might involve the PI being given
responsibility for developing space with the understanding that it would be
shared, as needed, with other projects. It is hoped that the options and the
choice were discussed before application submission. However, some of the
best-laid plans have been known to go awry. Promises of space to a unit or
department might not be realized within the time frame expected or to the
extent expected. It is important that the space situation be clarified early,
particularly when plans need to be made to make the space usable. Even if a
laboratory is not being set up, most space requires telephone installation,
ethernet lines for computer operation, and furniture selection and arrange-

ment, all of which require getting in queue by placing work orders. This is an example of a risk-free way to start moving the project forward by using informal information that the award will be received.

Personnel. Agreements need to be made about how the personnel requirements will be met for the project duration. Organizations differ regarding the extent PIs are given discretion over these matters. Policies might demand that graduate students be employed, or that full-time research assistants, already employed by the unit, be used on the project. It is important that the PI know what staffing options are available, such as research assistants, project coordinators, and data entry clerks, so that if necessary, the process for hiring new employees can be initiated with the appropriate human resources section.

Project budget. In our opinion, it is best to review the complete budget and budget justification, even if the notice of award with the final budget amount is not available. Systematically reviewing each budget item ensures that all parties have the same view of the project and required resources as well as the possible financial advantage entailed by support of the PI's time and possibly other department members' time.

Before committing funds, it is critical that a PI understands the extent to which he or she will have control over how the award is used. These items might have been discussed during the application process but in quite broad terms because of uncertainty about project funding and the reasonable expectation that organizational policies might be different at the time of the award. In addition, at the time of proposal submission, the importance of administrative detail might not have been fully understood by PIs because their plunge into the "small business world" had not yet occurred.

Publicity. PIs also should learn the extent of their discretion concerning initiating publicity about the project, responding to media requests for information, and participating in radio or television interviews. For projects that will generate program income, guidelines need to be developed for involving units/departments.

Discover the Business Manager's Role

Business managers know the policies and regulations governing receipts and expenditures related to the award, as well as who is responsible for the accounting procedures. As with immediate supervisors, we believe it is a good idea for the PI to meet with the business manager when it is known that the award will be received. Although some PIs prefer to make no plans until the award has actually been received, we believe that waiting can waste valuable start-up time. Arrangements for personnel, equipment, space renovation, and participant recruitment are just a few budget items that require considerable time to complete and can contribute to serious project delay. What PIs need to do is to start organizing the project work early without committing financial resources. A review of the application budget and budget justification with the business manager provides an opportunity to identify which tasks can be initiated early and to forestall problems down the road. Some budget categories cannot be modified, thus, these award restrictions need to be taken into account so that all available financial support is used.

Some funding sources permit expenditures to be made before an award is received, if the PI's organization agrees. The business manager can advise the PI about their organization's policy on preaward expenditures. Organizations that permit preaward expenditures take the risk of losing the funds should the award not be made. Finally, the business manager can provide general information about how the accounting system works. It is important that PIs have some idea of how bills for services and materials move through the system, which includes the authorization process, time lapse, and reimbursement procedures to project personnel when personal money is used for emergency purchases. If nothing else, PIs must be impressed with the need to allow the financial system to process requests; expectations for swift turnaround will not be met if the appropriate groundwork has not been laid or if the expectations are unreasonable for the system.

Most accounting requests arising from project funding are no different from the many other requests that the system regularly handles. However, some project requests might require special handling. The following are just a few situations that might be in this category. Discussing these situations with the business manager, as well as others that might be in this category, forestalls accounting nightmares during the project.

Personnel. There may be a need for short-term personnel, for personnel on an unusual schedule, or for project tasks that can be done at an hourly rate. The business manager can determine the cost of such personnel as compared with using regular position personnel. Sometimes the cost of having full-time personnel who might be fully engaged only 80% of time is less than hiring personnel from a different category.

Equipment. Equipment purchases or rentals may or may not be handled in a routine manner. For the business manager to be most helpful, the PI should have information about the equipment, vendors, hours of use, and possible alternatives to purchasing.

Space renovation. A PI planning to do space renovation must spend time with the business manager to learn the routes for paying the various kinds of bills associated with such a project. The more information the PI can provide to the business manager about the renovation (number of rooms, details of everything that needs to be done in each room) the more thorough will be the assessment of accounting needs.

Participant reimbursement. It is important that PIs establish a procedure for the reimbursement of project participants. The procedure used for participant incentives or payments must be designed to meet the accounting and project needs. For example, if the PI wants the reimbursement to represent appreciation for the participant's time and effort in the project, and encouragement for continued participation, it is not useful for the participant to receive it 6 months after the project has been completed.

Hospital charges. If a PI's project requires inpatient hospital care for participants, the associated costs must be determined as well as how they are calculated and billed. It is critical that the PI review all aspects of this kind of expense because of it potentially becoming very large very fast.

Accountant

The most important task is to establish the project account because no work can go forward until there is an account on which to draw funds. The processing of forms required to establish an account can consume more time than most PIs imagine. A delay in beginning the process can create significant bottlenecks later on. The accounting tasks are those directly related to project receipts and expenditures whether they be for salaries or purchase of regularly used items. Relevant to smooth project operation are the procedures for recording individual transactions, the data and authorizations required for transactions, the preferred timing of invoice submission, the appropriateness of a blanket purchase order, the procedures for requesting information about account status, the accounting periods, the possibility of interim reports, and the usual presentation format.

A meeting with an accountant to discuss the accounting tasks provides an opportunity for the PI to learn about the scope of the tasks as well as to forewarn the accountant of the potential work volume. Some projects require minimal accounting because the major costs are personnel costs and regularly occurring supply and other costs. Other projects are accounting intensive because they have daily or weekly receipts as well as multiple expenditures. Others are intensive because multiple purchases are made on a daily basis. Projects that provide food or other daily living items for participants are in this category. Sometimes during the project start-up phase the accounting process is unusually intensive because of the volume of daily purchases involved in establishing the project, but after the project is operational the volume becomes considerably less.

Discussing with the accountant the project and the expected pattern of purchases provides an opportunity for the PI and the accountant to establish work practices that lead to efficient use of funds and personnel. PIs who find the accounting practices cumbersome, intrusive, or time wasters can discuss these thoughts with the accountant. However, they should remember that accountants do not usually establish the practices and are not obligated to tailor the system to the PI's particular needs. Sometimes they can find ways to manage the system that mesh better with the PI's project, and they are happy to cooperate with PIs who try to understand the accounting dilemmas and are attempting to develop project systems that can efficiently mesh with basic accounting systems. PIs on a tight budget might consider regular weekly or biweekly account review sessions.

Build Relationships With Data Collection Intermediaries

Projects that rely on other organizations, departments, or units for accessing their participants need to establish procedures for this activity to run smoothly. It is advantageous to begin this early in the project permitting sufficient time to develop them and to do dry runs to identify and correct problems before the project is initiated. Even if pilot data were collected with the assistance of these organizations, and a procedure established, a PI must verify that they will be working with the same individuals (or that replacements understand the role required) and that the procedures are acceptable and as efficient as possible. With this understanding, there should be no inadvertent biasing with respect to potential participant availability other than that specified in the inclusion and exclusion criteria. Whether a new system is going to be initiated or an old system reviewed, the PI should request that a dry run be implemented, and he or she should carefully review each component of the process.

Learn About Personnel Policies

An understanding of regulations and procedures used by those responsible for human resources is required if PIs plan to employ staff. In the personnel area, as in other project areas, tasks that involve administrative activities take time. For example, if the creation of a new personnel position is necessary, the equal opportunity regulations requiring advertising the position for several weeks before filling it must be followed. Organizations may also have internal personnel policies such as initially advertising new positions within a unit or department before advertising more broadly within the organization, and only after not filling the position from within are efforts made to hire from outside the organization. A variety of internal regulations and priorities might come into play for some kinds of projects.

Another issue is employee safety. The National Institutes of Health (NIH) has requirements about compliance of the PI's organization with various employee-related assurances, and other funding sources might have such requirements as well. PIs need to determine where their responsibilities begin and end in this arena. It is important that the PI take the time to ferret out the requirements related specifically to his or her work, the individuals involved, and the paperwork accompanying the requirements. For example, PIs might find dealing with hazardous material issues fairly easy because of the surrounding publicity. On the other hand, depending on the individuals involved, and the recent regulations imposed by government authorities, satisfying the requirements could be quite time-consuming.

Stay in Contact With the Sponsored Projects Office

During the application process, investigators may have interacted with the sponsored projects office preaward staff. After funding, PIs need to become acquainted with the postaward staff. The postaward staff works with the business managers and accountants of the PI's unit and can also answer questions PIs have about expenditures, encumbrances, and timeline of award payments.

Application renewal information is also available from the sponsored projects office. These materials for submitting the first year's renewal should be obtained early so plans can be made to have the necessary information available. Many funding sources send the renewal materials to the PI a month or so before the renewal date. However, for those submitting a renewal for the first time, obtaining materials earlier can be very beneficial.

Collect Information on Project Materials Providers

Whatever the project's material needs, PIs need to investigate the service pathways and costs early. Because most PIs need to be cost conscious, time should be allowed to secure estimates from several providers, as well as information about their reliability, so that the best choice can be made to meet the project's ongoing needs in a timely manner.

Vendors

PIs should become familiar with the procedures used by vendors such as mode of delivery, time lag between ordering and delivery, warranty and replacement policies, and procedures for handling emergencies. Having information from several vendors and alternative sources of materials enables PIs to handle crises quickly and effectively.

Pharmacy

If the study requires pharmacy services, PIs need to visit the pharmacy to learn about its dispensing, record-keeping, and billing procedures. The dispensing procedures need to be scrutinized for vulnerability to error especially when study protocols afford unusual opportunities for error. In these cases, the standard procedures of a pharmacy may not meet the study requirements, and therefore, an arrangement needs to be made that satisfies both the pharmacy and the protocol requirements.

Hospital

PIs with projects that require inpatient or outpatient services need to make arrangements soon after receiving the award notice. This deflects any surprises in either services availability or cost at the time they are needed and provides time to seek out alternative options when required. Although PIs may have discussed this service requirement during application development, these discussions were probably not considered to be agreements. Also, it cannot be assumed that the hospital has not experienced personnel and policy changes.

Catering Services

Projects that require regular meals for their participants or special meals, if not to be jeopardized, must select a reliable catering service able to fill the specified dietary requirements. PIs cannot assume that because a business provides meals it can also accurately meet specific food or nutrient requests on either a regular or a sporadic basis.

Initiate Space and Technology Discussions

Space Renovation

Space renovation is probably one of the most difficult ventures associated with a funded project. The kinds and number of activities depend on the type of renovation and whether a room or a building is the target. We recommend that PIs approach renovation with the same attitude about detail and accuracy that they approach their science. Seek advice and information from an immediate supervisor, a business manager, and others who have had experience with kinds of decisions and activities associated with a renovation project. In our opinion, PIs need to oversee all aspects of the renovation, record all expenditures, log work completion dates, and assess the quality of completed work. The PI also must be prepared to be a troubleshooter and must, therefore, learn the areas of responsibility within which he or she can make decisions and which need to be referred to other organizational staff.

Space and Technology Sharing

The success a PI has with space sharing depends somewhat on the rigor of the agreement with the space owner, and on the reliability of those collecting data and their sensitivity to space-sharing issues. A formal agreement is perhaps not necessary, but it is our opinion that the requirements and use schedule should be outlined and perhaps posted so that all project personnel know about the arrangements. A vital aspect of technology sharing, not to be overlooked, is the cost of running the equipment, supplies, maintenance agreements, repair, and replacement.

The agreement needs to be jointly written by the space owner and the space lessor so that all items critical to each party are covered, and both parties understand the agreement. Written language is prone to ambiguity and it is best that the agreement represents as accurately as possible the understanding of each party. A indispensable aspect of this agreement is space security. Arrangements for securing or sharing keys must be specified and procedures for locking doors and cabinets outlined and procedures for monitoring security developed.

Learn About Parking and Transportation Policies

Parking. Parking arrangements must be made for project personnel and participants. Arrangements for personnel parking are usually not difficult, because organizational parking regulations will apply. For personnel requiring additional security measures because of their shift, the transportation unit can provide information about their safety policies. Most organizations now have standard procedures to ensure the safety of personnel en route to and from their vehicles. If participants require parking space, arrangements need to be timed to be in place when participants begin arriving. In addition, parking space availability for some participants requires special consideration, for example, elderly or handicapped persons. PIs in these instances need to learn the process for obtaining "special" parking permission. This is an example of a task that needs to be begun early so that arrangements are complete and operational by the time data collection begins.

Transportation. Multiple-site data collection and in-home data collection require transportation for data collection activities. The budget allowance for these costs is usually the determinant of the kind of arrangements used. PIs need to explore using their organization's transportation, personal transportation (and charging a mileage fee to the budget), and public transportation (charging the fare to the budget). If PIs elect to use their organization's transportation, they must contact the appropriate unit and determine the rules, regulations, and fees. Outline, in detail, the project's transportation needs so that the best and most cost-effective arrangements can be made.

Develop Computer Resources

Computer needs are ubiquitous, but computer resources are not. Assessment of the availability of computer resources needs to be done after space decisions have been made, and necessary procurement initiated soon after funding. Even though these resources are vital for most scientific work, they are usually not provided without cost to investigators. We have experienced a wide-ranging time lag from order placement to delivery whether the item was an ethernet port or a desktop computer.

Continue Relationships With Funding Source Contacts

Program Officer

The PI's funding source contact, for example, the program officer, is a resource for information about the PI's rights and responsibilities. The relationship with this person that might have begun during the application process should be continued after funding. During the second-to-last project year, discussions might begin about the next project and how the current project's findings can be used to choose the topic and strengthen the application. The program officer can also be helpful to PIs with NIH funding who are making plans to submit an administrative supplement. Because most of these require that at least 2 years remain on the current project, discussions about this might begin during the first project year.

Monitors or Multisite Coordinators

Contracts, cooperative agreements, and other multisite projects are assessed on a regular basis to assure similarity of procedures and validity of data. Depending on the funding source and the project, these assessments may occur on an annual basis, on a quarterly basis, or on some other schedule that suits the project and the funding source. PIs know what kinds of material are required during these assessments and are given sufficient notice of the assessment to prepare them. Although these assessments can produce tension for PIs and among project staff, they should remain calm and respond to questions and requests for information in a professional manner. Any disagreements with the monitors or coordinators need to be discussed, not ignored. It is important that the PI understand the basis for any ratings, conclusions, or recommendations that are felt to be unsatisfactory.

Be Prepared for the Food and Drug Administration (FDA)

PIs with contracts for clinical drug trials might be visited by FDA auditors. If a PI is called by the FDA for an audit, he or she should immediately call the contracting company, because only about 2 weeks' notice is given. The FDA generally wants to see evidence that the study of interest is being conscientiously run and that the data are of highest integrity. The PI is responsible for study progress and the well-being of the study participants. When the PI delegates the day-to-day involvement with participants to other clinicians, their qualifications, and ability to fill all aspects of that role for the particular study, must be documented. Documentation will be reviewed for completeness, including screening records, and all records will be expected to be up-to-date and faultlessly kept.

Use Postaward Organizational Support

Fiscal Management

Information about the funding source regulations and PI responsibilities can be obtained from the organizational office that handles funded projects.

Procedures and policies regarding such items as expenditures, encumbrances, and year-end balance disposition can be discussed with staff in this office, and arrangements usually can be worked out that are in the best interest of the project.

Conflict of Interest

The NIH and the National Science Foundation have placed responsibility for conflict of interest issues with the universities. PIs who have not reviewed the conflict of interest potential of a project need to determine their organization's policies.

> Under the rules, investigators are required to disclose to an official(s) designated by the institution a listing of Significant Financial Interests (and those of his/her spouse and dependent children) that would reasonably appear to be affected by the research proposed for funding by the PHS. The institutional official(s) will review those disclosures and determine whether any of the reported financial interest could directly and significantly affect the design, conduct, or reporting of the research and, if so, the institution must, prior to any expenditure of awarded funds, report the existence of such conflicting interest to the PHS Awarding Component and act to protect PHS-funded research from bias due to the conflict of interest. (NIH, 1995c; see also Public Health Service, 1996)

Continue and Strengthen Relationships With Investigators

Coinvestigators

During the project development phases, the coinvestigators' level of interest is usually as high as that of the PI. After the application has been submitted, however, they, like the PI, go on to other projects. Unless the PI keeps in touch throughout the months between submission and final review, interest in the project can wane. The point at which this becomes a problem is when co-PIs or investigators become involved in new projects and no longer have time for the project when it is funded. To avoid this occurrence, especially with difficult to replace investigators, regular communication between the PI and investigators should be established. This keeps the project in the forefront for all involved, and it also reassures investigators that the PI still has an interest in the project.

Co-PIs and investigators should be notified immediately whenever the PI gets information about the project's funding potential. Investigators often are also PIs on projects and consequently have busy schedules, which may change between application submission and funding. PIs need to review with investigators their project role that was outlined in the application's budget justification as well as the percent effort to be devoted to the project. It is best to follow these application guidelines. However, if they cannot be followed because of changed circumstances, the PI and the investigators need to agree how the project tasks will be apportioned, and with the help of the business manager, agree on a distribution of the funds awarded. The partnership aspect of the project must be highlighted to maintain enthusiasm and interest in the project to its conclusion. If it appears that the expected rewards of project participation are not going to occur, investigators will be swayed to participate in other projects and will be less available.

The community of investigators that are candidates for participation in projects is often very small. It is in everyone's best interest to organize communication and project tasks in a thoughtful and professional manner. A PI who is thoughtful of others' time, and efficient in the use of time, will be seen as a good investigator with which to work, and opportunities for collaboration will continue to be available.

Other PIs

PIs with contracts, multisite projects, or cooperative agreements will probably be required to attend PI meetings during which project issues are discussed. These meetings are opportunities for PIs to meet other investigators in their area of interest and exchange theoretical and methodological ideas. Besides these kinds of formal opportunities, funded PIs often contact each other for discussions about managing projects or personnel as well as about study-related topics such as methods, design, and statistical analysis. It is in a PI's interest to encourage these kinds of discussions and to contribute experiences and ideas as appropriate.

Selecting Project Personnel

The pool of individuals from which project personnel are chosen is heterogeneous. Individuals can be men or women; range in age from 16 to 65; have degrees or be seeking degrees in fine arts, social sciences, physical sciences, biological sciences, statistics, or mathematics; and be full-time or part-time work seekers. Within any unit or department of the primary discipline, heterogeneity is certainly dampened. However, with the need for projects to be multidisciplinary ventures, a wide range of skills and perspectives is needed. The dilemma for the PI is to select the personnel that will best meet the project's needs without undue amounts of skill training, content teaching, and explaining of concepts to enable recognition of problems that might occur. A strategy for selecting employees with the best skills profile for the job needs to be developed so that the most important aspects of the particular position will be carried out, and others can be met after minimal training and education. In reality, all available candidates will probably need a considerable amount of training before they are up to speed on the project's requirements and proficient enough to work independently with only sporadic supervision.

Action Strategies

Take Into Account the Consequences of Being a "Funded PI"

Being a funded PI entails responsibility as well as career advantages. This chapter focused on meetings that PIs need to schedule in addition to other time-consuming activities. Our action strategies will continue in this vein. A consequence, however, that is often not considered is that after funding, PIs are viewed in a different professional light than before funding. What this means is that they are sought after to give presentations, to be coinvestigators, to be mentors, to do workshops, and for other activities for which their funding has highlighted their expertise. Although this kind of attention is certainly complimentary and can help further a PI's career, we would like to offer a word of caution. PIs must not let themselves be overwhelmed by consenting to all requests. Although PIs would certainly make significant contributions, they must devise a priority system so that the requests to which they accede do not jeopardize the project or their obligations to their immediate unit.

Enter All Important Project Dates in a Calendar

Funded PIs learn quickly that their calendar is a necessary tool to be used faithfully for project success. Most projects run on subgoals, that is, the number of participants recruited, the number that have been screened, the number on which data are complete, or the next meeting for which a poster will be prepared. Each of these can only be achieved if the necessary intervening steps have been completed. It is these steps that must be entered in a calendar so that the PI can do or delegate tasks as required. An often overlooked important task is writing and thinking. PIs need to schedule their writing and thinking time, or as with any other task not scheduled, it will not be done on schedule.

Meet With the Business Manager

Ask specific questions related to perceived project needs, such as participant reimbursement, blanket purchase order for emergency purchases, and time lapse between request and check cutting.

Do Not Get Caught Up in Red Tape

A brief glance at this chapter is enough to persuade anyone that managing a project is going to entail red tape. Each of the organizational units discussed has policies and procedures, which when adhered to enable the unit to do its tasks efficiently and effectively. Clearly, experience shows that everyone does not agree on what those procedures and policy should be. It is this disagreement that leads to them being called "red tape." It is our experience that only rarely can we influence these policies and procedures, and then only after concerted time and effort; attempting to do this while trying to secure services for a funded project is, in our opinion, not a good idea. We recommend avoiding entanglements in policies and procedures unless absolutely necessary, becoming acquainted with the various organizational units as soon as possible, and limiting the number of negative interactions due to short timelines and crisis situations.

PART

Funded! Welcome to the
Small Business World

CHAPTER **6**

Designing an Organization
for the Project

Projects supported by external funding are usually larger than those supported by in-house resources. Externally funded projects, therefore, require a principal investigator (PI) to develop an organizational approach that includes the project's functional components to ensure that data, their analyses, and conclusions reached are accurate. An integral part of this organization is the people. Sapienza (1995) suggests an organization with reasonable working conditions and a supportive environment in which staff believe they are contributing to a valued outcome, are fairly compensated, and expected to meet reasonable challenges is viewed positively by employees.

A good fit among personal competencies, job demands, and organizational characteristics produces an organization that runs smoothly and is resilient. This requires that a PI provides leadership and have an interpersonal style that promotes a pace for project activities adequate to meet standing and unexpected deadlines. It also requires that communication channels, and procedures for staff performance evaluation, motivation, and training, be tailored to meet project needs.

Identify Project Functional Components

The major functional components of most funded projects are similar to those of any study: (a) administrative, (b) data collection, (c) data analysis and interpretation, and (d) dissemination of results. It is within these major components that each project's uniqueness becomes apparent. Several functional components are usually needed for a project involving data collection from participants, extensive data collection procedures, and complex data management and analysis. The administrative component might include a project manager, a recruitment group, and a computer support group to oversee all computer needs as well as handling the administrative programming needs such as reports, or a personnel database. Data collection staff might include a database manager, data collection personnel, and a data entry clerk. The data analysis and interpretation component usually includes a data analyst and a statistical assistant. The dissemination component might include clerical staff, a writer, content area professional staff, and investigators.

Table 6.1 presents selected project functions that require staffing and among which a communication system needs to be developed. This list is probably familiar to PIs if for no other reason than these kinds of activities were outlined in the application's project budget and budget justification. Although it is a familiar list, we are presenting it in a new light: as functional components of a project's organization. What can easily happen, because of a PI's familiarity with these activities, is that the project administration is perceived to be "similar to the work I ordinarily do." This can result in a PI not realizing the considerable impact that additional responsibilities inherent in a funded project will have on his or her day-to-day schedule. Plans must be made to facilitate smooth and efficient project operation.

Develop an Efficient Organizational Structure

Experienced investigators, using past models, might be able to quickly develop a project structure that encompasses all the project functions. New investigators probably arrive at the best structure by reviewing the project procedures, proposed budget, and budget justification. It is possible that when these materials are reviewed, the structure will be self-evident with functions and personnel clearly aligned. However, PIs might also decide that the proposed arrangement between the procedure requirements and the requested personnel is no longer viable.

In our opinion, two aspects of project structure are key to its successful completion. One aspect is that PIs must be comfortable with the project's organizational structure. If they are not, it will not be used with a possible outcome of turbulence among the project staff. As a consequence, PIs will begin to experience longer and longer days. The second aspect is that it must incorporate the project functions efficiently. Inefficiency is usually costly, and as a rule projects have tight budgets. For example, a different project structure should be used if a project includes significant recruitment because each participant is recruited individually, than if participants are recruited as groups, such as classes of students or the residents of a nursing home. If the recruitment process is simple and not labor intensive, it might be carried out by the project director or PI or by clerical staff under their direction. However, if it is complex it might require a coordinator and additional personnel. This is also an example of how an important function could be left to chance, or inadvertently be assigned a low priority, based on its size or location within the project's organizational structure. Note that the importance of function structure and size do not necessarily correspond. That is why we said "clerical staff under their direction." Clerical staff can be overwhelmed on any one day because of the variety of tasks they handle. On days, for example, when the telephone rings all day, clerical staff may not get to initializing or finalizing a recruitment arrangement, unless they have permission to give it priority over incoming calls.

Identify Necessary Personnel

Although all investigational projects include many of the functional components listed in Table 6.1, some projects do not require personnel other than the PI and part-time clerical support to complete the tasks. PIs, in this case, might believe that because they are going to be doing all the work, their usual work schedule and organizational plan will be adequate for project completion. It may be adequate. However, to ensure that recruitment proceeds at an acceptable pace, that data collection and entry do not lag, and that administrative reports are submitted on time, we suggest that PIs develop work and evaluation plans as if they were supervising other personnel. They will then have a check on their work performance even though their name would appear as the "manager" for each component. A top priority for PIs who decide to "wear all of the hats" is to develop a written work schedule that allows time for them to not only meet the funding source requirements but also to meet their own expectations for the data as a foundation for future projects and additional funding. In our opinion, vigilance must be exercised to keep the project work schedule protected from everyday demands, pressures, and new interests that can easily overrun the resolve to devote time to an ongoing project. A written schedule is a reminder to the PI of the project tasks, and it alerts others who might be inclined to usurp project time that the PI has project commitments.

Externally funded projects, however, usually require personnel. The characteristics of project staff and their duties are determined by the project's data collection methods, design, outcomes, and size. PIs need to be cautious about having more regular permanent personnel than are needed. Some

TABLE 6.1
Project Functions

A. Project administration
  1. Personnel
  2. Accounting
  3. Administrative and project supplies
  4. Word processing equipment and staff
  5. Housekeeping
B. Participants/subjects
  1. Human participants
    a. Recruitment
    b. Screening
    c. Monitoring
    d. Transportation
    e. Reimbursement
    f. Meals
    g. Pastime activities
  2. Animal subjects
    a. Vendor identification and purchasing
    b. Housing
    c. Daily care and maintenance
    d. Disposal
C. Data
  1. Data collection form development
  2. Data collection personnel
    a. One-on-one data collection

---

projects do not proceed at a steady pace, but wax and wane depending on a variety of issues, one of which is recruitment opportunities. PIs with such a project might find that employing part-time staff coinciding with project needs is efficient.

Attend to the Leadership Role

The PI of a funded project with project staff is not only the intellectual leader but also the manager, or what is commonly called the boss. To meet the project goals, and fulfill the promise to the funding source, a PI must exert leadership, as well as employ, train, and guide project staff in the required tasks. The responsibility for the successful completion of these tasks belongs to the PI, and the project staff are his or her responsibility. We have noticed that many PIs do not think of themselves as bosses, probably because of the autocratic, domineering stereotype that is associated with the role, and therefore do not realize the extent of their leadership responsibility.

TABLE 6.1
Continued

---

    b. Intervention leaders
  3. Data collection instruments (paper)
    a. Purchase
    b. Photocopying
    c. Design
    d. Master copy storage/maintenance
  4. Data collection equipment
    a. Identification of location and availability schedule
    b. Identification of vendor and purchase
    c. Maintenance (daily or agreement)
  5. Database design
  6. Data entry
  7. Software development for entry, storage, and backup
  8. Design backup procedures
  9. Storage arrangements for original data.
D. Data analysis
  1. Preliminary scan for accuracy and completeness
  2. Data analysis
  3. Results interpretation
E. Results dissemination
  1. Report results to sponsor
  2. Write journal articles
  3. Present papers at professional meetings

Zenger, Musselwhite, Hurson, and Perrin (1994) discuss several leadership styles that PIs can use. The traditional leadership style is the familiar *hierarchical structure* with team members performing technical tasks and relating to the leader one-on-one for problem solving and organizational communication. The leader develops solutions for problems, makes most decisions, and directs the project activities. Another structure is that of the leader as a *coordinator.* This is similar to the hierarchical structure because team members communicate on a one-to-one basis with the leader, but differs in that team members also communicate with each other, and project decisions, although made by the coordinator, are made in light of information from team members. A leader who chooses to lead with *collaboration* shares responsibility for decision making, planning, problem solving, and coordinating with others on the team. In this instance, the leader may spend less time on the day-to-day activities and more time on the broader organizational influences on the team and its successful performance. The *empowering leadership* role is used when the leader delegates responsibility for day-to-day decisions and activities and has a minor role in project tasks. Although still accountable for the team performance, the leader engages in activities related to the relationship between the team and the larger organization, removing barriers and securing resources required by the team for successful performance.

We find that PIs choose their management approach based on the project, their usual leadership style, and personality. If the project is large enough to require a project or study director, supervisory responsibilities are often with that position. The PI directly supervises the project director, provides leadership for project direction, and carries out administrative responsibilities associated with the project (the empowering leadership role). This model seems to work well, especially when there is frequent and clear communication between the PI and the project director, and when the project director develops job descriptions and clear expectations for the project staff.

Another option, whatever the project size, is to adopt a collegial interaction pattern. Within this approach, project staff are encouraged to be independent to pursue activities within their assigned area of work, and they are expected to need little if any direction. This model works fairly well when the project goals and the operational definitions for goal achievement are well defined and most of the staff are experienced in the area of the investigation, have previously worked on projects, and have a limited desire to build their own empire. If these conditions do not apply, particularly when the project staff include inexperienced personnel or there is a need for nonprofessional staff who are accustomed to working under direct supervision, this model can produce a work environment that is more turbulent. The turbulence arises when project staff are uncertain about job descriptions and the associated ambiguity of how their job performance is being evaluated.

Most PIs have some experience with directing the work of others, and some with administrative responsibilities. We believe it is a mistake to translate either of these approaches directly into the project organization. Funded projects usually include people who have different reasons for being part of the project. For example, graduate students and classified employees do the same work, but their motivation is different, and that difference should not be overlooked particularly when assigning tasks with uncertain durations. Career aspirations of professional staff may differ from the investigators', and therefore they may not be motivated by the same things. In addition to the heterogeneity in project personnel, procedures may require that daily work hours be irregular, that work days be irregular across weeks, and that work weeks be irregular across months. Consequently, the PI may not have contact with all project personnel each day, but must, nevertheless, have information on the project's progress. For these and other reasons, PIs probably cannot replicate a small business' or departmental organizational structure. However, we believe that PIs might find some of the basic guidelines suggested in the management literature worthy of their consideration (see action strategies at the end of this chapter). These suggestions can be a resource for developing ideas about style and activities that will enable PIs to enjoy their project and their relationships with project personnel as well as to ensure unquestionable outcomes.

Exhibit Leadership Characteristics

Reimold (1984) has seven suggestions for being a successful leader that we believe are useful for the PI to consider:

1. Develop professional expertise
2. Sharpen your communication skills
3. Cultivate enthusiasm
4. Respect your staff
5. Keep an open mind
6. Pay attention to accomplishment
7. Be accessible to your staff. (p. 29)

We will discuss each of these as we believe it applies to a funded project organization.

Develop Professional Expertise: Know What Is Being Done and How It Is Being Done

In the past, PIs were often capable of carrying out most project tasks themselves, but in this era of multidiscipline, multimethod, high-tech methodology projects, this is less likely to be the case. However, according to Reimold, it is not necessary for successful leaders to be technical experts, or be able to do the work themselves. What is required is that they know (a) what each employee is doing, (b) how she or he is doing it, (c) what results are expected, and (d) what major problems may arise. We would like to add that an ideal situation is one in which this information is available on a weekly or biweekly basis depending on the project phase and work flow. We believe that this knowledge enables a PI to spot indicators that forecast problems and deflect them. It also provides a check on how closely instructions are being followed and whether the expected outcome occurs. When the outcome expected by the PI does not occur, instructions need to be revisited and the interaction between the instructions and the project staff reviewed to determine where adjustments are needed.

Sharpen Your Communication Skills

Most PIs have at one time or another honed particular communication skills. In general, these areas include writing, speaking, listening, and seeing, which are important to project success. However, speaking, listening, and seeing are particularly important because of project complexity. A small lapse of attention in the middle of a procedural instruction can lead to the loss of weeks of collected data. A lapse of attention by staff can probably be eliminated by more skillful instructional communication. Project personnel often come from a variety of settings, and in each of these settings communication patterns and styles had become familiar and communication fidelity was high. In a new setting, the communication patterns and style may or may not be the same. PIs will be most effective in their communication with project personnel if they assume, for the first several weeks of the project, that they are more likely to be misunderstood, and to take nothing for granted. In addition, whenever possible, providing a hard copy of instructions as well as an oral presentation can aid understanding and memory.

Meetings

One example of something that might be taken for granted by PIs is that project meetings are interactive. That is, even though the PI chairs the meeting, he or she expect project personnel to make contributions to the discussion as they deem appropriate. Project personnel may not agree with the PI that the meetings are interactive, that is, the discussions are mutual and simultaneous rather than alternating—more like conversations than lectures. According to a discussion in Brand's *The Media Lab* (1987), a key feature of interaction is interruptibility. Some people, even though they do not object to being interrupted, have a presentation style that makes interruption nearly impossible. One thought follows quickly on the next, and a full stop in the conversation is never used. This presentation style takes on many characteristics of a lecture, which in general are not interruptible. To be interactive, the presentation must allow for frequent interruptions, at logical points, and at unplanned points. The speaker certainly would finish his or her word, might finish the sentence, and might finish the thought, but would definitely not go on longer. There is a risk in allowing this pattern of interruption. If the presenter has decided what is going to be said, and does not want the discussion to go in any other direction, either the comment is ignored, and the presenter picks up where he or she left off, or an explanation of why the direction is not being taken must be given. Whatever the choice, a distraction has occurred, and depending on the resolution of the interruption, project personnel will form opinions about whether the meetings are lectures or interactive discussions in which they can participate.

Rather than give a false impression about the interactive level of meetings, PIs probably should select a style suitable for each meeting's agenda.
Another option is to blend the lecture and interactive styles. Perhaps PIs
choose to have meetings that they control more tightly but would like some
interaction. This combination allows the opinions and ideas of the project
staff to be heard, but at specified times during the meeting. For example, the statement that questions and comments should be held until the
end of the presentation blends a conversational style with a lecture style. This
style also assures that the comments are considered in view of what was
presented, rather than the presentation changing direction as a reaction to
comments.

One-on-One Communication

We believe that a good definition of communication is supplied by
Reimold (1984), when she says that "the intended message is the one the
listener hears" (p. 20). Investigators are generally aware of the many barriers
to communication when designing instructions to their study participants, but
often do not carry over the same diligence when communicating with project
staff.

The behavioral aspects of communication interference include a speaker's
tone of voice, choice of words, and facial expression. For example, it can be
difficult to conceal impatience, tiredness, boredom, or frustration with the
world if not with the person to whom we are speaking. Unfortunately, the
listener does not know if they, or others, are at the root of the perceived
negative mood. It is particularly difficult for new employees to overlook these
behaviors when they are perceived in their supervisor. Misunderstandings
resulting from these situations are usually short lived when neither the
supervisor nor new employees leap to conclusions. However, employees can
become increasingly dissatisfied if they are routinely unable to discern that
they are not the source of their supervisor's negative mood.

Expectations about how sentences will end or thoughts will be completed
are also a common communication barrier. This barrier leads to selective
listening or not listening at all. Relying on expectations, rather than attending
to what is said, can have adverse consequences for the PI and the project staff.
A PI needs to be aware of this and take responsibility for detecting miscommunication by repeating material and asking questions and by being receptive
to questions when giving instructions or discussing project procedures and
ideas. This fosters an environment in which interaction can occur and miscommunication can be minimized.

Sometimes, in spite of best efforts, communication fails. Before this is
viewed as a personnel problem rather than a communication problem, consideration should be given to the PI's communication style. Communication

styles are often not conscious. The ways we ask questions, respond to questions, and express our wishes, unless purposefully analyzed and changed, are generally a function of our environmental, social, and employment experiences. People from different countries and different regions, as well as men and women, might have expression styles that do not produce predictable responses. Being in the age of a global community does not mean that we are in the age of a homogenized community. It is very likely that any group of people, even professionals within a particular discipline, is not homogeneous with respect to gender, region or country of birth, and culture. Therefore, it is risky to assume that styles of expression are common and not consider the possibility of miscommunication. Remember, it is the message received and understood that counts. Some insights into the different conversational styles of men and women are presented by Tannen (1994) in *Talking From 9 to 5*.

Bobbert (1992) recounts an incident that occurred shortly after he arrived in Kentucky. He requested a secretary to type a letter for him. She said, "I don't care to!" He typed the letter himself and was irritated with her. Only later did he learn that what she had meant was, "I don't mind doing it." Another kind of miscommunication is related to style—either direct or indirect as discussed by Tannen (1994) in her chapter "Why Don't You Say What You Mean?" An indirect style of making a request could be, "It might be a good idea if you think about helping Helen with recataloging the books tomorrow." Individuals accustomed to a direct communication style would think about helping Helen and either help her or not help her depending on their conclusion. Individuals accustomed to an indirect communication style would understand this request to be a direct order to help Helen. Either communication style is acceptable as long as everyone understands the style and can interpret it correctly. The longer a group works together, the better they become at high-fidelity communication. However, at the outset of a project many people are strangers, and during the course of a project personnel turnover can occur on a regular basis. This situation places the burden of communicating on those who are in leadership roles.

Initial communication is important. PIs often bring together people who have experience with the project procedures and interest in the content of the project, or whose backgrounds make them good candidates for developing expertise and interest quickly. Nevertheless, most new personnel have a lot to learn before they can become comfortable in their project position. To minimize the effect of their newness on the project and its operation, new personnel place a high priority on "fitting in," and most of the time they are successful. PIs need to remember that new personnel do not know everything they need to know, and new staff may not fully understand everything that goes on around them, whatever appearance they give. Brand (1987) labels what new employees might experience as "boggle": "Too much coming too fast to sort out. Too many named new things" (p. 15). Therefore, frequent and careful communication with project staff is particularly necessary during the early project stages, whenever a new phase is starting up, and with whoever is new to the project.

Cultivate Enthusiasm

Enthusiasm is contagious and promotes an environment in which good humor can thrive. Data collection, data entry, reliability checks, and other data-related activities are repeated with each participant. With large sample sizes, these tasks can become tedious and sight of the larger goal lost in the daily humdrum. A PI's enthusiasm and interest in daily project activities can help those engaged in tedious or difficult tasks appreciate the importance of each piece of the project to the larger picture. There are also times when projects do not proceed as expected or as desired. During these times, PIs and project personnel work very hard to modify procedures, find new personnel, search for new resources, and/or develop new software or instrumentation. These times can be perceived simply as tough, brain-draining, energy-sapping times during which everyone does what must be done, or they can be perceived as challenging times in which everyone is given an opportunity to push the creativity edge out a little more, celebrate the successes, and support one another in attempts that may or may not hold the answers. A good psychological work environment is as important to maintain as the physical environment with appropriate furniture and reliable equipment. The enthusiasm of PIs for their work and the project in particular has a direct positive influence on the morale of the group. Examples of other things that contribute to a group's high morale fall under Reimold's (1984) category of "respect your staff."

Respect Project Staff

Because projects have a relatively short life, 1 to 5 years, and because there often is no opportunity for promotion within the project, it is important that each individual understands that he or she is valued as a person and as a worker and that this is communicated by PIs on the first meeting with project personnel—essentially, when they are hired. In our opinion, organizations with policies that can take into account individual staff needs will be less turbulent and experience less turnover. The work concentration of projects, and the accountability of PIs to funding sources, generally mandates that each person fulfills the assigned tasks according to the project protocol. Thus, guidelines for work expectations need to be clearly delineated so project staff can be comfortable with their work and with the hours they work and have a predictable schedule. A broad guideline of "we work until the work is finished" is not adequate for obvious reasons. Project personnel have personal emergencies, or times of the year may be personally stressful for them (i.e., exams, children starting school, holiday times), and efforts to accommodate needs during these times are appreciated. In addition, when people realistically can make plans, the need for emergency measures can be reduced. PIs who can be flexible and equitable with their project staff, given the constraints placed on them by project demands, will be able to complete the project successfully.

PIs can fail to understand their employees' perspectives because of their own and the place of the project in their lives. PIs are engaged in the project because it is part of their life work and their careers, and it embodies much that they enjoy. It does not occur to them that some project personnel may be interested in doing an excellent job, sharpening job skills, and possibly even promotion, but still not be interested in the project as a career or the subject matter as their life work. It is important that PIs understand that many project positions are filled with this kind of employee and that they remember that project personnel have lives that are unrelated to the project. Careful consideration must be given to job descriptions and prospective personnel informed about the conditions under which they will be working. If PIs expect staff to cancel the remainder of their lives for the duration of the project, this needs to be stated at the time of employment.

It is difficult for many PIs to accept that they are project leaders and ultimately responsible for the complexion and characteristics of their project organization just as they are for integrity of the data, data analysis, and conclusions. A PI is not absolved from these responsibilities. Sometimes, rather than adopting the role of boss, PIs develop a paternalistic leadership style, which in our opinion, can lead to complications. Within their leadership role, PIs cannot be counselors and mentors for their project staff because there can be a conflict between what is best for the project and what is best for the individual's overall life goals. A PI might want to wear a mentor or counselor hat for some project staff, but this cannot be done within the context of the project, and a PI must be vigilant about letting the staff's personal long-term goals influence their duties, promotions, and monetary increases while working on the project.

Keep an Open Mind

Encourage project personnel to keep open but disciplined minds about their areas of expertise! Soliciting ideas on all project activities and tasks from all project personnel might be productive, but we believe that it can be a false perception. The issues that come into play when this arrangement is adopted are related to timing—how much time is available for a particular topic, procedure, or decision, and experience or expertise of the project personnel. We believe that the best interests of PIs and their project personnel are served by matching the experience and expertise of the group with the task. Including individuals in discussions, because they are part of the project, but for which they do not have the background or experience, can be a waste of time and can undermine morale.

Project PIs are inherently curious individuals and most of the time are comfortable with listening to a wide range of ideas and even suggestions and criticism directed at their work. Directing a project can be difficult because it requires rigid adherence to data collection procedures, and concomitantly developing a good working relationship and environment, which generally requires flexibility. To accomplish both of these requirements, PIs need to clearly identify the areas in which flexibility is not possible and areas in which flexibility is an option and then keep an open mind about suggestions concerning both of these areas. Many quantitative data collection procedures have little flexibility once they are established. Suggestions, however, about how they might be improved can be noted for future projects. If the project group is involved in determining procedures, their suggestions can be considered and incorporated as appropriate. Being open minded about suggestions directed at the project and its conduct can nurture morale and encourages project personnel to have an interest in the project's success.

However, PIs need to be cautious about encouraging all project personnel to be involved in decisions, design, and procedure development for the project. The PI, as a leader, must develop ways to maintain the focus of the project personnel and must not convey that anything takes precedence over their project tasks. Thus, it is important for PIs to be open minded, as they set boundaries for acceptable behavior, and encourage project personnel to cultivate a disciplined open-minded stance when they have suggestions. Suggested modifications to procedures, instruments, and work flow might be kept in a project log to ensure that none of the project personnel's ideas are lost.

Attend to Organizational Communication

Being attentive to suggestions regarding personnel issues is critical, especially for PIs who are managing their first project. PIs have been project personnel and have models from which to develop their own organizational scheme. However, what seems to work on paper does not always work in practice. Although some PIs have a repugnance for what can be called a chain of command, it is difficult to avoid. Today, the most popular organizational structure is flat. This is probably the structure that many PIs believe they have established, and therefore they also believe that they know what is going on within their project organization. Nevertheless, an attentive attitude, and a willingness to listen to project personnel about how the system works, especially in the early phases of a project, is key to developing a system that will work for the project, whatever its label. Here again, there are boundaries that need to be adhered to until they are perceived to be unreasonable.

Pay Attention to Accomplishments

An important aspect of positive project morale is the individuals' perceptions that they are making a contribution and are valued. Continued employment is a common indicator, but most people like a broader range of feedback about their performance. How the feedback is given depends on the PI. In an organization where employee evaluations are required on an annual or semiannual basis, employees get feedback about their performance over the specified period of time. For most, this is sufficient, and it has the advantages of being more macro- than microscopic. The small failings that everyone seems to experience are forgotten or seen as inconsequential in view of total accomplishments. On the other hand, this means that small successes are also forgotten.

An effort should be made to discuss important small successes during evaluations so they are not forgotten. Nonrecognition of apparently small successes can fuel employee discontent. Unfortunately, PIs are faced with the dilemma of identifying what the employee perceives as "small" and how that matches with what the PI perceives as "small." In this area of employer-employee relations, there are going to be errors until the PI becomes familiar with the project staff, with their individual work styles, and with their expectations of themselves and the PI.

Be Accessible to Project Staff

The extent to which a PI is accessible to project staff is largely dependent on the kind and scope of the project. Each project places different kinds of demands on the PI and on project personnel. No formula can be offered about how to regulate accessibility. PIs must communicate with all project staff and assure their availability in emergency situations. PIs must be available in the early stages of a new project and be patient with nonemergencies until ground rules are understood. PIs also must be visible to the project personnel. PIs who are never seen where the work is being done (data collected, data entered, work and participant schedules being developed) can be viewed as uninterested in both the project personnel and in the data. This perception puts data integrity at risk and makes retaining personnel difficult.

Project Implementation

Have an Orientation Meeting

Before beginning the project, an orientation meeting should focus on staff objectives. A copy of the project proposal helps overview the science and project-specific aims, but not necessarily the objectives for individuals and the group. It is important that the PI clarify staff objectives. These can include lab development, participant recruitment, data collection, data analysis, reports, articles, and presentations. Attainable objectives need to be set (e.g., 10 participants enrolled in the study within a 2-month period, or one article submitted for publication within 24 months after beginning the project).

The working schedules of the different personnel should also be discussed. If staff are working by the hour, they expect to be paid for the hours they work. If they cannot be paid for hours over 37 ½ or 40 hours a week but are allowed compensatory time, this should be stated. If there is a limit on the accumulated hours of compensatory time, this should be stated also. There are few hourly waged staff who are interested in donating large amounts of time. If this is an expectation, that should be discussed at the outset and people can than choose to stay or seek other employment. Staff who have no interest in donating time but remain with the project are likely to be disgruntled employees and the project will suffer in the long run. There should be a system for keeping track of hours worked, whether or not the official time sheet reflects these hours. Some projects require 10-hour days during some phases and 4-hour days during other phases, or 3-day weeks for some phases and 7-day weeks in other phases. These kinds of irregularities should be discussed and the manner in which they are handled on time sheets made clear. Although these situations are irregular with respect to other positions, they can be a normal project schedule.

The availability of vacation and sick leave should also be discussed. Sometimes vacations can only be scheduled at certain times if a project is going to remain operational. Procedures for covering project tasks during vacation times must be in place for tasks that need regular attention. It cannot be assumed that the project staff will, among themselves, assume responsibility for this task. Developing a procedure not only assures the PI that project tasks will be done but also assures the funding source that project details are receiving sufficient attention.

Monitoring Project Flow

Operations

It is critical that research project personnel meet as a group periodically. The schedule of planned meetings should be available, and it should be made clear who is required to attend each meeting. At least one meeting a month should include all project personnel. If the project requires coordination among different groups, the strategy should be explained. As the project develops, it will become clear whether the strategy is effective. If it proves not to be, changes should be made as soon as a more effective strategy can be developed. Sometimes it seems that most days are spent in meetings. Be sure that meetings only include those who need to attend. Circulate agenda and minutes to all personnel to keep everyone informed. Keep in mind that meetings are time wasters only when that is what they do. If meetings are planned to accomplish objectives, are closely focused, and conclude when the work has been done, they are not really meetings, in the usual sense of the word, but work sessions. We believe it is important that this distinction be made so that project staff do not mistakenly expect to not accomplish work at meetings.

Project co-principal investigators, investigators, collaborators, and consultants also need to be invited to participate in project operations. This invitation should include what is expected at the meeting and what will be expected of project coinvestigators or collaborators. Co-PIs should be encouraged to attend all project meetings when project phases with which they are involved are under way. Their presence establishes them as integral to the project and enables project staff to learn how to interact with them so that project goals are efficiently achieved.

Coinvestigators

The PI, in most instances, must also remain in touch on a regular basis with co-PIs and coinvestigators. Depending on their project role, this could be weekly, monthly, or periodic telephone calls. The intensiveness of this communication is dictated by project requirements. However, even if frequent contact is not required, it is recommended that the PI meet periodically with all project collaborators and investigators. These meetings can be used to update everyone on the project status, ensure that all aspects of data collection are proceeding, and serve as discussions for publications or presentations.

Developing Ideas

An important aspect of research projects is the opportunities they provide for developing ideas and new projects. New studies can begin with the funded project or are more feasible because of the project's environment. Ideas for such studies, or pilot studies, are easily and efficiently explored when the PI and collaborators and coinvestigators work together. Because of vested interests in project resources, it is advantageous to everyone to extend those resources to their limits in terms of research data as well as for developing a scientific knowledge base.

Action Strategies

Actively Seek Information on Management Styles and Procedures

PIs often do not understand that receiving an award does not automatically endow them with administrative prowess. The reason they do not understand this is that no one talks about the administrative requirements associated with receiving an award. Assumptions are made that the PI "will handle it." The same assumption, for example, is not made when a faculty member becomes a department head. Universities regularly conduct retreats for new administrators assuming that being a faculty member and being an administrator require different information and skills. Businesses also do not promote individuals into administrative positions without training. In our opinion, PIs should take advantage of training opportunities provided by their organization. For example, while their project is being reviewed, they might be able to attend a new administrator's retreat. If they cannot be included in this group, they can request that a retreat be organized for prospective project PIs.

Bookstores are a good source of management information. In the management area as in most areas, there is a selection of "self-help" volumes. PIs can choose information that seems to best fit their personal preferences. However, PIs who prefer to work without supervision and with limited accountability need to understand that their employees probably cannot achieve the project goals within such a system. Their search for guidance should be among materials that minimize supervision, but offer specific guidelines for managing loosely organized employees.

Professional seminar groups offer seminars on management, for example, about the fundamentals of effective project management in which the attendee might gain the critical skills needed to complete a project on time, on target, and within budget. Also offered are seminars on managerial skills, such as assertiveness and working with difficult people. These seminars can be useful to PIs as well as to project directors.

Review the Funding Source Requirements for Organizational Structure

Organizational structure and written procedures are often viewed as ways of placing restrictions on the project and project personnel. However, many times the structure and procedures permit greater overall freedom and productivity because time is not consumed in repeatedly making the same decisions. Written manuals are helpful for procedures that can usually be effectively handled routinely. Routine structures and approaches should be established such as regular meetings, or monitoring. In the project's early stages, there may be some false starts in this area, and there may be omissions, but with vigilance and cooperation of the project staff, effective strategies can be developed.

Grants or contracts can have requirements for organizational units, either implicitly or explicitly. When projects involve the Food and Drug Administration, for example, there can be a requirement that adverse events be discussed at regularly scheduled times.

Maintain Communication With Coinvestigators, Collaborators, and Consultants

The easiest contacts to maintain are those that occur regularly because the project stage demands the attention of coinvestigators or collaborators. However, although a coinvestigator is "waiting in the wings" so to speak, PIs should try to maintain regular contact, even if it is only a brief monthly call. Consultants, who routinely are involved only sporadically, need to be informed of the project's stage, its progress, and the issues that are arising around the consultant's area of expertise. Memos or written project summaries should be sent to consultants and to coinvestigators so that when they are asked to solve a problem or express an expert opinion they have an information base available. In our opinion, it is advisable that PIs provide ongoing and complete information to consultants rather than providing only what they think they need to be effective.

Recognize Work Style Diversity

Project personnel usually have different backgrounds, interests, and educational histories. All of these come together in the way each individual thinks, behaves, and completes objectives. It is our experience that there is often more than one way to accomplish a particular task. Brenstein (1996) suggests that recognizing work style diversity and attempting to accommodate different styles can foster a calm work environment. However, when a procedure has implications for data, interpretation, and scientific theory, the procedure must be standardized. We also believe that procedures need to be standardized to reduce the stress of ambiguity arising from less predictable situations. However, whenever an individual's preferred work style can be accommodated, we find it best to do so. This accommodation not only improves everyone's work environment but also becomes a catalyst for developing more effective or efficient standard procedures.

chapter 7

Establishing Financial Procedures

Principal investigators (PIs) understandably are quite impatient while wait-ing for the formal notice of award. Not all PIs may be aware of the many administrative details to be completed before the project can officially begin. This chapter discusses selected administrative and financial issues that need to be initially resolved.

Learning to Track Expenditures

One of the first important administrative tasks a newly funded PI must do is secure a project account number. All expenditures to conduct the project must reference the project's account number. This means that the first contact a PI must make after receiving an award is a department or unit business manager so that the administrative process can be set in motion for securing an account number. Without special arrangements in place, expenditures usually will not be covered by the awarding organization if they are made prior to an award and/or before the PI's organization assigns an account number.

Although most PIs are part of a larger organization that has accountants or business managers to assist with managing project awards, PIs are not relieved of accountability. Accountants or business managers may be sophis-ticated or naive about management of a project award. Universities and other awardee organizations often provide in-service workshops for accounting staff working with funded accounts. In our opinion, PIs should learn all they can about managing project funds, because they are fully aware of the work to be performed. Workshops can be a good source of information about project accounting. This knowledge will enable PIs to work effectively with those who handle the project accounts, recognize irregularities, and contribute to corrections.

In our opinion, the PI can delegate day-to-day fiscal matters, but must keep abreast of the cash flow on at least a monthly basis. This is particularly important during the early stages of the project, when cost overruns can easily occur because it appears that there are sufficient funds for everything, and near the end of the project year, when it is important that all funds are either spent or encumbered so that they are not vulnerable for return to the funding source. For example, many times PIs on projects for which participant recruitment is required are too optimistic about the number of individuals they can completely process in the first year. A similar scenario can occur with animal subjects if the supplier is unable to provide the projected number of animals for a project year. Subject costs of this nature could be encumbered before the project's year ends.

The budget worksheet that was used to develop the project budget is a good source of information about the kinds of expenses covered by the award and the planned time of the expenditures. This worksheet should be reviewed, and a scheme developed for tracking each item listed. If that worksheet is not available, the guidelines presented under action strategies in this chapter can be used.

Determine Current Personnel Costs

The most straightforward budget item is personnel. However, even this can present problems if organizational salaries have been adjusted upward, and if project personnel categories are entitled to increases. Personnel costs include salaries and fringe benefits (employee-related expenses). For students or individuals employed less than half time, these rates are considerably lower than for regular employees. Rates can range from 3% to 25% depending on the organization's benefits package and the personnel category. What this means is that although the proposed budget met the project's personnel needs, personnel employed may cost more than the amount awarded specifically for personnel. If the award is not sufficient to cover costs, alternative strategies have to be initiated for completing the project. These strategies vary with the PI's organization as well as with the availability of other resources from departments or units. Accountants or business managers, knowledgeable about project awards, as well as the PI's immediate supervisor, can be resources in this situation. Ultimately, the PI must find the wherewithal to complete the project work.

PIs often use project grants to reduce their teaching or clinical responsibilities. What apparently happens is that PIs carry out project work and their colleagues are reimbursed for doing extra teaching or clinical work. As a rule, only those who do project work can be paid with the project funds. If it is possible for others to be paid from the salary savings resulting from the project award, a PI needs to understand the relevant procedures so they can request implementation. The ease with which these arrangements can be made varies from one organization to the next.

Project personnel costs can be high, sometimes accounting for more than half of the yearly budget. Because of this large proportion, coupled with funding source regulations and the unstructured nature of many projects, accounting for project personnel effort should be flawless. The standard accounting practice of Research I universities for project personnel is commonly referred to as *effort reporting*. We suggest that PIs obtain a copy of their organization's effort reporting and policy guidelines so that they can be knowledgeable participants in managing this important portion of the project budget.

Make No Assumptions About Equipment Expense

PIs may think they are not responsible for scientific equipment and that they do not have to be concerned about this category's restrictions. Equipment is defined by the federal government as anything costing at least $5,000 with a useful life of more than 1 year. This definition is used, unless the awardee organization's definition differs. Equipment can include computers, top-of-the-line printers, and selected lab equipment depending on the cost and the grantee organization's guidelines. According to the National Institutes of Health (NIH) guidelines, equipment includes such things as furnishings and movable equipment, but equipment such as cabinets, a fume hood, a large autoclave, or biological safety cabinets can be charged as an alteration and renovation expense. The cost of insuring equipment purchased with project funds is an allowable expense only if it is not normally considered to be part of the organization's indirect cost rate whatever the source of the funds. These NIH guidelines can be used to question other funding sources about their policies.

Since 1990, the federal government has allowed equipment to be purchased in the final 6 months of a project (NIH, 1995b). However, all equipment charges to a grant project must be allowable as a direct cost, be reasonable, and be necessary to conduct grant activities. It is suggested that PIs review their funding source's policies on when equipment purchases are no longer allowed with grant funds. Equipment carries financial implications because indirect costs are not calculated on equipment. PIs interested in keeping project costs down may prefer a high value in the equipment category; administrators may prefer a low value.

Selecting a Vendor

PIs may believe that equipment can be bought from whomever they wish and for whatever price is agreed on. However, organizational arrangements with vendors, and the prices deemed appropriate, must be honored. In the best-case scenario, an "approved" vendor has what a PI wants at the price the PI can pay. Sometimes it is necessary to obtain bids and sometimes the particular make and model desired by a PI cannot be bought because of policy considerations. NIH awards require, whenever possible, that only American-made items be bought. Notices of grant and fellowship award include a footnote, which contains the following: "Pursuant to the NIH Revitalization Act (P.L. 103-43, June 10, 1993), section 2004, when purchasing equipment or products under this assistance award, the recipient should, whenever possible, purchase only American-made items" (NIH, 1996a).

Be Prepared to Negotiate

PIs may also find that although the proposal included the most recent equipment, budget realities can produce something less. This can be a problem if the affordable equipment cannot provide the data accuracy and reliability required by the project. An item frequently omitted in proposal budgets, which is associated with the price of equipment, is maintenance agreements. These must be budgeted as soon as the factory warranty expires, usually during the second year of the project.

Because projects are often funded 9 months or a year after being submitted, it is possible that additional equipment could be needed to keep the project at the cutting edge of science. PIs deal with this problem in a variety of ways. The first choice, usually, is to negotiate sharing available equipment. If this is not an option, buying the equipment should be explored.

Controlling Supply Expenditures

Supplies usually include disposable items and other items that are routinely used. Although it is important to monitor supply purchases and their use, watching this category too closely can have a negative influence on the morale of project staff. Availability of paper, pens, lab supplies, and other things that are needed on a daily basis contributes to a sense that the project and the project team are prospering and succeeding in attaining project objectives. However, these expenses can quickly skyrocket if there is no monitoring system. PIs need to achieve a balance of cost awareness and staff requirements. Sometimes it is realistic to buy things at a lower price that serve everyone's needs just as well as a higher-priced item. Staff can often be helpful because they are the supply users and often have an interest in what vendors have available. Their interest stems from curiosity about items that can simplify their tasks and from a common distaste for paying "too much" because of rigid organizational procedures. Establishing a routine for ordering supplies and maintaining lists of needed supplies can minimize the occurrence of shortages and the increased expense that generally results. A system for paying for last-minute purchases should be developed. Petty cash systems can be used, as can asking project staff to pay and be reimbursed. One effective approach is to use a blanket purchase order that enables staff to buy small items as needed using the purchase order number.

Purchasing Priorities and Planning

Expenditures need to be routinely balanced with the annual grant or contract award to prevent overspending. The proposed budget indicates a timeline for purchasing equipment, supplies, and hiring personnel. During the proposal process, yearly activities were carefully laid out on a reasonable timeline. However, to blindly assume that the plan was also realistic could be an error. At the beginning of the first year, and on a regular basis thereafter, yearly plans as well as the need for phasing in and phasing out personnel must be reviewed. This should enable PIs and accountants to make the best use of funds and for developing plans for encumbering or spending to avoid losing unused project funds. The frequency of account and financial review required depends on the project's activity profile.

Monitoring Financial Balances

PIs often are not as comfortable with accounting system printouts as they are with scientific data sheets. Therefore, a PI might not comprehend the importance of monitoring the balances in each category of their project budget. There are several reasons for PIs to review balances on a periodic basis, but the most important is that it is the only way to know what resources are available. There may be instances when project staff authorize charges to the project account. Also, with more than one person authorizing expenditures, errors can be made in account numbers, account numbers can be omitted, or an item might be charged to the project account when an arrangement had been made to have it covered by another department or agency. Accounts must be carefully monitored so that such instances are discovered and entries corrected.

Obviously, it is in the PI's best interest to monitor project accounts and institute a system with which they are comfortable. Some PIs work directly with the accountant or business manager by reviewing each item within each category. The review by category is important because each project expenditure has a category code attached to it. PIs need to know the balance for each category because money that has been awarded in a particular category may or may not be restricted to that category. Because fund use is regulated and restricted by category, it is not sufficient for PIs to only review the bottom line. They should also review each category balance to get a complete picture of the project's financial status.

PIs can delegate this detailed review to a project director, and only review the final results with the project director. In some cases, accountants and business managers can be relied on to automatically update PIs about the status of their project accounts. This is a great help, especially for PIs who do not want to face this task. We recommend that PIs not rely solely on automatic monitoring of their account balances, nor on the judgment of an individual not associated with the project.

Expanded Authority

Many PIs have learned that effective October 1, 1994, NIH has revised its implementation of expanded authorities. This means that the awardee organization can make some fiscal and project decisions without obtaining approval from the funding source. PIs should note that it is "some" and not "all" decisions. It also does not include all awards. For example, based on the following criteria, certain awards may be excluded:

> Grants that require close project monitoring or technical assistance, e.g., clinical trials, exceptional grantees, or certain large multi-project grants, may be excluded.
>
> Grantees that have a consistent pattern of failure to adhere to appropriate reporting or notification deadlines, may be excluded.

In addition, some grants, for example, centers and training grants, do not automatically receive expanded authorities, in whole or in part, due to the routine requirement for close project monitoring or technical assistance. Cooperative agreements, because of substantial programmatic involvement, are usually excluded from expanded authorities (NIH, 1994b).

Cost Sharing

Budgets can include cost sharing when it is required or when a PI believes that the application will be more competitive if cost sharing is included. Cost sharing might include a percentage of investigator effort, a percentage of total funding source costs, or a dollar amount. When cost sharing is included in an application it becomes a legal obligation. In addition, the record keeping associated with cost sharing can be extensive, unless the organization's standard accounting practices include the cost-sharing information. If a PI has included cost sharing in the budget, he or she needs to review the cost-sharing policy and guidelines of the organization and arrange to meet the reporting requirements of the funding source.

Indirect Costs

Indirect costs are costs charged by the awardee organization to cover the related cost of supporting a project. Universities negotiate an indirect cost rate with the federal government. The indirect cost rate that funding sources are willing to pay varies from zero to standard federal government negotiated rates. In universities, generally, a portion of the indirect costs can be returned to the college and the college in turn returns a portion to the PI's department or unit. The portion returned may or may not depend on the rate received. For example, in some instances if a rate less than the negotiated rate is received, the rate returned may be less than if the full federally negotiated rate were received. The use of the indirect costs also varies.

PIs need to discuss indirect costs with their immediate supervisors so that they know their indirect cost return, and if it is available for use on the project or for related pilot projects. Although it is important for PIs to know about the policies and distribution of indirect costs, unless total budgets are very large, the amount is small. For example, in the case of a university with a 40% to 50% indirect cost rate, the PI's department might receive about 5% to 10% with the remainder being distributed to the university and the college. Again, even though the amounts may not be large, PIs should know about financial arrangements associated with their funded project.

Salary Savings

The disposition of the PI's and investigators' salaries covered by the award is also an aspect about which PIs and investigators need to be well informed. For example, in some instances the PI's department might have access to these funds, along with the financial resources usually available for salaries. This could be the case if the PI's or investigators' salaries are paid by other sources and they are not expected to earn their salaries. Thus, the full amount of salary savings could be returned to the PI's or investigators' unit, or a portion, for example, perhaps 10% is returned to the department and the remainder to the college. Generally, when a larger portion is returned to the department, it is expected that operating costs and/or other costs will be paid by the department. Again, PIs and investigators need to know how these funds are distributed to determine what rights they might have to some portion of the funds to support pilot projects or project-related activities.

Subcontracts

PIs on subcontracts and PIs who have subcontractors also need to be attentive to accounting procedures, and monitor expenditures on these project components. Subcontract accounting might be the responsibility of the parent grant. In this case, all receipts and expenditures are processed by the parent grant organization. It is the responsibility of the contractor to inform the funded organization about receipts and expenditures and to remain within the awarded budget. Subcontractors might also receive the awarded amount in installments. Subcontractors subsequently process receipts and expenditures and return unused funds to the parent grant organization at the end of the project year. Whatever the subcontract arrangement, subcontract PIs need to be aware of the award's fiscal responsibilities, like the parent grant PI, and PIs with a subcontractor need to monitor the receipts and expenditures of the subcontract as closely as they do those of the parent grant.

Grants, Contracts, and Gifts

Grants, contracts, and gifts are all a source of project funds but each has different accounting rules, regulations, policies, and customs.

Grants. Grants require detailed accounting, but the PIs and investigators can decide the project items for which funds are used. For example, if the investigators agree that a different procedure or a different measurement method would obtain an outcome superior to that described in the application, they can make that change. Or if a new vendor is located that is geographically closer or more reliable, the change can be made and project funds can be used for materials. However, there are boundaries that cannot be exceeded by PIs when making changes in projects supported by the federal government, which are noted in Chapter 5. In general, grant funds support a particular outcome and within limits a funding source is willing to let PIs determine how that is best achieved.

Funding sources require periodic accounting reports from grantees. Disposition of funds that are not spent or encumbered varies with the funding source. Some funding sources require that any positive balance at the end of a budget year be returned; others allow balances to be carried over from year to year, and a final accounting can require a returning any unspent funds. Whatever the funding source policies, PIs should know them and keep records to document the use and planned use of funds for each budget period. As a general rule, funds received are to be used for the project. Therefore, the PI does not want to be required to return funds early in the project and be left short in the final year.

Contracts. Contracts are the most restrictive awards in terms of required expenditures and associated accounting. In most instances, contractors agree to perform a service for a specified cost, and the funding source is interested only in receiving the agreed on product. A detailed accounting system for all production expenditures must be used to avoid cost overruns and to provide a record of the actual product cost. Any costs in excess of the contract agreement are the contractor's responsibility. On the other hand, excess funds might not need to be returned to the funding source. Because of the detail involved in contractual arrangements, we recommend that PIs review the business proposal with their contract officer and accountant to ensure that they recover all allowable funds and that they fully understand the terms of their contractual responsibilities.

Gifts. Gifts are the most flexible source of project funds. Gifts are generally made to investigators with little specificity about their use. An area of interest is usually indicated, such as the development of a registry, or the study of patient-physician communication by disease or disorder. However, they generally provide no detail about the procedures to be followed or outcomes expected. Gifts usually do not require regular reporting to the funding source, nor do they generally require an accounting for how the money is spent. Gifts also do not have indirect costs, thus enabling the full amount of the gift to be used by the investigators for their project. Although the funding source does not require accounting for the financial award, PIs nevertheless need to keep records for themselves and their organization of how the money is used. We recommend that the detail be the same for all projects. The final decision on the extent of detail is, of course, the PI's unit and organization's requirements.

Action Strategies

Review the Planned Project Expenditures

A review of the planned project expenditures can provide a guide for the kinds of accounting categories required by the project. The worksheet used to develop the application budget can be adapted for this purpose. The budget outline provided here, with modifications made for particular project and organizational needs, can also be used. The following suggested guidelines include instructions about application submission requirements. However, we think that completing all possible information will be most useful even for review purposes.

Budget Worksheet Guidelines

It is the PI's responsibility to determine yearly costs of each project item for all budget categories. Table 7.1 presents the major categories usually found in a research budget, and examples of the kinds of multipliers that might be used to arrive at the various line-item totals.

The following guidelines might be helpful in budget calculations.

Personnel

1. It is recommended that names be associated with each project role/activity.
2. Percent effort is determined by the activities associated with the role.
3. The value used for base salary depends on the project start date.
    a. If the project is to begin in the current fiscal year, it is the current salary or the maximum allowed by the funding source, whichever is less.
    b. If the project is to begin in the next fiscal year, it is the current salary plus increments expected in the new year (e.g., promotions) plus 4% of that sum, or the maximum allowed by the funding source, whichever is less.
4. Use an appropriate inflation factor. The federal government currently accepts an inflation factor no greater than 4%.
5. The salary-requested computations depend on the project year. If the project year coincides with the awardee organization's fiscal year, for example, July 1-June 30, the salary requested equals the product of the base salary and percent effort. If the project year crosses fiscal years, for example, October 1-September 30, calculate the requested amount for each of the years and sum them. For example, if the project year begins October 1, 9 months of the requested salary is based on the current year's salary and 3 months on the next year's salary (current year plus expected promotions plus 4% of that sum).
6. Fringe benefits or employee-related expenses vary by personnel category. Check with an accountant to ascertain the appropriate rate. Also, note that some organizations do not use overall rates, but calculate the sum of the applicable benefits, social security, retirement, health insurance, and so on. Some examples of employee categories that might apply are regular faculty, clinical faculty, regular classified, temporary employees, and student employees.

TABLE 7.1

Examples of Budget Categories and Multipliers

Category	Category
Personnel	Supplies
Name	Drugs
Project role	Name (bottle/capsule)
Percent effort	Dosage each time
Base salary	Times per day
Inflation factor	No. of days
Salary requested	No. of subjects per group
Fringe rate	No. of groups
Fringe amount	No. of dosage units
Total requested	Unit price
Consultant	Computer supplies
Name	Type
Organization	Unit price
No. of days/hours	Quantity
Daily/hourly fee	Item no.
Per diem	
Lodging	Travel
Air/mileage cost	Name
	No. of trips
Equipment	Location
Item	Airfare/gas mileage
Model no.	No. of days
Quantity	Per diem
Price	Lodging/night
Vendor	
	Patient care costs
Supplies	Inpatient
Data collection material	No. of patients
Unit price	No. of days
No. of subjects per group	Day cost
Times per subject	
No. of groups	Outpatient
	Pharmacy

7. The fringe benefits equal the product of the salary requested and the fringe benefit rate, or the sum of the amounts calculated for each of the fringe benefit items.

8. Total requested is the sum of salary requested and fringe benefit amount.

TABLE 7.1
Continued

Category	Category
Lab supply costs	Drug dispensing fee
Unit price	Times per patient
Times per assessment	No. of patients
No. of assessments	
No. of subjects per group	Other expenses
No. of groups	Lab work
Total no. of units	No. of subjects per group
	No. of groups
Shipping supplies	No. of tests per subject
Type of unit	Price per test
Unit price	
Units needed	Project communication
	Type of unit
Other expenses	Unit cost
Physical evaluation	No. of units
No. of subjects per group	
No. of groups	Maintenance agreement
No. of evaluations per subject	Equipment
Fee per evaluation	Cost per year
Fringe rate	
Total price per evaluation	Photocopying
	Type of material
Subject costs	No. of subjects per group
Costs per unit	No. of groups
No. of types per subject	No. of pages per type
No. of units per subject	No. of subjects per group
No. of groups	Price per page
Advertising	Publication costs
Price per ad	No. of pages
No. of ads	Cost per page
	Manuscript review fee

Consultant Costs

It is important to realistically estimate each of the cost categories to avert shortfalls. In our opinion, it is most appropriate to determine the number of days or hours required and the fee expected by the consultant during the project development phase, rather than estimating this cost.

Equipment

Ordering information for buying equipment must be obtained. If the purchase is going to be made in a later project year, an inflation factor must be part of the expected cost.

Supplies

Determine the unit price from a catalog or supplier when possible. If estimates are used, base them on information from previous years or similar products. Because determining some of these costs requires considerable time, it is recommended that the budget development process be begun as early as possible in the application development process. Final costs can be determined after the research procedures are finalized and the number of groups and number of participants per group have been established. The final budget must be matched against the procedures of the final application to ensure that all categories are sufficiently funded. In our opinion, research can be jeopardized in the face of monetary shortfalls, which are difficult if not impossible to cover.

Travel

Include as much exact information as possible. If estimates are used, base them on previous travel.

Patient Care Costs

Inpatient: Use exact inpatient charges. These data can be obtained by contacting hospital officials.

Outpatient: Use exact pharmacy and lab charges when available. In university settings, Schools of Pharmacy and laboratory facilities are a source for information about these charges.

Other Expenses

See instructions regarding supplies. Again, we recommend that these items be specifically identified along with detailed cost information.

Consult "Commonly Asked Questions About Equipment Under Grants"

For additional information about equipment, such as who owns it and what happens to it when a PI relocates, refer to NIH (1995b).

Keep on Top of the Paperwork!

Projects initiate a stream of paperwork that seems to be an endless flow of details about project expenditures. PIs must keep meticulous records of expenses and receipts, plan to start developing financial status reports several weeks before their due date, and work with the project accountant to simplify procedures that seem too complicated to get done on time.

PIs with federal funding should also be knowledgeable about the Office of Management and Budget circulars. We are not suggesting that detailed knowledge is required, but PIs should have sufficient knowledge of policy changes to form intelligent questions for those who have the details.

chapter 8

Selecting Project Personnel

When we are at work, taking vacations, or at home sick, the process for recording our activities and producing our paycheck is nearly invisible. Everyone seems to know how the system works and his or her part in it; it appears to require little attention. Like many apparently effortless systems, the personnel system runs smoothly only when a good deal of thought and effort go into preliminary considerations.

Managing a project means that the principal investigator (PI) must not only be conscientious about the project's science and its data but also about project personnel and the related data. The personnel system and data are often not familiar to PIs, but working with them requires the same thoughtfulness, care, and accuracy as project descriptions and information. This chapter focuses on the administrative aspects of project positions and acquiring personnel. Although this chapter is written from the perspective of the PI, it should be noted that potential employees have personal preferences and agendas. PIs should, therefore, be as thorough as possible in writing job descriptions and discussing job expectations with potential employees to minimize the number of inappropriate agreements and resultant employee turnover.

Developing Job Descriptions

Although the relationship is not usually recognized, job descriptions are important to the successful completion of a project. PIs are often in organizations with a personnel unit that oversees the organization's positions and their descriptions. Some of the positions have titles that suggest it would be effective to use them as project job descriptions. We recommend that PIs do not automatically use standard or general job classification descriptions as the basis for hiring. PIs might need to develop several job descriptions for a single position to meet both their requirements and their organization's requirements. The first of these must be a detailed description of each position's project-specific responsibilities. The description can be used to determine whether there is a match between the project-position description and one already used by the PI's organization or whether a new position needs to be developed. Creating a new position is time-consuming and requires close collaboration with the personnel unit so the final description meets the project's and the organization's needs. In addition, new positions might require approval at various organizational levels. If the project timeline requires that a position be filled within the first month of the project, these procedures can be a real barrier to project activities. To avoid delays of this nature, we suggest that the PI begin developing an organization chart and job descriptions as soon as there is encouraging information about funding. This places a PI in a position to begin advertising and hiring as soon as the award is received.

The words *job description* are deceptively simple because a job description is often perceived only as a list of an employee's activities. What is not apparent are the ties each activity has to (a) the annual award, (b) the project's organizational structure, and (c) the data collection environment. The positions proposed in the budget's personnel category were determined by the kinds of project staff and amount of effort perceived to be required at the time the application was developed. Depending on the experience of the PI and the extent of specificity about the project tasks, the proposed positions may or may not be congruent with what the PI regards as imperative to implement the project. After a project is funded the positions are no longer hypothetical; they are part of an organizational structure with specified supervisory, communication, and project responsibilities. The major determinants of the position's salary range are related to the inclusion of supervisory and fiscal responsibilities. In general, positions that include significant supervisory and/or financial responsibilities are at the higher end of the salary distribution. Keep in mind that along with salary, the project is also responsible for each employee's fringe benefits (employee-related expenses). Depending on the PI's organization, these could be a flat rate for all employees, a variable rate depending on the position classification, or calculated as the sum of benefits (i.e., Social Security, Medicare, hospitalization, retirement, life insurance), and can be as much as 25% of the base salary.

Developing and writing a job description is only possible after there is a detailed outline of the project's organizational structure and a flowchart of the project activities. The project activity flowchart should, in our opinion, be the master list of all basic activities. This chart with its sequencing of activities is a tool for grouping activities by type and sequential contingencies. The sequential contingencies will flag instances of particular tasks requiring more than one individual. The groups of activity types need to be reviewed to determine which of them can comprise a position. In our experience, a project organization chart can be used to determine the supervisory levels required, the positions that need to be responsible for financial aspects, and the positions that will interact with administrative officers of the PI's organization (i.e., chair/head, dean, vice president for research, CEO), the media, or the public (including community organizations and participant recruitment). The PI's organization may have a specific classification with an associated salary range for positions that have these kinds of responsibilities. At the outset, PIs should design positions that best meet the project's objectives, and they should include all required positions. The position descriptions, as well as the number of positions, may have to be modified, but these initial plans should represent the ideal staffing for the project's successful completion.

Each job description must meet at least two criteria: (a) It is reasonable to expect a single individual to have the skill, experience, and personal style demanded by the tasks; and (b) the salary associated with the tasks is affordable. An example of a job description that might not meet the first criterion is one that emphasizes technical tasks that are usually conducted with little interpersonal interaction and require concentration and long attention spans, but also includes a data collection task that requires empathetic and prolonged interaction with project participants. These tasks probably cannot be effectively done by the same person. Examples of job descriptions that cannot meet the second criterion are those that include supervision or financial responsibilities because of the high remuneration level associated with them. For the most part, project budgets require that these tasks be centralized in one position, even though the organization chart might clearly indicate the need for several positions of this nature. In this case, the organization chart should not be changed, but the same individual is expected to carry out both supervisory and fiscal responsibilities. This requires an individual with broad project experience and knowledge, often called a project director. With very limited budgets, the best person to fill this position is the PI. The project director position is vital and must be a top budget priority, if the PI cannot fill the role.

Use Established Advertising Procedures

The process of advertising for employees varies by organization. PIs need to discuss personnel needs with their immediate supervisor and follow the established procedures. Commonly, advertising begins with PIs announcing within their unit the availability of project positions. This is usually done by posting the position requirements in a prominent place for a few weeks. Following this posting, the personnel unit disseminates a position announcement. Again, preference is given, for a specified time, to individuals already employed within the organization. The time varies, but can be as long as 6 weeks. The position is then opened to those outside of the PI's organization, with first opportunities going to individuals who already have applications on file. If this pool does not yield an employee, advertisements are placed in newspapers. We strongly encourage PIs to ascertain the aspects of the personnel advertising for which they are responsible. For example, they may be responsible for writing the newspaper description and the costs, but not for placing advertisements. Although it is particularly critical for PIs to know if they are responsible for the advertising costs, the other aspects can require considerable time and effort. The equal opportunity employer regulations must be followed throughout this process.

During all phases, the advertisements provide minimal information about the position. The first phase of advertising, within the PI's unit, will probably inspire people with appropriate qualifications and expectations to apply, because specific position information is informally available. PIs must follow all organizational procedures, even for candidates from their unit. When a potential candidate stops by to "talk with the PI about the position," the PI must be alert to the consequences of the conversation and be ready to ask, "Do you wish to be a candidate for the position?" rather than unwittingly becoming involved in an "applicant" interview that is outside the proper procedures.

The second advertising phase produces candidates that are generally appropriate but might not be specifically qualified because established position descriptions are used by personnel to screen applicants. Even when a project-specific new position description is used, personnel staff usually interpret requirements broadly to provide PIs with the best possible candidate selection. Also, the personnel unit has an obligation to expedite placement of staff laid off because of rightsizing. Some of these people may be only marginally suited for the position, but if the personnel unit recommends them for an interview, a PI must agree to review the individuals' files and possibly interview them. Most PIs find the group of heterogeneous applicants responding to the general position description includes several candidates warranting an interview. The advantage for the PI in hiring someone from a second advertising phase is the individual's familiarity with the organization as a whole, as well as having an information and support network. These are important considerations in view of the bureaucratic complexity that provides support to projects.

The third advertising phase initially provides candidates who have been on file with the personnel unit because of their interest in working within the larger organization, and only when none of these is hired is the position publicly advertised and these respondents evaluated for the PI. Applicants' files must be reviewed, and appropriate candidates interviewed during all phases of advertising. Summaries of the PI's conclusions about the interviewed candidates can become part of the organization's personnel file, and they are subject to review by a human resources committee. It is during these interviews that a PI will most appreciate the effort expended in developing the detailed, project-specific position description.

Conducting the Interview

Before beginning interviews of position candidates, PIs should get interview and hiring guidelines from their personnel unit. There are some questions that cannot be asked of an applicant, even if the answers will have an important influence on a candidate's ability to fulfill the job requirements. A PI also should not rely on the personnel unit to send only candidates that are suited for the position. It is the PI who knows the kinds of individuals who will best be able to do the required tasks and work with the project group. Sometimes PIs interview candidates alone and sometimes other project staff are included. In this case, not only the PI but everyone that participates in the interview may need to complete a summary of their impressions and conclusions for the personnel unit.

Match Skills and Expertise to Tasks

Projects often include common tasks or procedures as well as some that are project specific. PIs must recognize which tasks are project specific and focus on these when reviewing skills of prospective employees. For example, if the project requires developing an interactive database, some but not all people with data entry skills, and general computer literacy, will be able to do the job. In this case, a PI should consider in greater detail the skills required to develop the project database. Regardless of the project environment, an individual who has experience in developing interactive databases probably can do it and do it quickly. An individual with project experience, data entry and data collection skills, and experience with spreadsheet and statistical program software probably could do it, but not as quickly. An individual with basic computer skills and data entry experience, with or without project experience, will probably have a difficult time.

In our experience, the most successful personnel selection is made when PIs (a) select personnel who have the skills to do the advertised job; (b) discuss the range of specific tasks that might be included under the phrase "to do anything that needs to be done"; and (c) discuss, within the project context, the meaning of the phrase "and anything else I am requested to do," which frequently occurs in employer-employee agreements. Whether or not PIs want to accept the responsibility, employees know that their livelihood is in the PI's hands and strive to do what is required to obtain satisfactory evaluations. It is not fair, therefore, for PIs to hire an individual for one position, and then expect the person to fill other positions, or carry out other tasks as needed, without a preemployment discussion of that possibility. Sapienza (1995) provides detailed examples of the advantages of matching personnel to job expectations to the greatest extent feasible.

Match Personality to Project Requirements

The position's interpersonal requirements need to be considered as well as the specific position tasks. Thus, an applicant's personal qualities need to be considered. A person with dominant extrovert qualities is probably best placed in a position that requires considerable interaction with other project members, with potential project participants, and perhaps data collection. An assessment needs to be made of the ability of the applicant to be self-directed, if the position requires that, or to be able to follow instructions exactly, when that is required. This is where the position evaluation of whether the tasks included in the position could be completed by a single individual is most useful. Individuals who are self-directed, and problem solvers in the face of crises, might not be able to run a research protocol that tolerates no deviations. Individuals who are very good at interpersonal relations when collecting questionnaire and assessment data may not be successful recruiters because of the marketing aspects inherent in the activity. During the interviews, PIs need to be as specific as possible about the required tasks and avoid making decisions based on general questions such as "Do you think you are good with people?" A yes answer to that question might suggest the person could be a recruiter, but if another question were asked, "Do you think you could encourage people to participate in our project given the risks and benefits?" the answer might be no. The second question must, however, be asked if the PI is to avoid forming an opinion with insufficient evidence.

Project data is collected in a variety of settings from individuals with a variety of characteristics. Individuals collecting data must be able to understand the settings and their customs. PIs need to collect sufficient information, before interviewing potential project staff, to help determine the personnel characteristics that will be required for the project to be successful at the site. PIs must keep in mind that it is not only the data collection personnel that interact with people at the project site. Many of the project staff will have occasion to be at the site for a variety of reasons, and all must, therefore, understand the role of good relationships with the site. We find that when PIs are thorough in describing the position to prospective employees, usually only those who are qualified continue to express interest in it.

Consider Data Collection Site Characteristics

Data collection sites generally have unique characteristics. Whether the site is a rural town, a hospital waiting room, an interview room in a community agency, or a high-tech setting, data collection must be completed nonintrusively, by those who respect the customs and sensitivities of the site's inhabitants. Often PIs have been at the proposed data collection or recruitment site and have met many of the staff people. Even when this is the case, a PI must carefully assess the environment and the influence the current project will have on it and the environment will have on the project. To assume that a new project will fit in as well as others, in our opinion, is a serious error. For example, rural communities have histories that influence their reception and perception of individuals from other places. Some communities accept individuals only very similar to themselves, whereas others are more friendly to strangers. PIs need to assess the extent to which the setting inhabitants will react negatively to project personnel different from themselves. They should also assess whether the project's topic might make it unwelcome.

Hospitals have established customs about interactions among different kinds of personnel and with patients. If a hospital is a data collection site, PIs need to visit the site just as they would a community to determine whether particular kinds of people are going to be more successful in their interactions and data collection. Tolerance for research projects and data collection efforts can vary with the reasons for hospitalization. Data collection procedures that are viewed as unnecessarily intrusive, insensitive, or particularly burdensome may not be welcome. It is the PI's responsibility to prepare the hospital personnel for the project and correct misperceptions about data collection methods, importance, and usefulness.

Community agencies are environments with special requirements for data collection because of their close ties to the people of the community. The community agency staff can become protective of their clients, if they perceive an activity as being disruptive of an improved state that has been achieved only over time and with great effort. PIs are encouraged to also visit agencies and the data collection and/or participant recruitment space to be used. They must resist the temptation to make a telephone call to make the arrangements, and to do telephone introductions of the project staff, no matter how well acquainted they are with the agency personnel.

High-tech data collection sites also have unique requirements and procedures for those working in the environment. It is vital that PIs visit these sites and request information on all procedures including security and equipment sharing. If the PI is establishing such a site, complete manuals need to be prepared for the project staff as well as for anyone else who might share the space.

Consider Participant Idiosyncrasies

Data collection procedures can range from distributing a questionnaire to a group of several hundred people and monitoring the process to one-on-one data collection of material that is personal in nature or from individuals who have physical or mental disabilities. Project participants can influence the kinds of personal characteristics desirable in data collection staff. In most instances, PIs have collected data from similar participants and have a good grasp of the potential difficulties. The individual characteristics that will be an attribute in the specific situation must be actively sought. Reliance on a curriculum vitae or on general questions is probably not sufficient. Sometimes direct questions are required to discover how candidates assess their probability of success in new situations.

Provide Personnel Training

Project personnel must be trained if they are to be productive members of the project. For PIs to omit an initial training period is a serious oversight. Periodic refreshers might also be needed, particularly when staff are required to cover for each other, because skills used only occasionally need to be refreshed on a regular basis to maintain high levels of efficiency, accuracy, and effectiveness. The extent of training and its timing are dependent on the project and the kinds of activities involved. The training categories we have found useful are (a) project-specific training, which includes a complete introduction to the project functions, how they relate to each other, and the people filling the positions; (b) technology training; and (c) supervisory training.

Develop Project-Specific Training

Everyone involved with a project must have working knowledge of the project aims, the protocol, the time frames for work completion, and project staff responsibilities. Although more ordinarily thought of as "orientation," this kind of information should be included in the very first project meeting. Sometimes the first meeting is very light in tone and project staff introductions include only summaries of duties. In our opinion, each introduction should include time for project staff to ask questions about positions and tasks and how they relate to other project positions. Introductions of new staff as they come on board should also occur at project meetings and be extensive enough so that their role in the project is clear.

Each employee is entitled to project-specific task training. For example, individuals responsible for collecting data need to have several training sessions with the protocol, the instrument, or the method. Data processing and data entry individuals need to be trained in the computer program system and its role in the project. Individuals working at another site need to be introduced to the site by the PI or the project director and not simply "sent."

Promote Technology Training

Some new employees will not have all technical skills required to work at the level of expertise required by the project. An example of this is the use of computer software. Even though a staff member has significant computer skills, these skills may not include particular standard programs or applications and certainly will not include project-specific programs required for project work. Much of the training for working with standard programs can be done through seminars offered by commercial organizations. Computer software seminars, for example, word processing, spreadsheets, statistics, and Windows, are available. Although these seminars are targeted for a heterogeneous audience, the cost is usually reasonable, and skills learned can be transferred to the work environment. For project-specific program training, the program experts should schedule training sessions to coincide with project requirements, but provide sufficient lead time so that employees have time to do practice sessions.

Require Supervisory Training

Project staff in supervisory positions need to be prepared for a wide variety of situations. In our experience, the broader the perspective of the supervisor, the more likely success will be the outcome. Multiple training sources are one way to develop a broad perspective. PIs need to have training sessions with supervisory staff to develop a supervisory approach that reflects their personal work style and tone that can be applied throughout the project. In addition, other sources of supervisory training can be useful. Universities often have in-service courses that are available at no cost. These are useful for the information they provide about the regulations and policies of the larger organization and divert personnel problems arising from personnel regulation infractions. Commercial organizations offer material that is different from either the project level or the larger organization level. This material usually focuses on behaviors, interactions (e.g., negotiation and assertiveness), and management issues (e.g., dealing with difficult people). We have noticed that PIs sometimes believe that supervisory training is not necessary because the individual has "worked with people before," "supervised students," or "has several children." Although these situations can enhance an individual's ability to supervise, supervisors do not supervise colleagues, students, or children—they supervise employees. It is important that the distinction be made, and one way to emphasize it is to provide training so supervisors can learn the differences in style required by these various situations.

Discuss Ethics

The ethical issues associated with the project need to be discussed. We suggest at least two meetings with project staff to review the kinds of situations that might arise that require decisions and actions that could have ethical implications. The human and animal subject issues should be covered, and the ethics of data collection, data entry, data analysis, and interpretation should be another. Perhaps not all project personnel need be involved in all the meetings, but involving everyone contributes to the overall project unity and deepens the group's sense of commitment to conducting excellent research in a mindful way.

Provide Effective Supervision

All project staff for whom the PI is responsible require supervision. The complexity and time frame of the project, the number of different kinds of personnel as well as the number of the same kinds of personnel, and the work style of the PI are factors influencing the selected supervision plan. It is a serious error for the PI to believe that because project positions have been filled with competent, trustworthy, energetic people that supervision tasks can be eliminated.

Projects with large staff often require several levels of supervision, because the supervisory workload is too much for a single individual. With this plan, however, individuals who supervise others often need to be trained. Even if supervisors have had supervisory experience in other settings, providing training sessions that are designed specifically to meet the situations likely to arise within the project establishes staff performance norms.

In our opinion, establishing performance norms is a critical ingredient for a smooth-running project, even when the project staff is the PI and one other person. Establishing norms is necessary for quality assurance, and neglecting to place these kinds of activities at the forefront of the project operation can lead to unpleasant discoveries later on. In addition, they can provide a basis for evaluating requests for salary raises and job reclassifications whenever they occur and serve as guidelines for promotion decisions. Without established norms, there are no criteria for these evaluations that both the PI and staff can use to govern work and advancement expectations.

Action Strategies

Make a List of Supervisory Training Resources

A list of available training for supervisors should include that provided by the project and by the PI's organization and courses offered by commercial organizations.

Compile a List of Project Tasks Requiring Additional Staff Training

Use the project job descriptions to make a list of activities that might not be incorporated in usual training. This might include, for example, training on the use of specific computer software or a project-specific data collection method. Most computer applications now use a Windows environment. However, it is still a relatively new addition to computer options and many people do not have extensive experience with Windows. Another factor that can play an important role is whether Macintosh computers will be used. People who are highly computer literate may not be familiar with the Macintosh system or be only familiar with the Macintosh system. Data collection methods specific to the project must be reviewed with staff. Novel methods may require extensive training, as might methods requiring detail or that have small error tolerances. Not to be overlooked, however, is training for individuals using familiar methods but for which project data requires small deviations from standard procedures. Practice sessions are particularly important in this instance to assure that "old habits do not creep in," invalidating the date.

Read the Employee Handbook

It is important that PIs have general knowledge of the larger organization's rules and regulations governing employees. PIs will develop some project-specific regulations; however, these cannot violate the larger organization's rules and regulations.

Determine the Daily Time Schedules of
Employees Before Interviewing Candidates

Employees want to know how many hours a day or week they are expected to work, and the time of day they will work. If they are not given that information by the PI, they will ask others in the project, or employees in other departments. Employees who obtain scheduling information in this way may or may not have the correct information, but they will assume it is correct and behave accordingly. Difficult situations can be averted by stating when and how many hours employees are expected to work.

Develop Time Sheets That Reflect Project
Structure and Budget Categories

Keeping time sheets is not anyone's favorite task, but it is a necessary part of employment, and critical for projects because of limited resources. Time sheets serve two valuable functions. First, they help employees keep track of their time so that they can be fairly compensated for overtime and make efficient use of their vacation and sick leave. Second, if properly designed, they can provide the PI with accurate information about the cost of the various project components. For example, rather than have a research assistant enter 80 hours on a time sheet for a 2-week work period, entries could be made by important and costly project functions. In this case, the time sheet might include items such as participant recruiting, participant screening, data entry, or community liaison. A single-time-sheet design would be used by all project staff, but each would only use the categories relevant to that person. The PI could then, for example, quickly check on the personnel cost of recruiting up to a particular day, and make decisions about how future recruitment efforts should be distributed, given budget constraints.

Find Out the Benefits to Which
Project Employees Are Entitled

Benefits, such as health insurance, life insurance, retirement contributions, vacation and sick leave time, are all important to employees. In many organizations, human resources personnel can review these benefits with new employees. PIs should make sure that employees attend these discussions so that they are informed. If a PI is responsible for informing employees of their benefits, the PI needs to gather the information and distribute it. We do not think it is a good idea to have this information transmitted on an informal basis, such as during discussions about other project matters, or while walking to a meeting.

cHAptER 9

Communicating With Organizations and With the Scientific Community

Communication is an important theme during the project application process and during the life of the funded project. The organizations and individuals associated with the project have a vested interest in its successful completion, and in the events associated with its progress. It is easy for principal investigators (PIs) to overlook the importance of developing communication channels while experiencing the excitement and apprehension often accompanying the reality of implementing a funded project. Nevertheless, information must flow from the PI to associated organizations and coinvestigators, as well as to news and scientific media. This chapter discusses some of the individuals and organizations PIs should include in their communication network.

Tell Those Associated With the Project About Funding

PI's Immediate Supervisor

Although the PI's immediate supervisor may have other means of learning about the funding status of unit projects, it is important that he or she also learns about it from the PI. Although a simple memo is an efficient method of communicating this information and becomes part of the project's permanent record, in our opinion, it is important that PIs discuss the award with their immediate supervisor. It is unwise for PIs to assume that their immediate supervisor knows all about the project, and its ramifications for the unit, and will take action on the project's behalf. During this discussion, PIs can briefly review their project, discuss their time commitments to the project and outside of the project, and refresh their supervisor's memory about the unit's financial, material, and personnel commitments. Although it is best to have this discussion as soon as the PI has informal information about funding, it is critical that it be scheduled soon after receiving the notice of award. This enables a PI to include revisions in the project plan that might be required by the unit's changing circumstances. It should be no surprise that some modification of the agreement might be needed because it could have been made more than a year before, and perhaps with a different person. However, in most instances, externally funded projects are valued, and PIs receive as much support as can reasonably be provided.

PIs need to provide their supervisor and other administrative personnel with basic project information. This might include the following and any additional information required by the unit.

Names of all project personnel including coinvestigators and project staff
Percent effort of all project personnel
Title of project
Funding source
Funding source's project identification number
Dates for entire project period
Direct costs and indirect costs approved for entire project period year by year
Current year (annual) direct costs and indirect costs awarded
Abstract

This kind of information, which is also an indicator of the unit's productivity, can be an important part of an annual report because a strong external funding base is often associated with increased status. Funding information is also useful as an indicator of faculty interests and departmental prosperity, during the recruitment of graduate students, postdoctoral fellows, and residents. Because of its potential wide use, we suggest a copy of this information also be given to others such as the business manager, those responsible for student recruitment, and research development personnel.

Colleagues

Other people with whom communication about the award must be a high priority are those who contributed to developing the application. Investigators who submit one application often submit more. It is a good idea to develop a mutual support structure, which can simplify the submission process for everyone. Informing those who contributed to the application about the project implementation plans facilitates formation of such a support structure. Colleagues who have received funding and who have experienced budget cuts will be particularly interested in the award amount and how the shortfall, if any, is going to affect the project's science. This usually doesn't require extensive memos or meetings. PIs probably know their colleagues well enough to know how each of them would like to be informed. For example, some might be interested only in whether it was funded and the final award approved. Others might also be interested in knowing something about the early data collection or when an abstract or poster might be presented. Colleagues also have an interest in supplementing their information about the application process so they can improve their chances of being funded by avoiding pitfalls discussed in the project's review comments. Colleagues who have contributed to the application have demonstrated an interest and begun a relationship that, if fostered, can facilitate efficient and effective grant applications.

Coinvestigators

Project coinvestigators need a copy of the items listed above for their files and for use on their curricula vitae and "other support" reporting for future grant applications. They also need the information for their unit's administrative personnel and for planning activities during the project's duration. PIs should also send coinvestigators and consultants a copy of the complete application, if they do not already have one, and the reviewers' comments when they are available. It is particularly important that coinvestigators have a copy of the reviewers' comments because even funded projects have negative comments. Negative comments can result in project modifications in which the coinvestigators have an interest. Whether or not project modifications arise from these comments, they are useful in preparing future proposals.

In our opinion, the PI needs to formulate a tentative implementation plan and convene a meeting of project personnel to discuss implementation, the reviewer comments if available, and possible project changes resulting from them. It is best that this meeting occurs soon after it is known that the project will be funded. It may not be possible to immediately set project activities in motion, but it is important that the PI begins building a project group that works well together. Projects may not develop in a serene atmosphere. PIs must, therefore, take advantage of all opportunities to bring the group together for meaningful activities so that it will mature before project work begins. Another reason for meeting soon after receiving the award is to signal that steady, forward movement, rather than procrastination or bursts of activity followed by inactivity, is to be the project's tone and style. Coinvestigators will not hesitate to arrange schedules to accommodate the project if it is unmistakable that the PI is energetic about the project development and interested in setting achievable goals and timelines.

Discuss the Schedule for Publications and Their Authorship

Publications are the lifeblood of an academic career whether or not they are first authored. However, investigators actively seek publications on which they can be first author because they have the most professional weight. Externally funded projects generally provide opportunities for a variety of publications with different emphases. Project PIs and coinvestigators need to agree on who will author specific publications and the author order soon after the notice of award is received. Ideally, agreement about these issues was reached at the time of application submission. Frequently, however, because of the stiff funding competition, many investigators perceive such agreements as premature and a waste of time and effort. However, even if an agreement was reached, review and possible modification are necessary to include what has transpired in each of the investigators' careers as well as project changes that might result from the reviewers' comments and budget cuts.

In view of the importance of publications, authorship issues can be a source of conflict. There are some guidelines, although few disciplines have specified criteria for authorship (American Psychological Association, 1994). Articles that might be useful, if this is a difficult issue for PIs and investigators to resolve, are those by Digiusto (1994) and Huth (1986a, 1986b). Digiusto had colleagues assign points from 1 to 6 to 13 types of contributions that might be relevant to authorship issues, none of which received 6 points. Those that received 3 to 5 points as their maximum value were "thinking up the idea" (5 points), "drafting a manuscript" (5 points), "preparing a grant application" (4 points), "creative input" (4 points), "directly supervising or coordinating the work" (4 points), "statistical analysis" (4 points), "revising a manuscript critically" (3 points), and "actually recording or collecting data" (3 points). "Being a director or chairperson," "lending one's name and reputation," "providing essential resources," and "repetitive or routine work" received a maximum value of 1 point each.

Whatever the criteria selected for deciding authorship issues, we recommend that sufficient time be allowed to discover differences of opinion or custom so that agreements can be worked out before the reports are due and publication deadlines imminent. PIs and investigators are in the best position to know what arrangements will be most suitable. It is imperative, however, that expectations and deadlines for article materials be developed. In addition, a meeting should be set for a future date, in 6 months or so, to review the schedule and the investigators' writing progress. Needless to say, it is best if these meetings can be conducted in a collegial manner so that serious disagreements do not occur. It is to be hoped that the many opportunities investigators have to meet will enable understandings that promote working toward equitable solutions under potentially difficult conditions.

The Media

Some projects, because of their size or subject matter, capture media attention. In most instances, public relations offices provide the media with project information and arrange interviews, radio shows, or television presentations. It is also possible that the PI wants to generate local interest in the project to ensure a sufficient pool of volunteers from which to recruit participants. Before arranging to publicize the project, investigators need to discuss the procedures for press releases and radio and television presentations with their public relations office. Keep in mind that material designed to recruit participants generally needs to receive human subjects committee (IRB) approval, and the press release material designed for this purpose might need to be approved before publication.

Project Year 1 Activities

After the project is under way, communications for the first 8 or 9 months are primarily those related to conducting the project. Communication with the project group is ongoing and new channels are devised as needed. The project's accountant establishes guidelines for organizing and reporting expenditures. PIs need to understand and adhere to these guidelines to avoid infractions. The requirements for the protection of subjects were met to obtain funding. However, whenever consent forms are revised, because of changes in the project protocol, they must be submitted for IRB approval.

Funding Source

The PI, during Month 8 or 9 of the first year, begins to communicate with the funding source to secure the second-year funding. Usually, this noncompeting continuation application recounts the previous year's progress and outlines second-year plans and budget requirements. This is an important task, and a PI must not assume that he or she will receive the second year's award. It is as important to carefully follow the instructions for the second year's application as it was for the original application. In general, the application requirements are brief. Reviewers are interested in any major project changes anticipated in the second year as a function of the first year's findings. They want to see evidence of the project's progress during the first year including publications and data presentations. They are also interested in implementation and administrative plans for the second year particularly if they deviate from the first year's. Funding sources usually require a detailed budget only when major project changes are planned resulting in a budget that significantly deviates from that submitted with the original application. We recommend that PIs prepare a detailed budget for their records even if the funding source does not require one. Although the primary purpose of preparing the budget is to estimate the coming year's project costs, it also serves to focus attention on the details of planned activities for the coming year and can be used to identify operational problems.

New Coinvestigators

PIs should send reminders, sometime during the latter part of the first year, to coinvestigators who will be initiating their project work in the second year. They should also meet to discuss the new project activities and the investigator's role and personnel needs. It is also suggested that the entire project group meet with coinvestigators to facilitate their specific project activities. New data collection staff or technicians, who might be added at this time, also need to be introduced to the group as well as any new procedures to aid a smooth transition.

Accountant

It is critical that the PI review the project's first-year expenditures before the year ends. It is the PI's responsibility to monitor the project category account balances. Accountants may or may not take responsibility for advising PIs about excessive positive balances near the end of a project year. The disposition of remaining funds can be critical to the final success of the project. PIs cannot assume that the money awarded in the first year will remain available for the project if not spent in the award year. Nonexpended funds, restricted by the funding source, are usually subject to return. Funds not used, but encumbered in the first year, are often not subject to being returned to the funding source. Arrangements, therefore, for encumbering and carrying over funds need to be made before the year's end to allow the paperwork to be completed. If communication has been ongoing with the accountant, as we suggest, there will be no surprises and both the PI and the accountant will have plans for remaining balances.

Data Publication Decisions

At the end of the first year of the project, the PI should review the data that have been collected and plan analyses. In most cases, sufficient data are not collected during the first year to warrant conclusions. Nevertheless, this should not be assumed. The PI should review the data, particularly if they have been collected and managed by an independent section of the project group. The PI and coinvestigators, with the consultation of the project staff, need to decide whether the data are ready to be analyzed, where they will be presented, how they will be presented, and who will present.

Activities of Project Year 2 and Succeeding Years

When the notice of award for the second year is received, a PI should update the project information provided at the beginning of the first year and distribute it to the administrative staff of the units as well as to project coinvestigators and consultants. For most projects, this is the year when data collection is in full swing with the possibility of future presentations and publications.

Scientific Community

Schedule Publications and Presentations

Projected presentations and publications should be identified and outlined by the PI and coinvestigators. Some writing can usually be completed before data are available; abstracts can be written and posters can be planned. During this time, it is important that everyone be aware of what is being prepared and how responsibilities are distributed. It is also important that investigators fulfill their publication commitments. We have discovered that some individuals are skilled at some publication aspects but find other aspects difficult. Unfortunately, these individuals do not refrain from volunteering for the writing tasks—they just do not write. This can create frustration and increased work for others. We would rather an individual not make a commitment if he or she is not going to deliver the product, so other arrangements can then be made.

When individuals are working together for the first time on a funded project, it can be a trying time for investigators, particularly when first authorship is being decided. Although initial agreements may not be feasible, an attempt should be made to adhere to them before renegotiating a new agreement. If there were no agreements, but all investigators had assumptions about who would be first author, these assumptions must be openly discussed to arrive at agreements that meet individual needs. For some projects, it is at the end of the second year that the funding source expects evidence that the data collected during the first 2 years have been published, if not in final form, at least in preliminary form. To do this, agreements among the coinvestigators must be concluded for publications to proceed. If the PI has maintained close communication with the coinvestigators, and involved them in the everyday conduct of the project, everyone will have a fair idea of what publications are expected.

Agreement also needs to be reached on when the results should be released to the public and scientific community. An article by Relman (1990) discusses the roles and responsibilities in publishing biomedical research. His position on publication timing is that "there are good reasons why authors should in most cases delay public announcement of their work until the publication of their data in scientific literature, or at least until they have presented their results at a scientific meeting" (p. 25).

Consider Hosting Conferences

Projects can usually benefit from a conference, which might include regional and national scientists. If preliminary data suggest this could be beneficial, plans should be made early so there is time to make arrangements and the participants have time to prepare presentations. Conference funding might be available through the project budget, through a special conference grant, or from the PI's organization. The conference format depends on the subject matter, willingness of scientists to participate, and available funds. The word *conference* suggests a rather large undertaking. However, it need not be large. A conference can be one or two eminent scientists who visit the project site and spend time discussing findings, giving presentations to students, or reviewing data. These kinds of conferences can be used to incorporate project findings into the scientific knowledge base, because other scientists will review findings, discuss analysis strategies, and posit possible interpretations.

Submit Subject Protection Documentation on Time

Reviews of the subject protection documents occur annually. PIs are required to provide information, and approval is renewed if the review board finds no problems. It is important that this is not neglected, because it is required by many funding sources before they award the next year's funds. PIs also need to consider how the heightened awareness of issues relating to participants, as demonstrated by the National Institutes of Health (NIH) announcements "Informed Consent in Clinical Mental Health Research"

(1995d) and "Informed Consent in Research Involving Human Participants" (1996e), can affect their projects.

Develop a Partnership With the Media

Like the initial funding year, the second and succeeding years of the project might also generate media interest, or the PI might seek media exposure to maintain local interest and sufficient participant volunteers. Even though PIs in the second and succeeding years may be more experienced with the project and perhaps with the media, press releases should be cleared with the public relations office or other designated persons. Because universities are dynamic and responsive to public concerns and events, priorities and policies can change. The assumption, therefore, cannot be made that what was appropriate remains appropriate.

Action Strategies

Getting Credit Within the Investigators' Organizations

Establish a system for updating and distributing the project information so that the PI and coinvestigators receive credit for their work and have access to advantages associated with being actively engaged in externally funded projects. The following information might be included and any other items considered important to the PI's organization.

Names of all project personnel including coinvestigators and project staff
Percent effort of all project personnel
Title of project
Funding source
Funding source's project identification number
Dates for entire project period
Direct costs and indirect costs approved for entire project period year by year
Current year (annual) direct costs and indirect costs awarded
Abstract

Make Plans for Developing Publications and Presentations

After a project is funded, we suggest that the PI meet with coinvestigators to discuss publications, presentations, and authorship. Although the list will change as the data are collected and analyzed, many of the agreements will remain viable throughout the project and publication preparation. Two sources that we have found useful to help with preparing publications in addition to the American Psychological Association and the American Medical Association style manuals are

> *Successful Publishing in Scholarly Journals.* Bruce A. Thyer, Sage, Thousand Oaks, CA, 1994
>
> *Writing Papers in Psychology.* 3rd ed. Ralph L. Rosnow and Mimi Rosnow, Brooks/Cole, New York, 1995

Give Appropriate Credit on All Publications

Be sure to include an acknowledgment statement and disclaimer as appropriate for all project publications. The following is suggested for projects funded by the NIH and can be used as a model for projects funded by others.

> "This publication was made possible by Grant (grant number) from (name of awarding agency)" and "Its contents are solely the responsibility of the author(s) and do not necessarily represent the official views of the (name of awarding agency)."

It should also be noted that the Public Health Service requires that three reprints of publications resulting from work performed under a PHS grant-supported project or activity must be submitted to the PHS awarding office.

Think About the Media's Role

Actively consider the role of the media for your project's success. If the media can play a role, we suggest that PIs not hesitate to contact media representatives. Media can be important from both short-term and long-term perspectives. In the short term, media exposure can help participant recruitment as well as foster a positive relationship between the community and projects that are highly visible in the community. In the long-term perspective, talking with media people can foster community appreciation of research in general. Because much of research is publicly funded, feedback about what those funds are producing can facilitate congressional support for research budgets.

Many scientists fear that their findings or scientific positions will not be represented accurately or will be trivialized by the media. Communication with the public requires that complex scientific issues be framed so nonscientists as well as scientists in other fields can understand them. Carol Ezzell, science editor for the *Journal of NIH Research*, recommends that calls from journalists be taken. "If they haven't done their homework, tell them so, and that you'll speak with them once they have. If a journalist breaks his or her word to you, don't speak to that person again. But don't forsake the public— including scientists outside of your field—by blindly refusing to speak even with knowledgeable, honest journalists" (Ezzell, 1996, p. 10).

Make Plans to Meet With the Project Accountant

Meet with the project's accountant soon after it is known the award will be received. Each organization has rules and regulations that accountants must follow. Learn as much as possible about the restrictions placed on the funds and the kinds of things that can be done to have the regulations work to the project's advantage. Some of the most troublesome restrictions do not allow funds to be transferred between certain categories, or be carried forward to the next year. Another restriction that is sometimes overlooked is in the personnel area where funds are restricted to a particular type of personnel function for the award year. In other words, if that position is not filled during that year, or is filled for only part of the year, unused funds must be returned.

PART IV

Continuing a Project
by Submitting a
Competitive Application

CHAPTER 10

Strategies to Identify a Continuation Project

Funded principal investigators (PIs) often find that their success is accompanied by excitement and collegial respect. Also with funding comes visibility as an active PI, both at home and at professional meetings, which can result in a plethora of requests that require time and effort. A PI can be the target of requests to be a coinvestigator, an informal consultant, a mentor, a guest lecturer, and a presubmission application reviewer. It is during this time that investigators might also be recruited as reviewers for foundations and federal government grant applications. As a consequence of this attention, PIs can become too busy to give sufficient time and thought to their competing continuation. This chapter focuses on strategies that might be used to develop a next project.

Do Not Delay Plans for a Continuation Project

In our opinion, plans for developing a continuation project should be initiated during the second to last project year. Although this might be early for several reasons, including the fact that publications have not been accepted and that data may not yet be analyzed, in our opinion, PIs should not delay planning the next project. PIs submitting their first competing continuation might not realize that the task is not a simple and straightforward exercise. PIs submitting their second or third competing continuation, although enjoying the benefits of funding, may have forgotten the difficult challenges they successfully faced with their submissions.

Funded PIs achieved peak application performance, but with the final project year in sight they are faced with the realization that success is not final and that the feat must be repeated. Reviewers have different expectations of funded PIs than of nonfunded investigators. A funded PI is assumed to be an accomplished and active scientist and validation of this is sought in the new application. Although it would be wonderful if funded PIs could leap from one funded application peak to the next, without entering a valley of preparation and review, that is not possible. The competing continuation application must be as excellent as the prior application in all respects. The project plan must be as thoroughly developed and described, and the idea must also be original, compelling, and significant. The criteria of original and compelling are often the most difficult to meet with a competing continuation proposal, because the previous project made the train of thought, concepts, and associated ideas familiar. The previous project also narrowed the field of significant projects because of the results and because the investigator must stay within the boundaries of its broad, long-term objectives. PIs planning a second or possibly a third competing continuation might find the task even more difficult.

Actively Seek Intellectual Exchange

Campbell, Daft, and Hulin (1982) identified antecedents of research. The antecedents of significant research they labeled as activity, convergence, intuition, theory, and real world. Those of not-so-significant research they labeled as expedience, method, motivation, and lack of theory.

Ideas associated with significant contributions are most often generated by investigators engaged in a variety of activities that encourage conversations with their colleagues. Developing a project plan with a significant contribution is usually preferred by investigators and, as with most high goals, is rarely achieved without the help of others. Frequent interactions with colleagues and students set the stage for opportunities to test ideas. These conversations are also a source of a variety of scientific opinions and assertions that, if not precisely relevant, can nevertheless lead to development of questions and hypotheses through associational thinking. For these reasons, an environment in which interactions occur might be better than an isolated one for creative and integrated thinking.

With a reasonable level of collegial interaction, a PI can develop material in new ways. For example, an idea from one discipline might be combined with a method from another. The variety of issues in today's world begging to be researched calls for not only multidisciplinary projects but also interdisciplinary projects in which the disciplines become opaque. In our opinion, opportunities to assess the plausibility of converging ideas and methods are more likely to occur for investigators who continue to interact with their colleagues. PIs who attempt to broaden their knowledge of disciplines related to their interests, while they are thinking about their competing continuation, might also discover new collaboration avenues.

Investigators can find it difficult to devote the required time to a project that is driven solely by logic with no "fire to know" on their part. In our opinion, they need to be aware of their sense that the project "is just what is needed" and that the methods are "a surefire way to tease out that result" and use that information to fuel their writing. Although a strong belief in the project's significance to the particular scientific area helps a PI write strong projects, this belief, if followed blindly, can also be misleading. The emotional component of an idea is not a necessary and a sufficient criterion for its ability to become a competitive project. However, we would like to reiterate that when investigators have little attachment to a project or its ideas, they are not likely to give it the attention required to write a competitive application.

Projects based in theory are usually more intellectually engaging because of the broad implications for supporting hypotheses and knowledge base expansion. These projects are often motivated by a desire to explain a phenomenon. However, investigators sometimes neglect the possible theoretical implications when studies are designed to be predictive, or designed to enable a particular phenomenon to be observed. In most cases, there is theory underlying variable choices or procedures. These theories need to be presented and explored just like those associated with explanatory projects.

Projects developed for submission to a funding source must have an outcome that is highly relevant to some aspect of the project's "real world." Not all projects contribute to the same reality. Some contribute to the real world of medicine, others to the real world of the justice system, and others to the real world of microbiology. The reality to which a project contributes must be defined by the investigator, and that definition must fit what a reviewer would devise from the information provided in the application. Therefore, the definition must be a "real world" definition that is reasonably within the project's domain. This reality is usually that addressed in the project's broad, long-term objectives.

Not-so-significant projects are often the result of investigators being required to be actively involved in projects, trying to increase their number of publications, or being involved in a project because it offers opportunities for spin-off projects. Within a scientific area, there is often a need to validate, evaluate, or demonstrate phenomena. These efforts could be viewed as scientific housekeeping. The projects are not interesting to most because there is little doubt about the results. Although the work must be done, these investigations are usually not fundable, and they are not seen as contributing to strengthening a scientific area, despite the importance of substantiating basic assumptions.

Powerful methods are usually developed in response to a need to demonstrate specific phenomena. This development becomes intellectually stimulating and a time-consuming project in and of itself. With an elegant method in hand, investigators sometimes focus on projects that use the elegant method and enlist coinvestigators with expertise in the content area. The key factor to whether a strong project results from this strategy is how well the method, content, and scientific-area issues can be related. When investigators find that a particular method meets their data needs to advance theory or practice, it is imperative that the project be described in a manner that leaves no doubt that the theory associated with the content, not method, is the driving force.

Projects initiated to develop a new method belong in a different area of investigation and theory. The sole purpose of these projects is to test and refine a method or procedure so that it can be used to collect data under specified conditions for specified purposes. Investigators must be clear about their purpose, not attempt to develop the method and collect content data in the same project, and incorporate the literature and theory leading to the proposed methodological development.

Opportunities to participate in projects often come to investigators because of their expertise. These projects may or may not be interesting, but participation might be important to an investigator for a variety of reasons. It is doubtful that a significant project will result if investigators do not develop an intellectual interest in the project but merely lend expertise. Although it is difficult to describe how enthusiasm is expressed in a project plan, its lack is noticeable. In our experience, investigators with enthusiasm for a project engage in more creative thought, as well as more critical thought, and it may be this consequence that is apparent in a project plan. Projects completed with little enthusiasm may be successfully completed, and may fill a scientific need, but they generally do not engender enthusiasm and may not be seeds for future scientific advances.

Insufficient attention to prior theory, or project aspects that might require modification of current theory, produces a project that makes little, if any, contribution. In our opinion, whether the focus is the project's content, instruments, methods, or procedures, the theoretical base must be included in the project development and specified in the proposal. Investigators who are conducting studies that focus on method development must be particularly diligent in describing the project's theoretical underpinnings.

The Search for a Next Significant Project

Identifying an acceptable competing continuation project can be difficult. The reasons for this vary, but investigators share the unexpected frustration. We, therefore, suggest that the competing continuation be part of an investigator's "to do" list well before the current project's end date. For the most part, progress toward identifying an appropriate project occurs in small steps and with erratic progress. Broad swings of ideas, methods, and interests are characteristics of the early efforts to define a project. During this time, we suggest that investigators keep careful notes of their thoughts and discussions, and develop written refinements of promising ideas. It is not unusual for an idea to be appealing and feasible until it is committed to paper when theoretical and logical flaws are revealed. Further discussion about thinking is noted in Chapter 16. Some avenues used by investigators to assess the pros and cons of ideas and directions for the competing continuation are discussed below.

Review the Future Directions of the Previous Application

The first thing to do, in our opinion, is to review the Future Directions (or Future Projects) section of the previous application. The ideas for future projects generated while the application was being developed represent previous interests based on the project's planned data. The suggested projects are usually stated in broad terms and each might embrace several projects. These ideas need to be critically mined for viable competing continuation projects. We suggest that a list be developed of all potential projects that are included in the application's Future Projects section. This list will probably include projects that are interesting in their own right as well as those that validate strongly held assumptions and fill in some missing pieces. With project results in hand, reassess each project's potential as a credible next step in the research line, as an important scientific contribution to the project's broad, long-term objectives, and its feasibility. PIs also need to consider the impact of their project's results and of other research on the originality and importance of the suggested projects.

Investigate Collaborative Potential

Current project coinvestigators may not be appropriate coinvestigators on a new project. It is crucial that the project include only investigators with a specific role and with the required credentials. On the other hand, all project requirements must be filled. For example, if there is an evaluation component in the new project, a coinvestigator must have the credentials to design, implement, and interpret the data. Unfortunately, this requirement is often a serious restriction for PIs because the needed expertise is not available at their site. Sometimes this difficulty can be overcome by using off-site consultants. In our opinion, however, it is preferable for PIs to remain with projects that are feasible within their environment and centered in their area of expertise.

The dilemma faced by PIs is whether to design a project in which they have intense interest and superior expertise or one with different combinations of these attributes. The decision is not easy. The PI's experience with collaborators, however, must carry significant weight. If the only choice of a collaborator for a particular project, either on site or off site, is one who has a reputation for procrastination or excessive time commitments, the project's attractiveness might diminish. This is a strong possibility if another project can be designed without the risks of working with a collaborator who might slow the project's progress, even though the PI is less enthusiastic about the project.

Do an Equipment and Procedure Inventory

Another consideration that must be revisited in these times of tight resources is the equipment required to collect and analyze data. In our opinion, it is preferable that a PI not embark on a project that requires high-tech instrumentation if it is not available on site. For example, projects with biological components might require lab procedures that are expensive, require extremely rigorous levels of accuracy, or are vulnerable to deterioration within very short time spans. The use of magnetic resonance imaging and positron emission tomography (PET), for example, are instances of data collection methods that may provide information about a particular area of investigation but to which the PI does not have access, or the available equipment is no longer state of the art and will not provide high-quality and precise data. Without access to adequate, accurate, and acceptable data collection tools, some projects are impossible.

Take a Program Approach

If using a linear approach for defining the next project does not produce a viable topic, try taking a program-of-research approach. New investigators do not usually think about their research as part of a larger body of related projects that can be thought of as a program. If the "next step" from the current project might not be interesting to a funding source, and needs to be pursued by other means, a related project might be a good choice. This is where the broad, long-term project objectives are important. Theoretically, any project that fits within the overall objective and that has not been discredited by the current project's findings could be an original and interesting line of investigation. It is important when submitting a project that is clearly not the next step to develop a strong rationale for the project as a parallel activity to the current project, stating clearly the contribution of the converging outcomes.

Review the Questions That the Current Project Has Raised

Any questions raised by a current project could be the source of a new application. Solutions to these kinds of questions are sometimes more difficult to sell, because they might be obtained through simple approaches or methods, such as adding a group to the study but essentially replicating the current project. If the questions raised are of this type, but their answers are imperative to conceptually move the project forward, a project should be designed to achieve those ends and test hypotheses associated with new specific aims.

Review the Funding Source's Mission and Interests

Along with the criteria demanded by the scientific community, a competing continuation must be within the funding source's mission and interests. Having been funded does not give investigators free rein to deviate from the funding source's mission. After identifying one or more viable potential projects, a PI should consult with the funding source contact to get assistance with a decision. This advice should be taken seriously and not discounted if an investigator disagrees with it. However, before following any advice, investigators need to be sure that they have communicated their ideas, the project's purpose, and the benefits of the outcomes. If the funding source agrees to review a preproposal or a concept paper, take advantage of the opportunity.

Budget Considerations

Some funding sources permit competing continuation projects to exceed the prior project's budget only by a specified inflation factor. In view of inflation and the need to use improved technology and current methods, this restriction can be a serious limitation. It is when budget computations on a potential project are more than the specified amount that a PI should consider not submitting the project as a competing continuation but as a new project. Very often a PI cannot carry out the project he or she wishes within the budget restrictions. In addition, a high scientific price is often associated with attempts to fit the project to the budget. In our opinion, potential project budgets should be carefully calculated because the availability of funds can be an important variable in the decision about which project should be developed.

Project Feasibility and Doability

Investigators need to assess their resources for each potential project. Several factors are relevant. New consultants need to be located and recruited. The current project's consultants may also be unavailable for a second project. If they are relocating, a PI should consider having them remain with the project, although off site. If off-site consultants are included, a strong case needs to be made to persuade the reviewers that the attention, interest, and contribution of the off-site consultants will not vary from their on-site productivity. Data collection for the new project might require equipment that may have to be bought or upgraded if the project is to be successful. Subject availability is also a key concern. If the project requires subjects that are not common, decisions must be made about the appropriateness of recruiting the first project's subjects for the second project. If subjects are considered a vulnerable population, regulations and policies may have changed since the first project's data collection, making recruitment difficult, if not impossible. The importance of staying abreast of the current public policy issues was brought home when New York state stopped psychiatric research using "incapable" patients in state-run facilities (K.H., 1996). Another example is the current support for a bill designed to protect families and children by requiring a single standard of written parental consent before a minor can complete a federally funded survey or questionnaire ("Bill Threatens," 1995; L.S., 1996).

Action Strategies

Review Funding Source Requirements

Review funding source requirements as carefully when planning a competing continuation as when the original submission was planned. Some funding sources do not fund competing continuations and may not fund the same investigator for two sequential funding cycles. If the original funding source does not fund competing continuations or a second project for the same investigator, a new funding source must be found and its requirements obtained. Keep in mind that funding sources usually require competing continuations to include an extensive section about the previous project's accomplishments and their relationship to the proposed project. Reviewers are not only interested in the results but also evidence that the PI is able to publish results, is conducting the project in a manner that foretells a successful conclusion, and that the PI is able to incorporate unexpected results into the ongoing project as well as into the proposed project.

Determine Budget Restrictions

Budget restrictions can play an important role in the competing continuation submission. Although PIs are often tempted to submit a continuing study as a new application, there are advantages to submitting a competing continuation in spite of the budgetary limitations' influence on the project design and size. The important thing for investigators to realize is that there usually are restrictions, and not assume that because they were funded, they are no longer required to meet funding source restrictions.

Include New Pilot Data

Important information for the funding source is the current project's results and their implications. However, it might be necessary that other pilot data be included to support the new project, particularly if the new project does not directly follow the current project.

Review the Reviewers' Comments From the Current Study Again

The reviewers' comments can provide information about a reasonable course of action. Although the application was funded, some negative comments were made. Some of these could be about procedures or design that were considered when the project was implemented; others may have targeted the project's contribution to theory, its long-term value, or included suggestions for alternative designs or methodologies that were not appropriate for the project. These comments are a small window into how reviewers understood the project, and the broad, long-term objectives in which it belonged. PIs should consider these comments and use them, as appropriate, to guide the new project.

Discuss New Project Plans With the Funding Source Contact

Funding source contacts can help PIs make decisions about the best direction for their next project. Discussions with funding source personnel can often provide insight into more efficient and competitive project presentation approaches.

Select a Project That Will Be Viable for at Least 18 Months

Another feature of the competing continuation project is that it must remain viable, interesting, and doable for at least 18 months if the application is not funded on the first submission and a revised application can be prepared in time for the very next deadline. This, of course, is an optimistic timetable, and often at least one cycle is missed. Whether investigators can maintain interest in the project and keep their program active depends on the breadth of the program and the investigator. Because most lines of investigation incorporate aspects that require pilot work, many investigators use the time between awards to secure funds for pilot research from foundations or by participating in other projects that provide opportunities for collecting additional data. Publications also need to be developed quickly. Resubmissions are usually strengthened by inclusion of new pilot data and publications. However, keep in mind that the time between receiving reviewer comments and the next receipt date is often short—8 weeks or less. It is, therefore, imperative that investigators not get deeply committed to other projects during the apparent "down" time. During the application review period, investigators must maintain their intellectual enthusiasm for the project and maintain their contact with coinvestigators to sustain their interest and commitment.

Review Information on What to Write and How to Write It

Review Chapters 13 and 14 with an eye to evaluating the application while it is in progress, as well as the final application. It is critical that the competing continuation be as well prepared as the prior application. Although the reviewers know that the PI has been previously funded, they consider each application for its potential contribution to the mission of the funding source.

Include a Cover Letter

A cover letter provides an opportunity to help funding source staff direct the application to the most appropriate reviewers. Funding sources hold the right to make the decision about reviewer assignment, but they usually consider recommendations. Funding sources want to keep their review section membership flexible, to ease the burden for reviewers and to provide appropriate reviews. In this review climate, it is more important, in our opinion, than in previous years, for PIs to include a cover letter. This letter should include the following: (a) application identification, for example, title and a number if one has been assigned by the funding source; (b) a statement about the specific area of inquiry, such as "This application focuses on . . . "; and

(c) the aspects of the investigation that require particular expertise for proper evaluation.

Whenever possible, a particular review group recommendation should be made. It is not always possible for a PI to know what the appropriate review group might be. If that is the case, then a review group recommendation cannot be included. The difficulty with locating the appropriate group is that the group titles alone do not provide sufficient information about the group's particular expertise. PIs can seek information about review groups and membership, however, rather than specifically request a section that might not be appropriate. It would be better, in our opinion, to rely on the objectives, procedures, and cover letter information to assist funding source staff to direct the application. However, if the PI believes that the previous review group was appropriate and that it can also accurately review the competing continuation's content, request that it be sent to the same group. If the proposal has unique characteristics that might require ad hoc reviewers, suggest specialists that might serve.

cHAPTER 11

Selecting a Funding Mechanism for a Continuation Project

Securing funding to continue projects can be as difficult as obtaining the initial funding. After investing time and energy in a funded project, investigators usually have an interest in continuing the specific line of research and expanding it to address associated issues. Investigators who desire to keep their research program active may have to seek out a variety of funding sources and mechanisms. For these reasons, we recommend that investigators begin their plans for maintaining funding for their research program early in the second to last year of their award. This chapter briefly discusses some of the options available and their advantages and disadvantages.

Continuing the Line of Research

Competing continuation or renewal applications are applications that continue and extend the work started with an initial or continuation award. Continuation applications include regular research applications, program projects, and center applications that are usually planned to maintain the line of research. Some funding organizations provide special procedures for such applications, and others treat continuations as new applications. If a principal investigator's (PI's) funding source offers special considerations for competing continuations, the advantages need to be investigated. When the option is available, most often PIs use the continuation approach because of advantages accruing from having an award in the specific area of investigation and being perceived as a mature investigator. Although the success rate for competing continuations is very encouraging to PIs—for National Institutes of Health (NIH) a 40.8% success rate for FY 1996 (Rhein, 1996a)—it is clearly not 100%, but every possible advantage needs to be used.

Competing continuation applications must not only meet the high standards of the previous application, but they must also be viewed as continuing to contribute significantly to the particular knowledge area. Designing a project that meets all the requirements can be difficult for the first competing continuation application, and it can become more difficult with each succeeding competing continuation. Therefore, we suggest that investigators have serious conversations with their funding source contact to examine whether the area of the potential application is generally appropriate and specifically if there is an interest in the design and the proposed measures.

The NIH recognizes competing continuations and has some requirements unique to the NIH. Investigators need to review the application instructions to determine the kinds of special application procedures required by their funding source for their particular kind of submission. For the regular research grant, the NIH requires that the same title as the previous application be used and that the proposal extends the research. There are also a few special application procedures that apply primarily to the application's administrative aspects. These include a progress report as part of the Preliminary Studies/Progress Report section. In addition to the beginning and ending dates of the prior award, the application must include (a) a summary of the previous application's specific aims and the importance of the findings; (b) a discussion of changes in specific aims as a result of budget reductions; (c) an enrollment report of research participants by gender, race, and ethnicity by each relevant funded study and for studies that will be continued; and (d) a succinct account of published and unpublished results, indicating progress toward their achievement, as well as a list of the titles and complete references for all publications, manuscripts submitted or accepted for publication, patents, and other printed materials resulting from the project since its last competitive review.

The National Science Foundation (NSF; 1995) offers two formats for renewing proposals with a regular research grant. The "traditional" renewal is developed as fully as an initial application, and it must include results from the prior work. The "accomplishment-based renewal" (ABR) proposal is a second alternative. With an ABR, the project description is replaced by copies of no more than six reprints of publications resulting from the research supported by NSF during the preceding 3- to 5-year period. These publications can include those from research supported by other sources that is closely related to the NSF-supported research. A brief summary of no more than four pages of the proposed research plan must also be submitted. The NSF also offers an NSF-initiated 2-year extension for special creativity. The purpose of these extensions is to offer the most creative investigators an extended opportunity to aggressively pursue adventurous, "high risk" opportunities in the same general research area, but not necessarily covered by the current proposal. Investigators are informed of the availability of this option a year before their grant expires.

Budgetary considerations are usually significant with a competing continuation if the funding source restricts the budget to the level approved in the prior project plus an inflation factor. This limitation can be restrictive for the first competing continuation, but becomes a more significant problem with each succeeding application because the projects were completed with budgets based on a budget that was less than adequate 6 years before. These restrictions often make it necessary to use several sources of funding, such as private and internal, and perhaps several different mechanisms, for example, a small grant, an equipment grant, or an internal career development grant. What we see most often when combining application mechanisms and/or funding sources is not possible, is investigators designing smaller projects. In the past, investigators were able to secure support from their organization to pursue high-quality research projects. Today, however, most investigators find that this is no longer a viable option.

A New Project Application Within a Personal Program of Research

Regular Investigator-Initiated Research Application (R01)

Submitting the next application as a new regular research application rather than as a competing continuation is a necessity if the funding source does not recognize continuation applications. This is also an option for PIs who have the continuation alternative. Submitting a new application is the only option when neither the current project's findings nor the broad, long-term objectives can support a continuation project or when a project requires a budget that exceeds the restrictions resulting from the prior award. One of the major disadvantages of a new application is the lower success rate of these applications. The NIH's rate for new submissions of R01s in 1994, for example, was 18.2% (Rhein, 1996a). PIs should discuss the advantages and disadvantages of initiating a new area of research with colleagues and coinvestigators. In our opinion, this could be a reasonable choice for investigators whose interests have changed over the course of their funded research. It is also a reasonable choice if data sources become unavailable, which can be the case when children or other vulnerable populations are included. For example, HR 12711, known as the Family Privacy Protection Act of 1995, requires

parental consent before asking questions about such things as political affiliations; psychological problems; illegal, antisocial, or self-incriminating behavior; religious affiliations or beliefs; and so forth ("Bill Threatens," 1995).

Interactive Research Project Grant (IRPG)

The IRPG is a viable option for research programs that require multiple
data collection in several projects. This mechanism, offered by the NIH,
enables investigators to develop at least two related lines of investigation
simultaneously. These are projects that do not require extensive shared physical facilities and could be accomplished independently, but for which collaboration is scientifically important. For example, this mechanism is an effective
means to fund applications for focused clinical research and related correlative
laboratory studies (NIH, 1995f).

Other Alternatives for Maintaining Funding

Small Grants

When investigators need to examine their hypotheses with additional
pilot data, small grants are often a possible funding mechanism. Small grants
from foundations are sometimes available expressly for pilot work, and
sometimes the federal government has a particular interest that incorporates
a small grant program. Investigators need to investigate the availability of
opportunities that coincide with their interests and research needs. The experienced investigator who is interested in continuing ongoing research cannot
use the regular NIH small grant program unless funding is specifically
required to test new methods or techniques that will be incorporated in a future
application. These small grants, like many small grants, are usually limited to
$25,000 to $50,000 per year for 1 or 2 years.

Program Project Grants

Participating either as an investigator or a project PI on a program project
grant could enable an investigator to secure funding for a pilot project that
would keep the research program active for 1 or 2 years and provide the data
required for a full application. Investigators should be aware of the research
of their colleagues so that they do not miss opportunities to either collaborate
in ongoing plans or initiate a plan that would be seen as advantageous to other
investigators. The advantage of program project collaborations is that the

mechanism is designed for projects that require shared physical resources and are theoretically related. These are important advantages for investigators who are seeking a route to obtaining data that are important to a theoretical area but are not sufficiently influential to be funded as a regular research project.

Career Awards

Career awards can be a source of funds for investigators who have received funding for several continuation applications and do not need research funding but need released time from their nonresearch obligations. Career awards are available through the NIH K-awards, the NSF, and larger foundations. The NIH Independent Scientist Award (K02), for example, provides support for newly independent scientists who can demonstrate the need for a period of intensive research focus as a means of enhancing their research careers. The candidate must have peer-reviewed independent research support at the time the award is made. These awards can provide funds from 2 to 5 years. They support some salary and fringe benefits for the PI; limited research support; tuition, fees, and books related to career development; and a low indirect cost rate (the NIH rate is 8%). No support is usually available for ancillary personnel such as clerical, technical, or administrative assistance. The review criteria can include candidate qualifications, the career development plan, the research plan, and the environment and institutional commitment.

Action Strategies

Design the Next Funded Project in Advance of the Current Project's Termination

Take time to focus on the project's scientific future taking into account the funding and scientific environments, which are continually developing. Investigators need to remain current about the kinds of funding opportunities available, funding source interests, and the scientific development in their field of interest as well as that in closely related fields.

Develop Back-Up Funding to Avoid Research Program Shutdown

Although applications can be funded on first submission, this is not the rule. Investigators need to develop back-up plans with colleagues, their supervisors, and their organizations to provide operational funds while waiting for funding. Some organizations have funds that are reserved specifically for investigators while they are applying for continuation funds.

Use a Variety of Resources to Meet Scientific Needs

Do not perseverate on one type of mechanism, one funding source, or one funding plan. As an overall strategy, we suggest that investigators apply to foundations for pilot projects, be aware of opportunities for collaborating on funded projects with colleagues, and investigate related-discipline funding for opportunities. For example, an investigator funded by the National Institute of Mental Health might also have research of interest to the justice system.

Be Alert for Contract Offerings

For experienced investigators, contracts can be a way of funding parts of an active research program. The primary advantage of submitting proposals for contracts is the short turnaround time. Usually, the time between the announcement and the receipt date is short, sometimes only 35 days, and the time between receipt date and notice of award is also usually brief. This mechanism can be used by investigators who are active in an area of research and whose specific interests coincide with that of the funding source. Contracts often are restricted to a specific topic, such as a disease, treatment, or product (e.g., tissue samples, data sets). Some of the important disadvantages are the creativity restrictions, detailed reporting requirements, and level of funding. However, there are also contract announcements that afford investigators greater leeway. For example, a funding source might be interested in proposals that are restricted to a particular area such as consequences of smoking, but that is the only restriction placed on investigators. In this instance, projects about the physiological, psychological, environmental, or policy consequences of smoking would be acceptable. These funding sources do, however, require the administrative work customarily associated with contracts.

We suggest that investigators examine the funding source requirements before either accepting or rejecting the idea of submitting a contract proposal in response to a call for proposals. This funding method does require more administrative effort. The budget should be meticulously calculated so that the desire to get funded does not produce a net loss later. In addition, investigators need to be willing to stand firm on an offer the funding source views as too high. Although some contracts permit scientific and creative leeway for investigators, this does not release investigators from being constrained within the boundaries set by the funding source.

PART V

Application Preparation

chapter 12

What to Include in a
Project Application

This chapter provides an overview of the application's components and discusses several in more detail. The best information available to investigators about the application components expected by reviewers is provided by the funding source. This information can range from a cryptic statement— "Present a description of the project and provide a cost estimate"—to a detailed description of information required in each part of the application. The instructions might also include the information about what to exclude, which could include appendixes, publications, manuscripts, and letters of support from individuals not involved in the project.

Each application part provides new information about the project and the investigators. Investigators submit the strongest applications when they reflect on how they can make each part contribute to the overall quality of their application and will produce an application that makes a strong case for the importance of the project and the ability of the investigators to complete the project successfully. In most instances, funding sources require information that can be placed under headings such as Title, Specific Aims (Objectives), Background and Significance (Literature Review or Conceptual Framework), Preliminary Studies (Previous Work), Design and Methods, Abstract, and Literature Cited. In addition, supporting documentation is generally required. In some instances, the requirements are limited to curricula vitae or biographical sketches for the principal investigator (PI) and investigators. In other instances, additional materials such as reporting other funding sources for the

PI and key investigators, description of the project environment detailing the resources available, budget for the entire project as well as a detailed budget for the first year, budget justification, cover page or letter, and evidence of adherence to specific regulations are required.

Do Not Neglect Parts of the Project Plan

Title

It is common for investigators to write titles with little thought to the consequences of their word choice or the word order. In our opinion, it is an error to disregard a title's potential power. The title can play a role in reviewer selection and can be used by reviewers to identify the project's content area. A carefully crafted title communicates effectively and can correctly guide a reviewer's expectations. A worst-case scenario is for reviewers to respond to a title with excitement only to feel let down when they discover that the project is not what they expected. We believe that effective titles are short, interesting, informative, and have first words that provide information about the project's content.

Specific Aims (Objectives)

The Specific Aims and/or Objectives section presents the project's goals. An effective presentation of these goals includes statements at three levels of generality: the broad, long-term goals of the project area, the specific aims of the proposed project, and the study hypotheses or questions generated by the specific aims. An optional description that can be used in this section is a brief statement of the project's rationale. Inclusion of this statement depends on the discipline and the area of investigation. For some proposals, a rationale statement might be considered needless repetition of what everyone in the content area knows. Keep in mind, however, that the project plan should educate the reviewer not only about the content but also about the investigator's knowledge about the project's place in the broader area of investigation. In our opinion, it is desirable to limit the Specific Aims section to one single-spaced page or less. For some projects, presenting a list of the overall or long-term objectives, the specific aims, and the hypotheses or questions without additional supporting material is sufficient. The discipline and project type determine whether this is a compelling presentation. However, it is our experience that a combination of lists with brief discussion paragraphs provides more information for the reviewer and is also a familiar presentation format for many investigators.

Brief Rationale Statement

The purpose of a brief rationale statement for the project is to provide information about the current conditions or positive consequences of the proposed project. This rationale statement should establish the social, economic, educational, health, or scientific context for the project and its relationship to the funding source's mission. For example, this might be developed in terms of costs incurred by unsolved problems, contributions to scientific knowledge, or perhaps the need for data that can be used for intervention strategies. Because one of the characteristics of a successful application is that it is original, it must be assumed that the investigator's line of thought and reasoning will not be immediately obvious to others. Whether a project contributes to scientific knowledge or applies current knowledge to new populations or to previously hidden problems, a rationale statement placing the project in its context relieves the reviewer of the task of reconstructing the PI's train of thought.

Broad, Long-Term Objectives

The overall long-term project objective should be the broadest use of the findings. Reaching this objective is achieved only through extensive investigation of multiple aspects of the problem. New investigators when they write this objective have a tendency either to have too broad an objective or to constrain it too narrowly. The long-term objective needs to be broad enough to justify the project efforts, yet narrow enough so that it is evident that the proposed project's activities are integral to achieving it.

Specific Aims

Specific aims or objectives are statements about the project outcomes. They specify and operationalize the project focus. They are statements of the problem to be solved or how the project's findings will be used. These statements are not hypotheses; they are not tested; they are not descriptions of the methods through which outcomes will be achieved. For example, "The aims of this research are to divide the population into socioeconomic status groups and to survey the parents in each of these groups to determine the health-care needs of children" is not a statement of specific aims; it is a statement about design and data collection methods. A specific aim of this project might be stated as follows: "The specific aim of this research is to determine how parents' perception of children's health care needs differ from health care use as reported by community health agencies."

Hypotheses or Questions

Hypotheses or questions should originate in a knowledge base, and that knowledge base must be presented in the project proposal. We suggest that hypotheses should not be formed on the basis of a comment such as "It would be interesting to see what happens when variable X is included." It is our opinion that the inclusion of variables in hypotheses or questions should be supported by theory or experience. Kerlinger (1964) points out that hypotheses must express a relationship and be testable. They must include, therefore, at least two measurable, or potentially measurable, variables and their relationship. We prefer that substantive hypotheses be used in this section of the project plan rather than statistical hypotheses. Hypotheses or questions direct the project's design and the data collection methods and the substantive hypotheses clearly state the outcomes expected by the PI. Whether hypotheses or questions are used depends on the project. A quantitative study might have hypotheses and questions, whereas qualitative studies generally use questions rather than hypotheses. Usually, study designs do not support inclusion of both hypotheses and questions. However, if a study includes both quantitative and qualitative components, then hypotheses and questions appropriate to the objectives need to be stated.

Literature Review

The purpose of the literature review is to build a case for the practical or theoretical importance of the proposed project. The most effective literature reviews demonstrate the investigator's understanding of the subject matter and compellingly justify the need for the investigation. This section is analogous to the summing up statement of an attorney before a jury. Literature reviews that are not exhaustive but contain a carefully selected literature that undoubtedly forms the basis for the proposed projects are most likely to lead reviewers to the same conclusion as the investigators. Therefore, we suggest that the application should present only the literature pertinent to the project in a thoughtful and integrated way. The literature review should be written in a manner that persuades the reviewer that the investigators have a solid grasp of the subject matter and that the related studies and theoretical formulations have been read with a critical and integrative attitude. It is suggested that the following three elements be included in this section: rationale for the research, theoretical position (if appropriate), and review of investigations inspiring the current project. For the most part, if each hypothesis or question presented in the specific aims has a literature, it is recommended that the literature review be presented in the same order as the hypotheses or questions. A book that might be useful in overcoming some obstacles encountered in writing the literature review is Cooper's (1989) *Integrating Research: A Guide for Literature Reviews,* even though it focuses on writing review articles rather than Literature Review sections.

Research Rationale

This section amplifies the rationale for conducting the project presented in the Specific Aims section. The literature review pertinent to the rationale should play a role in determining the importance and urgency of the proposed project. The information presented should be adequate to provide the complete context. However, investigators should refrain from mentioning every article ever written. We recommend that they do not simply present a list of referenced facts and figures but develop their own conclusions based on the data and their relationships. Many projects arise out of prior investigations believed to have conclusions that are faulty or narrow. When this is the case, the reasons for believing that the conclusions drawn are faulty or narrow should be explained and alternatives described in detail. It is a serious error for PIs to fail to state their conclusions, because it compels reviewers to draw their own, which may or may not be congruent with the PI's conclusions. Statements of how the proposed project will influence the current social, economic, educational, health, or scientific situation should be incorporated.

Theoretical Position

Whenever a project is based on one or more theories, a brief discussion of these theoretical positions needs to be presented. In our opinion, a clear discussion of the scientific rationale is imperative. Draw out the relationships between the project hypotheses and the theory. Do not introduce or discuss a theoretical position and then never refer to it again. Whenever there is a potential for confounding from issues closely associated with the experimental treatment or intervention effects, a PI should discuss how these will be minimized, and how interpretations will be handled.

Review of Research Inspiring the Current Project

In our opinion, investigators must read as much of the literature relevant to their topic as possible. The reviewers, however, have no interest in reading abstracts of all of these articles or the details of each study. Knowledge acquired by PIs through a thorough review of the pertinent literature facilitates writing a concise and effective review of the material directly related to the project variables; to write not only words but to communicate thoughts. A literature review frequently progresses from general background information, such as early studies and early theory testing, through amplification studies emphasizing either populations or variables, to current investigations that have sparked the PI's interest, and subsequently to the proposed project. We suggest that general background information, information about the trends that have been established, and a description of the customary project and statistical methodology be included. As the brief historical description of the science becomes more current, greater attention is given to changing methodology (particularly if the project proposes to change it), sample size (especially if sample sizes are small for the type of project), and project design. The studies for which most detail is required are those that surround those gaps that the proposed project is designed to fill, or the conclusions that are the basis of new hypotheses or questions.

In some areas of investigation, such as randomized clinical trials and others using experimental designs, investigators can use quantitative literature reviews. In these reviews, data from previous studies are pooled and these pooled data analyzed. This technique, called meta-analysis or CI (combination of information) (National Research Council, 1992), might be used in conjunction with a qualitative review. Its use, however, must be governed by the conventions of the research area, and the composition of the review group. Unless a new investigator knows he or she would be considered remiss for not including a quantitative review, the investigator should seek advice from colleagues before including it as a part of the application literature review.

Characteristics of the Literature Review

The literature review must be focused. Ruthlessly exercise discipline to exclude excursions into related research areas. The articles included must be directly related to the project's stated objectives. We emphasize that every article that makes a particular point need not be cited separately. A sentence such as "Evidence that this is the case can be found in several research reports, the most impressive of which are . . . " might be used. Be certain to cite current research, and whenever possible research reported by review group members. Do not perturb reviewers by not including literature that is reasonably expected, or by presenting the literature in a list, rather than in an integrated, persuasive style that leads to justifying the proposed research as the next step.

We would like to give a word of warning about using the results of investigations reported by review group members. Because the review group consists of investigators interested in topics similar to the one being proposed, it is reasonable to assume that some of their findings are relevant. These are the findings that cannot fail to be mentioned, but because relevance is most apparent to PIs, it may be important to discuss the criteria used to determine the relevancy of the work. However, if findings are clearly not relevant, the author, now reviewer, will certainly know that and may exact a penalty.

Preliminary Studies

The purpose of the Preliminary Studies section is to provide reviewers with evidence of the PI's ability to successfully complete a project such as the one proposed. Write this section so it presents the relationship between prior work and the proposed project and also documents how the investigators' previous project experience will be used in the proposed project. The information in this section will help inspire confidence in reviewers about the PI's experience and competence to pursue the proposed project. List the titles and complete references of appropriate publications and manuscripts accepted for publication.

The strongest preliminary data are pilot data collected by the PI for the proposed project. A brief description of the PI's projects that lay the groundwork for the proposed study helps reviewers assess competence. In our opinion, the entire study, as published, should not be reported, but rather a summary of those highlights that buttress the reviewer's perception of the PI's ability to carry out the proposed investigation, with specified subjects, using the proposed methodology and data, and applying the selected data retrieval instruments. As in the literature review, avoid a seemingly endless list of project titles, procedures, and data. In many cases, a list of the citations for the published studies discussed is permitted in this section.

Because the Preliminary Studies section recounts prior work required for the successful conduct of the entire proposed project, not just that which is the responsibility of the PI, work of the coinvestigators should also be included. Keep in mind the purpose of this section. It is here that investigators are building a case to document that they can successfully complete research projects and are competent and knowledgeable about the requirements of the proposed project. If complicated instrumentation is required, provide evidence that pretests have been conducted and that back-up support is available should instrument failure occur. For example, if electronic or photo imaging is used for data collection, describe in detail the procedures previously used and the reliability of the measures. With this kind of methodology, details are particularly important in instances in which subtle position changes of the patient (subject) influence the image and consequently the data.

Research Design and Methods

The Research Design and Methods section describes the project design, procedures, and statistical analyses that will be used to accomplish the project's specific aims. The section includes the components of a journal article: design, participants/subjects, instruments, procedures, and statistical analyses.

Project Design

The design, experimental or other, must be clearly described. A statement that a "split plot," a "regression discontinuity," or a "focus group" design will be used is not sufficient. Some designs are unique to a discipline or content area, and designs used in common across disciplines may have different labels. Therefore, it is helpful to the reviewers to describe the design in a way that clearly demonstrates its applicability to the project's hypotheses. In experimental or quasi-experimental research, comparison or control groups must be given as much attention as the experimental or intervention group(s). It is critical to be able to determine the effectiveness of the research manipulation or the intervention. Generally, simple designs are preferred. Qualitative study designs need to be as carefully described as quantitative designs. As with a quantitative description, designs need to be described in a way that is understood across disciplines and by investigators favoring quantitative or qualitative paradigms.

Participants/Subjects

Describe relevant subject characteristics. Specify the ways in which the subject characteristics and the sample will be selected for testing the hypotheses. Sometimes it is necessary to use samples of convenience. When this is the case, the significance of the method of subject selection for data interpretation should be discussed. It is important to defend the appropriateness of the sampling procedure in spite of shortcomings. We suggest that information be included about projected attrition rates and, if significant, the corrective procedures to be used.

When people are studied, describe in as much detail as possible the expectation for including minority groups and/or women as participants. Include data on minority rates in the population from which participants will be drawn and the recruitment procedures for minority and women participants. These issues are discussed further in Chapter 15. Include oversampling plans whenever the proportion of minorities in the population is low and discuss how oversampling will not invalidate conclusions. If the proposed project cannot accommodate minorities or are gender specific, discuss the reasons. When an investigation requires exclusion criteria, do not describe them in general terms, but provide an operational definition of how the criteria will be applied. For example, if individuals with cerebrovascular or cardiovascular complications are to be excluded, give detailed information about how the presence of the complications is determined and the range of measurement values used to exclude potential participants.

Although it is more difficult in qualitative studies to be precise about the number of individuals or subjects that will be interviewed or will participate in other ways, estimates need to be presented. It is important that reviewers have an idea of the size of the data collection effort. An estimate by the PI provides reasonable guidelines for reviewers to use in their project assessment.

Data Collection Instruments and Data Characteristics

Describe the data collection instruments, including reliability and validity information when appropriate. If one instrument has been chosen over another, or if a decision has been made not to upgrade an instrument, describe why the instrument selected is appropriate for the proposed project. The range of technology used for data collection continues to expand. If data collection incorporates cutting-edge technology, or technology that has not previously been used, greater effort must be made to describe how the collected information will be used for data analyses, and the inferences that will be made. The outcome measures for intervention evaluations must be related to the intervention rather than to the idiosyncrasies of the intervention participants. For data collected over time, both short-term and long-term data collection procedures should be justified. A discussion of the adequacy of data collection over the short term provides reviewers with a rationale for data collection over a brief period. When data collection extends over a long period, for example, several weeks, months, or a year, a discussion of the strategy for providing incentives for participants to remain in the study should be included. The potential negative or positive effects on the data of repeated meetings between study data collection staff and the participants should be discussed. Although it is common in longitudinal studies to use the same data collection instrument on multiple occasions, both positive and negative effects of this for the proposed project should be reviewed.

We suggest PIs not include plans for collecting data that will not be analyzed or that play only a cursory explanatory role. The amount of work expected from each subject—called respondent burden—is a concern of many reviewers. Thus, it is advisable that only data directly related to the project's hypotheses be collected. This focused data collection communicates that the PI has a solid grasp on the study parameters and does not wish to burden subjects with excessive data collection procedures. Reviewers will question, and perhaps react negatively, to collecting data on variables only remotely associated with the project topic.

Procedure

Describe the proposed data collection procedures in sufficient detail for reviewers to understand them in general terms. "A telephone survey will be conducted to collect data on . . . " is not sufficient detail. In this case, describe the interviewer training procedures, their instructions for entering respondent replies, and procedures for immediately capturing missed data. "Participant observation will be used to collect data on . . . " is not sufficient detail. The label *participant observation* is one of many labels applied to procedures that invoke a plethora of detail for those familiar with them, but provide very little or incorrect information for those in other disciplines or those familiar with other study procedures. Although the description need not go into microscopic detail, it must be sufficient for someone unfamiliar with the procedure to duplicate the major aspects and imagine the data collection environment.

If there are alternative procedures in the literature, indicate the ways in which the procedure selected is most appropriate for the project. If there is a possibility that something can go awry, discuss it and present the alternative action to be taken. Particularly vulnerable to modification are recruitment procedures because results are not always as anticipated. These procedures have a direct effect on the composition of the proposed sample and need to be designed so that the final results are not biased. Reviewers are interested in the details of the planned procedures, especially if they entail oversampling, and for modifications if planned procedures are inadequate, but they also welcome descriptions of alternative procedures that will not bias the results.

Whenever data collection requires training, for example, data coders, interviewers, recruiters, or intervention leaders, present a careful description of the training procedures and of the trainers' credentials. The detail required is dependent on the uniqueness of the project role or task being described. If there are standard practices, the description can be brief and referenced; otherwise, include sufficient detail to assure reviewers that training will be adequate. If data collection is associated with the occurrence of an event, such as the death of a spouse or the first visit to the physician, a detailed discussion of the event identification and appropriateness of the timing for data collection is imperative.

Data Management

Describe the plans for recording initial data and entering data for analysis and storage. It is critical that data entry, retrieval, and storage be given serious consideration, because some data entry and storage systems are more vulnerable to data loss than others. Whenever possible, include a detailed description of the proposed system and the factors that the design incorporates, such as research procedures and staff work style. When data confidentiality is an issue, detail the procedures that will be used to ensure confidentiality without compromising data integrity. If a data management center is to be used, include a description and credentials in the application.

Statistical Approach or Analysis Method

This section describes the statistical approach and related data analyses at a reasonable level of detail. The Data Analysis section should include descriptive statistics, data checks for outlying data with a discussion of how outliers will be handled, and data transformations expected to be used, such as log transformations. Present the specific statistic to be used, for example, Pearson's r, tetrachoric, or polyserial correlation, or the kind of factor analysis rotation, for example, varimax or promax, rather than a general label.

The greater the complexity of the statistical analyses, the more important it is to discuss their rationale and include details. Care with regard to these discussions communicates the PI's ability to handle whatever statistical problems might arise. Associating the statistical tests with their specific aims and hypotheses is extremely helpful to reviewers. The threads tying statistical tests to hypotheses are not always easy to follow, and misunderstandings can be deflected by carefully specifying the associations. The same issues arise when multiple data sets are analyzed. We also suggest that a discussion of expected results and their interpretation be included.

Statistical power. Statistical power is the ability of a statistical test to detect the effect size of interest. Important information for reviewers is a section indicating that the selected sample size is sufficient to detect a meaningful effect size, given the study's statistical design. Include the chosen alpha level, the effect size required, and the estimated standard deviation. When the analysis requires a variety of comparisons among groups, requiring several statistical tests, include information on statistical power for all the major analyses.

Project Timeline

A project timeline describes the time frame for the procedures presented in the project plan. This timeline needs to be realistic! If only 2 years are allowed by the sponsor and the project requires 2 years, report writing will need to be completed after the funded period. Although start-up time is routinely underestimated, serious underestimation may generate uneasiness in reviewers about the conduct of the entire project.

The project timeline is also a template for what is presented in the budget, year by year. The time frame within which data collection occurs dictates the yearly data collection expenses. We suggest careful attention to the availability of participants or subjects or other data sources year by year and the feasibility of collecting data on all those available.

Protection of Human and Animal Subjects

Although it often appears that investigators pay attention to the protection of human and animal subjects only after an application has been submitted, that is not so. The criteria for the protection of human and animal subjects must be met within the project procedures. The human participant information that needs to be provided is a complete description of the population and data sources, an outline of recruitment and informed consent procedures, a description of the risks to participants and how they will be minimized, and why they are reasonable in relation to the anticipated benefits to the participants and for the importance of knowledge that is expected. The animal subject information that needs to be provided is complete animal identification, justification of animal choice, veterinary care procedures, subject distress issues, and euthanasia procedures.

Abstract

The abstract is vitally important because it, like the title, is used as a summary for what is being proposed and how it will be done. It must, therefore, communicate the content of the proposed project succinctly and accurately, without reference to the entire application. Because some decisions about the application may be made only on the basis of the abstract, it is an important writing task and must not be dashed off in the last minutes before the application goes into the mail. Abstract length should conform to that required by the funding source. If no instructions are provided, in our opinion, a reasonable length is about 250 words, approximately one double-spaced page. The abstract should include the project's broad, long-term objectives and specific aims. The importance of the project should be outlined. This needs to be done in sufficient detail so that someone reading only the abstract can be persuaded that the project is worthwhile. Sufficient background information needs to be provided to place the proposed project in a scientific context. The PI's previous work can be cited if it leads to the current project. We recommend that the design and methods for achieving the project objectives be incorporated. A statement of the relationship of the project to the mission of the funding source is an important component of the abstract.

The importance of clarity and efficiency in stating this relationship cannot be overestimated. Figure 12.1 presents a sample abstract using the PHS 398 form.

Literature Cited

This section is often viewed as tedious and difficult because of the detail involved in each citation. It is important, however, to be as conscientious about it as about every other section. References that are incorrect or incomplete, misspelled names, omitted citations, or citations included for articles not referenced can all be viewed as indications of carelessness. Complete citations should be used, including title, names of all authors, journal volume number, page numbers, and year of publication, book publishers, place of publication, volume number, and publication year. Use a standard citation style such as that of the American Psychological Association (APA) style manual. Some citation styles do not include the title. It is our opinion that these styles are not appropriate for project applications, unless application instructions state that titles be omitted.

Include All Requested Supporting Documents

Most application forms require materials in addition to the project proposal. The most commonly required information is the budget and a budget justification. However, other documents often required are those (a) attesting to the PI's and coinvestigators' ability including curricula vitae and biographical sketches (see Figure 12.2 for a sample biographical sketch using the PHS 398 form), (b) outlining the other financial resources available to them for other projects and from other sources, and (c) substantiating the ability of the proposed project's environment to support the project.

Budget

Budget information includes the estimated costs for all project components that account for the direct costs, a narrative justifying these costs, and a statement of indirect costs or overhead requested by the applicant organization. Budget items are determined by the proposed project and the indirect cost agreement negotiated by the PI's organization, or the funding source guidelines detailing allowable costs. Budget categories generally include personnel, consultants, equipment, travel, supplies, and a miscellaneous category. In most instances, each of these categories requires a justification paragraph. Grant budgets should be a reasonable estimate of what the project

BB   Principal Investigator/Program Director *(Last, first, middle):* Winnit, Carol L.

DESCRIPTION. State the application's broad, long-term objectives and specific aims, making reference to the health relatedness of the project. Describe concisely the research design and methods for achieving these goals. Avoid summaries of past accomplishments and the use of the first person. This description is meant to serve as a succinct and accurate description of the proposed work when separated from the application. If the application is funded, this description, as is, will become public information. Therefore, do not include proprietary/confidential information. DO NOT EXCEED THE SPACE PROVIDED.

Rural communities, like urban communities, experience problems associated with drug abuse and drug dependence. However, existing treatment interventions are not tailored for rural settings. The overall aim of this three-year project is to modify an existing social skills behavioral therapy for rural population, refine the therapy, develop a manual, train and supervise therapists, and pilot test the structured behavioral outpatient rural therapy to treat rural drug abusers and drug dependents as Stage I Research for NIDA's Behavioral Therapies Development Program. Year One and part of the second year will involve rural treatment program therapists, university clinical staff, recovering patients, and the project team in modifying the existing behavioral therapy for use with rural drug abusers/dependents. A focus group will be convened by project staff to develop an initial draft manual. In Year Two instrumentation will be finalized after preliminary testing. The draft manual will also be finalized for the pilot test. Therapists will be selected competitively for the pilot test. In Year Three, therapy will be delivered by manual-trained therapists at three sites. At least one day of on-site therapist supervision will be given monthly and supervision sessions will be provided weekly during the comparative pilot test in Year Three. A total of n patients who meet DSM-IV criteria for drug abuse/dependence will enter the comparative pilot test. With a drop-out rate of about 20%, this will assure n patients with n patients in each of the two groups (therapy as usual and social skills behavioral therapy) for data analysis. The level of psychiatric severity assessed will be included as a variable for the analyses as will the presence or absence of antisocial personality. Patients will be matched by gender, race-ethnicity, and educational level.

PERFORMANCE SITE(S) *(organization, city, state)*

KEY PERSONNEL. See instructions on Page 11. *Use continuation pages as needed* to provide the required information in the format shown below.

Name   Organization   Role on Project

Figure 12.1. Sample Abstract

FF   Principal Investigator/Program Director *(Last, first, middle):* Winnit, Carol L.

BIOGRAPHICAL SKETCH

Provide the following information for the key personnel in the order listed on Form Page 2.
Photocopy this page or follow this format for each person.

NAME	POSITION TITLE
Carol L. Winnit	Professor

EDUCATION/TRAINING *(Begin with baccalaureate or other initial professional education, such as nursing, and include postdoctoral training.)*

INSTITUTION AND LOCATION	DEGREE *(if applicable)*	YEAR(s)	FIELD OF STUDY
College, Anywhere, US	B.S.	1965	Social Science
University, Somewhere, US	M.S	1967	Psychology
University, Somewhere, US	Ph.D.	1971	Psychology

RESEARCH AND PROFESSIONAL EXPERIENCE: Concluding with present position, list, in chronological order, previous employment, experience, and honors. Include present membership on any Federal Government public advisory committee. List, in chronological order, the titles, all authors, and complete references to all publications during the past three years and to representative earlier publications pertinent to this application. If the list of publications in the last three years exceeds two pages, select the most pertinent publications. DO NOT EXCEED TWO PAGES.

PROFESSIONAL EXPERIENCE

SELECTED PUBLICATIONS:

Figure 12.2. Sample Biographical Sketch

will cost. Underestimates not only are potentially detrimental to project completion but might also be a signal to reviewers that the PI is naive about the scope of the proposed project. An excessive overestimation also invites the latter view. Because budget reductions have become an expected occurrence from many funding sources including the federal government, and the decreasing ability of awardee organizations to pick up unexpected project expenses, careful attention to all project details is critical so that sufficient financial support is requested. "Good research requires an adequate budget. To passively accept a large reduction of an appropriate budget is to compromise the quality of the research" (Ogden, 1991, p. 47). Different strategies have been used by PIs to avoid serious funding shortfalls. PIs should be sure that all personnel and materials required to complete the project are included in the budget, and they should also be sure that succeeding years of the budget include not only increases for inflation but that known cost increases for specific items be factored into the costs. Figure 12.3 is a sample first-year budget page and Figure 12.4 a sample entire project period budget page from the PHS 398 application.

Personnel

Personnel includes those individuals who will be providing a specific service required by the project. Refer to the application instructions for guidelines on the definition of personnel. The PHS 398 form defines personnel as those individuals who are employed by the PI's organization. Individuals who fill a project role but are employed elsewhere are defined as consultants or subcontractors. Costs for personnel include salaries and fringe benefits, proportional to time required by the project. (Note that some funding sources will allow technician or research assistant salaries, but not PI or other investigator salaries.) If the project crosses fiscal years, be sure to weight the salaries and fringe benefits accordingly. The names and percent effort for investigators who donate time to the project are also listed in the personnel or consultant section of the budget, including their names and project roles.

PI, co-PI, and other investigators. In most cases, it is preferable that the PI's effort contribution be at least 20%. Co-PIs and other investigators are to be included in the project only when their expertise is required for its successful conduct, and their effort contribution must reflect their project role. Efforts of 2.5% or 5%, or 6 to 12 work days per year, are appropriate for investigators who are regarded as consultants, but generally not for investigators who will be doing project management, instrument design, or data collection.

Statistician. It is imperative, in our opinion, that statistical consultation be included in the budget. This service can be provided either by an investigator who qualifies as a statistical expert or by including a statistician.

Research assistant/staff effort. Research assistant/staff effort is determined by activities outlined in the Procedure section and the time required to conduct project activities. These roles can include interviewers, recruiters, research nurses, data entry clerks, coding clerks, transcribing clerks, programmers, lab technicians, or medical technicians. It is important to include adequate and qualified personnel to conduct all of the data collection tasks. Secretarial help, although often required on projects, is usually not considered an acceptable use of project money, whereas a project that requires a significant amount of coordination within the project and individuals outside of the project could request an administrative assistant for these activities. In cases where the PI's organization does not have the resources to fill these kinds of project needs, include the position in the budget and write a strong justification for it.

Consultants

Consultants are experts who provide advice and other substantive assistance to the PI and others on the project on an ongoing basis. Consultant travel, per diem, and lodging expenses usually are included in the budget as well as a consulting fee for each year of the project.

Equipment

The rules about the cost of items in the equipment category vary with the funding source. The National Institutes of Health (NIH) reserves this category for equipment that costs $5,000 or more per unit with a useful life of more than 1 year. However, the NIH accepts the definition of the applicant organization if it has a lower unit cost. In general, it is recommended that equipment that costs several thousand dollars not be included within a project application but be obtained with a separate application. Equipment items such as tape recorders and transcribing equipment that cost less than the minimum specified by the funding source generally are listed as "other."

Travel

Travel to professional meetings by the PI and co-PI to present findings is a customary budget item. However, it is prudent to keep the cost of travel as reasonable as possible and to limit trips to one per year for the PI and co-PIs.

DD | Principal Investigator/Program Director (Last, first, middle): Winnit, Carol L.

DETAILED BUDGET FOR INITIAL BUDGET PERIOD DIRECT COSTS ONLY	FROM 7/1/98	THROUGH 6/30/99

| PERSONNEL (Applicant organization only) | | TYPE APPT. (months) | % EFFORT ON PROJ. | INST. BASE SALARY | DOLLAR AMOUNT REQUESTED (omit cents) | | |
NAME	ROLE ON PROJECT				SALARY REQUESTED	FRINGE BENEFITS	TOTALS
Carol L. Winnit, Ph.D.	Principal Investigator	12	25	90,000	22,500	5,175	27,675
Brian Ford, Ph.D.	Co-Invest	12	15	65,000	9,750	2,242	11,992
Shirley Riley, Ph.D.	Co-Invest	12	15	57,000	8,550	1,966	10,516
Clarence Smith	Med.Tech.	12	100	25,000	25,000	5,750	30,750
SUBTOTALS ⟶					65,800	15,133	80,933

CONSULTANT COSTS John Seemore, Ph.D., Johns Hopkins University School of
Medicine; one 3-day trip @ $750 air fare and $500 per diem | 2,250

EQUIPMENT (Itemize)

Shock generator $1,500 | 1,500

SUPPLIES (Itemize by category)
Lab supplies $750
Computer supplies $500
Assessment schedules $600 | 1,850

TRAVEL
One Professional Meeting for P.I. | 2,000

| PATIENT CARE COSTS | INPATIENT | 0 |
| | OUTPATIENT | 0 |

ALTERATIONS AND RENOVATIONS (Itemize by category) | 0

OTHER EXPENSES (Itemize by category)
Participant costs 30 @ $25 = $750   Photocopying of rating scales:
Publication costs $700   4 ratings @ 15 pages @ $ .08 for
Long distance calls $500   30 participants = $144 | 2,094

SUBTOTAL DIRECT COSTS FOR INITIAL BUDGET PERIOD	$ 90,627

| CONSORTIUM/CONTRACTUAL COSTS | DIRECT COSTS | 0 |
| | INDIRECT COSTS | 0 |

TOTAL DIRECT COSTS FOR INITIAL BUDGET PERIOD (Item 7a, Face Page) ⟶	$ 90,627

PHS 398 (Rev. 5/95)   (Form Page 4) Page _____   DD
Number pages consecutively at the bottom throughout the application. Do not use suffixes such as 3a, 3b..

EE   Principal Investigator/Program Director *(Last, first, middle):* Winnit, Carol L.

BUDGET FOR ENTIRE PROPOSED PERIOD OF SUPPORT
DIRECT COSTS ONLY

BUDGET CATEGORY TOTALS		INITIAL BUDGET PERIOD *(from Form Page 4)*	ADDITIONAL YEARS OF SUPPORT REQUESTED			
			2nd	3rd	4th	5th
PERSONNEL: *Salary and fringe benefits* Applicant organization only		80,933	84,170	87,537		
CONSULTANT COSTS		2,250	2,340	2,433		
EQUIPMENT		1,500	0	0		
SUPPLIES		1,850	1,924	2,000		
TRAVEL		2,000	2,080	2,163		
PATIENT CARE COSTS	INPATIENT	0	0	0		
	OUTPATIENT	0	0	0		
ALTERATIONS AND RENOVATIONS		0	0	0		
OTHER EXPENSES		2,094	2,177	2,264		
SUBTOTAL DIRECT COSTS		90,627	92,691	96,397		
CONSORTIUM/ CONTRACTUAL COSTS	DIRECT	0	0	0		
	INDIRECT	0	0	0		
TOTAL DIRECT COSTS		90,627	92,691	96,397		

TOTAL DIRECT COSTS FOR ENTIRE PROPOSED PERIOD OF SUPPORT *(Item 8a, Face Page)* → $ 279,715

JUSTIFICATION. Follow the budget justification instructions exactly. Use continuation pages as needed.

Figure 12.4. Sample Summary Budget

Investigators on the project usually do not receive travel funds from the budget. For multisite projects, travel fees for co-PIs to attend annual project meetings should also be included in the budget, as should mandatory meetings associated with contracts and cooperative agreements.

Supplies

This category includes all disposable items. In our opinion, it is best to organize these items by categories, such as office supplies, lab supplies, computer supplies, glassware, or chemicals. When the cost per category is $1,000 or more, we recommend that costs be itemized within each category to provide reviewers with the most accurate picture of the scope of the project plans. If animals are involved, describe them as completely as possible, including the species, the number to be used, the unit purchase cost, the unit care cost, and the number of care days.

Other or Miscellaneous

This category is for budget items not contained within the above budget categories. These expenses may include participant reimbursement, long-distance telephone charges, mainframe computing time, postage for mail surveys, lab charges, publication costs, page charges, books, rentals and leases, equipment maintenance, and minor fee-for-service contracts such as one-time programmer fee. It is important that all of the expenses associated with the data collection be included. If there is no budget item, reviewers cannot assume the work will be done.

Indirect Costs

Indirect costs are costs paid by the funding source to the applicant organization to support the project. In general, indirect costs are based on the costs for utilities, building and lab maintenance, secretarial support, research support personnel, graduate student support, and upkeep of libraries. Although indirect costs are often overlooked as being part of the project budget, they do increase the total amount and become part of the project costs. Indirect costs can become very important in the design of a project with a funding cap that includes both the direct and indirect costs.

Budget Justification

Each budget item does not need to be justified, but it is a good idea to write a justification paragraph for each primary budget category, at the level of detail required for communicating the importance of the expenditure and the basis for the budget.

Biographical Sketches

Biographical sketches are generally required for all key project personnel. Key personnel are those involved directly in the project. Biographical sketches must be written and prepared according to the instructions provided by the funding source. In general, this includes the individual's formal credentials and a list of publications. Even if a page limitation is not placed on biographical information, we recommend limiting it to two pages. We also suggest that an exhaustive list of recent publications not be included, but a selection of recent publications relevant to the proposed project. Figure 12.2 is a sample biographical sketch page from the PHS 398 application.

Other Support

Other support information is often required for all key personnel. Other support includes financial assistance for current projects in which the PI or coinvestigators are involved. The information usually required by funding sources includes the project title, duration, award amount, funding source, amount of effort committed, a brief project description, and a statement about extent of overlap with the proposed project.

Resources and Environment

This section requires special attention because it substantiates the ability of the PI's setting to support the proposed project. The funding source may provide categories for required information. However, if categories are not provided, we suggest including pertinent information about laboratory facilities, clinical facilities and access patterns, animal care facilities, computer facilities, office space, available technology, or other special facilities on which the project will rely. Information about the availability of necessary equipment, together with information about location, availability, maintenance plans for vulnerable equipment, and related information, assures reviewers that a project can be completed. If the project requires major equipment and this equipment is not included in the budget, it is critical that it be mentioned in this section so reviewers are assured of its availability. Additional general information can also increase the reviewers' confidence in the ability of the PI's setting to support the project. For example, the availability of colleagues, the fall-back technology arrangements that are regularly in place, and the regular consulting resources available, such as statisticians or computer programmers, can be reviewed and discussed. The length of this section should be established by the number and extent of resources described and application instructions.

Program Income

Some projects have the potential for generating income for PIs and their organizations. Funding sources vary in their requirements for reporting income earned as a result of their project funding. Regulations also often vary between profit and nonprofit award recipients.

Appendixes

When an application is submitted with the PHS 398 packet, an appendix cannot include material essential to the evaluation of the project. In our opinion, an appendix should only be used to give expanded information about something that is fully explained in the text. Reviewers may or may not read the appendixes.

Action Strategies

Review Project Plan for Completeness

After reviewing the specific aims and hypotheses that reflect what the project is intended to accomplish, ask a colleague to review the procedure and other research sections for omissions. Familiarity with procedures and subject characteristics can result in a sketchy description that is insufficient for the reviewer to visualize what is planned. We recommend that reviews by colleagues be delayed until a good command of the project is attained, so that suggestions for including other variables and different procedures can be useful. Listen to these suggestions, and use what is appropriate, but do not feel compelled to significantly modify the plan unless a colleague points out a fatal flaw. If this happens, go back to the drawing board.

Read journal articles to learn what information is customarily provided on participants or subjects, what procedural details are included, and the extent of instrumentation detail for the specific research area. This probably is what reviewers also consider customary information. Include at least the minimum material generally found and present it in a conventional and lucid manner. Compare the funding source instructions point by point with the project plan. Be particularly attentive to policies about inclusion of women and minority populations as participants, investigators, and project personnel.

Recognize Funded Grants and Funded PIs as Resources

Looking through a funded project application can provide a general idea of what a completed application looks like. However, do not use an application to determine the funding source rules. For these rules, the funding source application materials must be used, if for no other reason than that they might be quite different, even from one funding cycle to the next.

Talking with currently successful PIs can also be helpful. The information obtained from these conversations, however, cannot be substituted for reading the funding source's application materials and guidelines. Also, remember that the experiences of a person whose application was reviewed during a previous cycle may not necessarily be the same as someone with an application reviewed in the current cycle.

chapter 13

Writing to Be Competitive

This chapter focuses on writing a well-organized and persuasive grant application. It presents strategies that can enhance the clarity of the project plan and evoke thought in the reviewer as well as intellectual excitement and urgency about the project's potential. The reviewer's situation of having only the application from which to mentally construct the project and glean answers to questions places high priority on clear, concise communication, as well as on the ability to be persuasive about the project's importance.

Communication Flow

The importance of honing communication skills has been discussed in other chapters. Communicating with collaborators, project personnel, administrative officials, staff, and funding personnel is a continuing process during project development and implementation. These communication situations, whether written or oral, require that investigators attend to feedback to assess what is being heard and that they also provide feedback so they can move forward with confidence. The hallmark of these situations is that they are interactive and that this enables the best work to be done. For example, clarification about issues in a written document can be requested, and conversations can be followed with written documents to crystallize the agreements and thoughts with a request for feedback about the accuracy of perceptions. During all phases of application development, there are opportunities to read material, to ask for clarification, and to follow a conversation with written suggestions. Thus, in our opinion, up to the point of submission the grant application process is interactive with the availability of all types of communication technology.

After submission, however, the application stands alone without opportunities for clarification by telephone, fax, or e-mail. Reviewers can review only what is presented. Further explanations, expansions, or definitions are usually not possible. Reviewers assume that the written descriptions of the rationale, the project plan, and the plans for using the data are congruent with the thoughts, conclusions, and plans of the principal investigator (PI). What this means is that reviewers are not likely to say, "This is what is written here, but I'll bet what is really meant is . . . , otherwise it just won't work." It also means that the PI's words are like spotlights lighting up a reviewer's information about the topic area. Thus, reviewers use this information to understand the thoughts and to draw the best conclusions they can, on the basis of the information provided.

Miscommunication

Miscommunication occurs swiftly, often surprisingly, and usually considerable effort is required to get a reviewer's thoughts back on track. For example, if an application has the simple intent of having a reviewer think "square," several critical pieces of information must be provided, for example, the angle of the corners, the relative length of the sides, and the shape that the lines form. It would be easy to leave out information about the length of the sides. A reviewer can still probably conclude that the discussion is about a rectangle, and then assume equal sides, and call it a square, or the reviewer can decide that opposite sides are equal but adjacent sides are unequal and call it a rectangle. If the reviewer makes the correct choice, no harm has been done by incomplete information. However, if reviewers make the incorrect choice much of the remaining information could be unintelligible because they are starting with an incorrect information base. Our example is simple, but with a little thought one can think of many more variables that have not been discussed but could have an important bearing on the reviewer's conclusions. The purpose of this example is to emphasize the difficulty of achieving 100% fidelity when using words to transmit thoughts and to encourage investigators to be relentless in searching out incomplete or ambiguous information in their proposals.

Meeting the Reviewers' Needs

The text of a project plan must provide sufficient and appropriate information to enable reviewers to construct a mental image of the project as it will be implemented. An investigator's goal is to achieve this with sufficient clarity to leave no uncertainty in the reviewer's mind. Each reviewer reads an application differently, just as we all read research articles in our own way. The reviewer, just like us, makes judgments about the material presented, how the material is presented, and what material is omitted. As much as we desire to be unfailingly objective about reported research, we often do not achieve this goal because the writer fails to meet our expectations, and because of our frustration at not being able to comprehend designs quickly, the relevance of statistics, and the reasonableness of conclusions. We believe that PIs need to do what Price (1981) suggests writers do for any reader, that is, "do not ask him to understand everything at once . . . give him a way to organize many different facts . . . let him feel forward movement" (p. 67).

Application reviewers, although striving for objectivity, are nevertheless vulnerable to influence from the frustrations and failed expectations described above as well as to the conditions under which they conduct their review. Investigators, because they want reviewers to be energized and enthusiastic about their project plans, must make their projects readily understood. That means presenting the plan so that it does not require the level of work needed for understanding a journal article. Investigators carry the burden of effective, persuasive, and efficient communication that enables a reviewer to understand and appreciate the significance of the proposed project. Their writing style should permit the reviewer to focus on the project rather than succumb to distraction and confusion prompted by complicated sentences and paragraphs. Their goal is to keep the reviewer's head nodding up and down—it is hoped that the document will produce few furrowed brows. Remember, the application is the only information that the reviewer has about the project. It is in the PI's best interest, therefore, to make it as easy to read and easy to follow as possible. It is to some suggestions of how this might be done that we now turn.

Physical Appearance

Some reviewers, before beginning a serious review, quickly page through the project plan to determine how difficult it is to read and follow. In our opinion, an easily read project plan is one with the following elements:

- Double spacing between paragraphs of moderate length
- Main section headings and paragraph headings as appropriate
- Main sections arranged and headed according to application instructions

- ■ Paragraph headings designed to provide information about the placement of the topic within the overall document

- ■ Moderate to short sentences with minimal use of semicolons

Organizational Plan

A well-organized project plan allows the reviewer easily to find answers to questions of intellectual curiosity such as "I wonder how . . . is handled?" or "What was included . . . ?" A plan in which answers are easy to find basks in a brighter light than the one in which questions can only be answered by reading large sections or the entire narrative. Easy access to materials is promoted by careful organization and by highlighting the organization with the judicious use of meaningful section and paragraph headings.

The first level of organization is that required by the funding source. For example, the organization of the PHS 398 packet begins with Specific Aims, followed by Background and Significance, Preliminary Studies, and Research Design and Methods sections. The plan for organizing information within each of these sections should follow the same pattern for all sections whenever possible. In our opinion, the material should be ordered in a way most likely to engage the thought process of reviewers and that enables them to understand the validity of the arguments presented. It must be assumed that this train of thought is novel to the reviewer. Care, therefore, must be taken to include all relevant pieces of information and to exclude information not integral to the arguments. The order and quality of information must preclude intrusion of prior conclusions about the literature's implications that are embedded in the reviewer's frame of reference. If there is no content-driven order, present the most exciting or most productive aspects first.

The Specific Aims section establishes the information pattern for the associated hypotheses. The order is determined by the nature of the project. When the project is concerned with a problem, the problem might be stated followed by the specific aims and related hypotheses. When the project is to make a point, it might be stated, and followed by statements of the activities associated with its proof. The order must reveal the importance and scientific potential of the project.

The Background and Significance section contains groundwork for the proposed specific aims and should be easily related to them. In our opinion, the literature review should not be a catalog. It should help the reviewer understand the correct order, by using both transitional and topic sentences. It is critical that this section be a well-ordered and integrated presentation of prior research. This section cannot just be a collection of facts or words. The facts and words must be presented so that they engender and communicate thought.

The Research Design and Methods section should also follow the order begun in the Specific Aims section. Place descriptions of procedures that studies have in common before the individual study descriptions. This overview can then be referenced in each study's presentation, followed by the study's unique variations.

Statistical tests of the hypotheses should be presented in the same order as the hypotheses were presented in the Specific Aims section. A statement linking statistical tests to hypotheses should be included whenever possible. Sometimes this is cumbersome to do because one analysis tests several hypotheses. It is more difficult to elucidate how conclusions are reached when this is the case, but it is nevertheless important to present unambiguous statements for the reviewer, even at the expense of repetition.

Finally, headings can be used as a proposal map. Because of this, it is not a good plan to use identical headings in different sections of the project plan. If a reviewer puts your application aside and returns to a page with headings that are duplicated in different sections, there will be confusion about the section being read. Deflect this kind of confusion by using unambiguous headings throughout the proposal.

Maintain Focus

A competitive proposal is written so the reviewer remains focused on content and thought. A focused proposal establishes reviewer expectations and meets them from the wording of the title to the conclusion about expected statistical results. Focus is achieved through scrutiny of sentence structure, content, and wording.

Sentence Structure

Because an application is a long document, reading it should be made as easy as possible by structuring sentences to promote comprehension. For example, one way to facilitate comprehension is to begin multiclause sentences with the most important clause.

Simple Sentence Structure

Simple sentence structure is highly valued by many readers. We are all familiar with the person who begins talking and does not let anyone else speak.

The speaker elaborates elaborations and, without a signal, launches into a new topic. We have come across this in applications with long, complex sentences, showered with semicolons and allusions to other topics. The interruptibility factor is absent in these applications. We also find material easier to understand when the author allows space, as it were, for thought. Sometimes long sentences cannot be avoided, such as one that includes a list of variables. If variable descriptions are also needed, use additional sentences for elaboration. Some repetition will occur, but it is better to repeat than to entangle the reader in multiple clauses. Crisp and direct statements are easily understood, convey the impression of clear thought, give an application an orderly and structured appearance, and permit thoughts, rather than words, to dominate. Unnecessary sentence complexity will not enhance the scholarly impression of the application.

Active Voice

Active voice sentences are more interesting and simpler and are recommended whenever possible. Active verbs aid understanding because they communicate who is acting. We do not suggest that only active voice sentences be used, but that they be considered and used whenever possible.

Completeness and Content

The major sections (e.g., Specific Aims, or Introduction, Background and Significance, Research Design and Methods), although each presents a single aspect of the project, should also contain enough information from the other sections to enable the reviewer to piece together the application's logic and argument. When this is done, each section can be read alone with a high level of understanding. The Specific Aims, or Introduction, section provides limited information about the theoretical underpinning of the project but clearly states the hypotheses. The literature review extends and expands the underlying arguments for the hypotheses and contributes further information about the scientific content of the project. However, to be persuasive, this section must also mention the study hypotheses or questions posed. The Research Design and Methods section outlines how the data will be collected and analyzed to test the hypotheses that were presented in the first section.

Each paragraph should contain sufficient information for the reviewer to arrive at the correct interpretation within the context of the application. Because some reviewers are not experts in the scientific area, it is important to provide more information than might be required in a journal article. Keep in mind that communication can be fragile because readers draw conclusions based on their experiences. Thus, it is our opinion that a project application is not the place to use slang, culturally driven expressions, or unnecessary jargon.

Another area in which content and completeness are important is comparisons. Be sure the sentence is completed whenever comparative wording is used. Although it seems that no one would write a sentence such as "There are a greater number of x cells," understood comparisons are commonly used. In a project plan, it is important to complete sentences so that there is no question about the comparison. Comparison sentences should clarify what is being compared with what: "There are a greater number of x cells than y cells." Implied comparisons might be acceptable, but they can cause confusion, unless all reviewers have equal knowledge of the project topic.

Word Usage

Words That Influence Content Perception

Some words assist in directing a reader's attention and conclusions and others distract. The following are some examples of word usage that influences how a reader views a document.

The words former and latter. The content of each sentence, paragraph, or section should be as complete as possible. The words *former* and *latter* should be avoided. Using these words requires a reviewer to search for the former or latter or recall the referred to material. In the same vein, the custom of referring readers to "Chapter 1, Figure 1," should be avoided. If it is important that the reviewer see the figure again, repeat it! If it is not valuable enough to be repeated, then choose the place where it needs to be included and handle future situations differently. Reviewers are not happy with proposals that require 10 fingers and perhaps more to keep track of all the places the writer sends them. Keep information together. If, however, it is not possible to eliminate references to other parts of the document, it is preferred that they be descriptive, such as "Chapter 1, Figure 1." The need for descriptive references places a premium on using meaningful paragraph headings, because they are the guideposts for a reader.

Words such as strength and shortcoming. Use the words *strength, advantage, weakness,* or *shortcoming* when these words characterize the discussion topic. Do not assume the reviewer will correctly label procedures, studies, or analyses as a strength, weakness, or shortcoming. The inclusion of these words elaborates the information provided and provides a check for reviewers of their conclusions. These kinds of words, which direct reviewers' views toward the PI's, are important for an accurate judgment of the scientific contribution of the project.

Jargon

One of the meanings assigned to jargon by Webster is the technical terminology of a special activity or group. Technical terminology is used to communicate precisely and efficiently within a scientific or other specialty area. In our opinion, jargon should be used in a project proposal only when there is no other word choice that will accurately communicate.

The application's audience determines whether the use of jargon is appropriate. For example, if a proposal is written in response to a request for application (RFA) or a request for proposal (RFP), both situations in which the reviewers will be very knowledgeable in the area targeted, jargon is acceptable if needed. In fact, the use of jargon in communication with individuals within a scientific area is appropriate for the fine distinctions it makes possible. However, with the current climate of multidisciplinary research, jargon should be used only when there is no other choice. Relman (1990) recommends that jargon be limited in journal articles. He comments that "obscure, badly written reports full of jargon and highly technical language discourage comprehension by all but those closest to the field" (p. 24). In view of the possible scientific heterogeneity of review groups, applications are more likely to be competitive when effort is made to render them understandable to a wide audience.

Synonyms

Using synonyms usually produces a more interesting document than one in which there is word repetition. However, the use of synonyms in a project plan can result in ambiguity. Individuals outside a particular area of investigation might not know when differences are not important and when a new variable or concept is being introduced. A reviewer might wonder when one or the other term appears: "Is this another group? I don't remember seeing it mentioned before? Did I miss it? Guess I'd better go back and hunt for it." This is not the way to create a positive frame of mind in the reviewer. Good communication, in our opinion, is achieved by the use of only one of the terms throughout the application. In summary, because of the confusion that can arise with synonyms we recommend that they not be used for words that are integral to the project science. In this case, variety is not welcome. Using the same word repeatedly makes it clear what is being studied, the methods used, or the analysis proposed. The science presented will be clearly visible and more likely to excite the reviewer's intellect than if obscured by attempts at verbal variety.

Simple Words

We recommend simple words. Long, complex sentences filled with multisyllabic words increase the reading difficulty of written material. The purpose of the words in an application is to *communicate good science.* Reviewers want to learn about the project, not about the breadth and depth of the PI's vocabulary. Each sentence should be crafted to express ideas and precipitate thought. Another reason for use of simple words is the application's audience. The easier an application is to read, the more possible it is for the reviewer to maintain a positive state of mind, especially those for whom English is a second language and those in other scientific areas.

Malapropisms

Malapropisms, the misuse of words, can pop up in the most unexpected places. Whatever their reason for appearing, when they appear they can be a serious distraction from the material in which they are embedded. Because these kinds of miswordings are difficult for the writer to detect, the possibility of their being in an application is just one more good reason to have someone else read the entire application before it is submitted.

Unnecessary Words

Whenever possible, avoid using unnecessary words. Unnecessary words can be pruned from writing by searching out instances where (a) fewer words can be used to express a thought, for example, "The room, desks, and computers where individuals work to collect data" could be expressed as "The data collection site"; (b) conciseness can be improved, for example, "Although it is generally believed that the open-ended interview questions are difficult to code, an efficient process can be designed" could be expressed as "Open-ended interview questions need not be as difficult to code as rumored"; (c) two words of identical meaning are used together; and (d) using the active voice would improve communication and conciseness.

The following are some examples (for more wordy phrases, see Strunk & White, 1979, p. 24):

despite the fact that	although
this is a study that	this study

Because the writing in a project plan carries a heavy communication burden, careful consideration must be given to what constitutes wordiness or use of unnecessary words. It is unwise to "sacrifice concreteness and vividness for conciseness and brevity" (Watkins & Dillingham, 1992, p. 38).

Avoid Padding

Padding may be the function of a writing style that includes unnecessary words and/or redundancy. Redundancy is repetition of the same thought, not the use of synonyms for concepts integral to the project. We recommend that it be said once and said right. If it is necessary to write a sentence that starts with "In other words, . . . " suspect that the writing may be redundant. However, if the thought cannot be communicated in any other way, be redundant. When redundancy arises from an attempt to communicate a thought before it is completely formed, it can be removed during editing. However, be wary about editing out apparently redundant statements without thinking about them and their context. Perhaps the statement needs to be elaborated, not repeated, for the reviewer to grasp its meaning and significance.

We suggest that extra material should not be included in the project plan simply to extend it to the maximum number of pages allowed. If the narrative is short, and if all pertinent information is included, leave it that way. Reviewers usually do not complain about a short, well-written project plan that communicates the maximum information in the fewest possible words. A project plan that exceeds the page limits should be checked for padding. The excess length might be the result of redundancy, use of unnecessary words, or the inclusion of tangential material. After eliminating redundancy and unnecessary words, check the material carefully for inclusion of tangential material. The development of a tightly designed project incorporates numerous tangential information threads. These threads deepen the investigator's comprehension of the project and enable him or her to present it in a clear, concise manner, but they are not, of themselves, important to the reviewer. Including them in the document can give an unfocused appearance to the plan and can contribute significantly to the project's page length. Be vigilant and avoid including material of this nature.

Action Strategies

Do Not Single Out a Particular Reviewer

We believe investigators should not focus the application's writing and communication style on particular individuals who are believed to be on the review panel. It is prudent for investigators to use any information they have about members of the review group so that they use words and phrases in the proposal that the reviewers customarily see and use. Keep in mind, however, that review group members are scientists with careers, usually in academia; they are likely to be middle aged; and probably a good number of them have families. When these circumstances are taken into account, a reasonable assumption is that a reviewer might be on sabbatical, on a family vacation, recovering from a serious illness, taking care of an ill parent, or adjusting to an appointment as department head during a particular review cycle. This means they will not be able to review applications for that cycle. Also keep in mind that environmental conditions, such as the blizzard of 1996, can drastically change the makeup of a review group. Because of these kinds of circumstances, we advise investigators to write a clear, concise, and persuasive application, but not to write it directly to please any single reviewer.

Monitor the Application's First Impression

Gain a slight edge by making sure that the first impression made by your application is a good one. First impressions can become hard-core reality, whether they be favorable or unfavorable. Follow the funding source rules for structure. Be sure that the application is complete, that the entire application meets high standards of neatness and accuracy, and that a brief perusal reveals that it is well organized and easy to access.

Spell Check

Be sure to use the word processing spell check program, but remember that it only checks spelling. Sometimes the wrong word is entered, but spelled correctly. PIs should proofread the application themselves and have someone else proofread it to be sure that the words are those intended and that they are spelled correctly.

Grammar Check

The application's grammar need not be perfect, but it should be good. Good grammar helps communicate good science. Poor grammar can be a barrier to understanding and to the reviewers' positive frame of mind. We suggest using a word processing grammar package, or using a grammar consultant to read it to improve communication with the reviewer.

Write Drafts

Write drafts! Ordinarily, it is not possible to write more than a few drafts, sometimes only two, but that does not mean that the first draft must be the first written thoughts. Fortunately, most investigators do a lot of writing, including memos and summaries for collaborators as the project plan develops. Save these materials and edit them. Ideas will take shape more quickly if they are subjected to scrutiny in written form. Any project notes should be saved. They might qualify for inclusion in the first draft of the proposal.

Do Not Use a Complicated Presentation Pattern

It is advisable, most of the time, to follow the often given advice to "say it once." However, because an application is long, complex reference to other parts of the application often force reviewers to turn back to previous pages to refresh their memory. This paper shuffling can often be avoided by briefly summarizing what reviewers would find if they turned to the specified page of the application. Although this is difficult when the intention is to direct a reader to a graph or complicated table, a narrative summary of what the reader would note in the graph or table allows a choice of reviewing or not reviewing the graph or table.

It is also helpful to keep the structure of the information presentation as simple as possible. Investigators who need to label paragraphs alphanumerically, for example, a.I.A.1, should reconsider the structure of the material and/or reassess the need for identifying paragraphs at this level of detail. In general, we believe that descriptive paragraph headings help a reader to quickly grasp the organization of the proposal as well as providing a quick overview. However, discipline convention and the type of application play a role in this matter as in all application matters.

Review Books on Writing

Several of the books we have used are listed below. Investigators with favorites might dust them off and review what are believed to be effective writing habits and styles.

The Elements of Grammar. Margaret Shertzer, Macmillan, New York, 1986

The Elements of Style. 3rd ed. William Strunk, Jr. and E. B. White, Macmillan, New York, 1979

The Plain English Guide. Martin Cutts, Oxford University Press, New York, 1995

Power Language. Jeffrey McQuain, Houghton Mifflin, Boston, 1996

Practical English Handbook. 9th ed. Floyd C. Watkins and William B. Dillingham, Houghton Mifflin, Dallas, TX, 1992

Attend a Grammar Workshop

Take advantage of any in-house writing or grammar workshops offered or select one from among those found in the usual "junk" mail we all receive. These are usually 1-day events and hit the highlights of problems with opportunities for discussion of specific types of situations. These workshops are targeted to help people with grammar and are usually not helpful for writing.

Grammar, spelling, and typographical errors. Grammatical errors, spelling errors, and typographical errors should be eliminated from the final document. It is difficult to eliminate all such errors and many times, in spite of a PI's conscientious attention, some errors are present in a submitted application.

Citation errors. The reference list must be accurate and include all literature cited within the application's text. This is not a trivial requirement, and every effort should be made to have the reference list complete and also free from inaccuracy and misspellings.

![decorative bar]

Seeing It Through the Reviewers' Eyes

A competitive application must be pleasing to the reviewers' eyes and exciting to their intellect. These qualities must dominate the application so that they are apparent even under the most intense reviewing circumstances. Reviewers are scientists who have ongoing research projects, classes to teach, service commitments to meet, and administrative duties vying for their attention. Scientists who volunteer to be reviewers have a commitment to developing scientific knowledge and are usually very busy people. Therefore, an application must be written in an appealing and persuasive style that promotes understanding and enthusiasm.

Review Before Submission

A comprehensive review can, of course, be completed anytime during project development and probably should be done several times. However, in our experience, we find that a rigorous review several weeks before the submission uncovers important omissions that diminish the application's quality. These are not minor errors in wording and formatting that are usually found in the review done just before putting the application in the mail. These are omissions and lapses that might lead reviewers to decide the proposal is flawed. Doing this review several weeks before submission allows investigators time to make any needed corrections and improvements in whatever shortcomings they discover and to have time to evaluate the changes. Most investigators, because they have worked on the application over the past 6 to

9 months, are saturated with the material and do not want to face the work this review usually uncovers. In some instances, finding the time and energy to make the modifications seems impossible. There is no question that the review might produce more work; on the other hand, it might also bring renewed confidence in the project and the content of the application. It is imperative that principal investigators (PIs) apply the same high standards to all aspects of the application as they apply to pursuing impeccable science.

Take the Reviewers' Perspective

We believe it is important to take the reviewers' perspective so minor errors and omissions in either the administrative or scientific application aspects are not glossed over, and major shortcomings are faced. Administrative errors, for example, must be changed, however much work is entailed, because a reviewer's response is not likely to be "well, they did the best they could!" It is more likely to be "they didn't follow directions." All science must be clear, jargon used only when necessary, and no assumptions made about the reviewers' knowledge base. Thinking "anyone in the area will know what that means . . . or why I came to that conclusion" is risky. Reviewers appreciate precise language and complete information for their own value, and because they provide information about the PI's knowledge. Completing this kind of review in an orderly fashion is likely to give the best results. Start, therefore, at the beginning with the announcement to which the application responds.

Make the Application Pleasing to the Reviewers' Eyes

Reviewers receive the same information as PIs along with guidelines to assist them with developing their recommendation. This practice makes applications that meet funding source instructions more attractive than those that do not. Although different sections of the application may be differentially weighted in the final analysis, these weights are not a license for PIs to deviate from the instructions.

We recommend that the funding source information be reviewed to affirm that the proposed project meets their requirements. A funding source selected early in the development of an application might not be as appropriate after the application is complete. Examples of influential changes include the participant or subject pool, the project costs, the overhead costs, and the earliest starting date. Projects that begin as a small grant or pilot project but develop into a full project may be larger than appropriate for a selected funding source. A comparison of the funding source's requirements with the final written application can provide opportunity for correcting deviations as well as providing assurance that the application meets the reviewers' expectations.

Make a Superb First Impression

An application's appearance makes the first impression on a reviewer. It is essential, therefore, that investigators examine it critically. How does it look? Does its appearance conform to that indicated in the instructions? Does it look neat? Is all the information provided? Blank spaces, where reviewers expect information, can begin murmurs of dissatisfaction and raise red flags for reviewers.

The more detailed the funding source instructions, the easier it is to produce an application that is pleasing to the reviewers' eyes. They have expectations about an application's appearance, and an application that meets those expectations is pleasing. If detailed instructions are not provided, the reviewers' expectations are likely to coincide with what they think is important information, and the order in which they are accustomed to seeing it or presenting it in their applications. In this case, use the items presented in this chapter to produce an application that makes a solid first impression.

Cover Pages

Cover pages are usually required. Applications either include a form with detailed instructions or requirements for a cover page are stated in general terms. Instructions, when provided, can also give directions about appearance and content.

Check the completed cover page. Does its appearance coincide with the funding source's instructions? Check the recommendations for type size or number of allowable characters for the cover page items. Notice that the recommended type size might be different in different parts of the application. Use the recommended left, right, top, and bottom margins. The left margin is particularly important to be correct because applications might be bound by the funding source. Does the title meet all restrictions? Is it precise and efficient?

The requested cover page items fill funding source information needs and must be completed, even when the PI cannot imagine that the information could be useful. Complete each item accurately, neatly, and within the specified space constraints. Unbelievable as it may seem, funding sources have trouble corresponding with investigators because they provide incomplete or inaccurate addresses and telephone numbers. If signatures are required, be sure they are in the right place. This page should be completed so that reviewers will be positively impressed as they quickly glance at it.

Abstract

Be sure the abstract follows instructions provided, including the number of words and the type size. If there are no instructions, the abstract should be brief. We recommend that it be no more than 250 words and include at least the broad, long-term objectives and the specific aims of the project, and a concise description of the research design and methods. Commonly, a moderate type size, 10 to 12 points, and six lines per vertical inch is used.

Personnel Information

Provide the personnel information requested for each individual on the project. Complete information should be provided for each individual, even when it is similar for several individuals. The information request may seem unreasonable, but funding sources have their own database requirements.

Table of Contents

The table of contents provides two kinds of information for the reviewers. It lists the application components, and it presents the order in which contents appear in the application. Applications may or may not include a preprinted table of contents. If one is provided, use it! If none is provided, develop one based on the organization of materials in the instructions. Check the table of contents for accuracy of the order and of the page numbers. Some funding sources do not permit using page numbers such as 3a, 3b. Under these circumstances, if pages have been added after numbering, all pages must be renumbered and the table of contents modified accordingly. We recommend that a table of contents that lists each application component and its page number be included even if not specifically requested by the funding source. A complete table of contents aids the efficiency of a reviewer and is appreciated. A separate table of contents preceding the project plan is an added feature that is helpful to reviewers. However, this would have to be placed within the page limit of the project plan and, therefore, is not usually provided.

Budget

Review the budget to verify that it meets funding source guidelines. If a budget form is provided, it must be used and information neatly entered in the spaces provided. If categories are not applicable, or if there are no dollar amounts, use dashes, zeros, or write "not applicable" so that it is clear that the item has not been overlooked. Do not forget to include all personnel mentioned in the project. If they are donating their time, indicate that, but do not omit them from the budget. Neatly typed, complete budget pages and a budget justification with paragraph headings create a good impression.

Supporting Documents

Biographical sketches and information about other external support for projects for the PI and each investigator should be included. A good impression is not made with a barely legible, hastily modified, biographical sketch that has obviously been culled from another application. Check supporting documents to be certain they have been prepared as carefully as the project plan, following the guidelines for type size and page limitations. Present the information about other external project funds consistently to make it easy for reviewers to understand.

Another set of supporting documents describes the PI's organization and the environment in which the project will be conducted. Complete this information as neatly and carefully as the rest of the application. There is no way to tell when a reviewer will look at any one of these pages. They should contain enough information to be understandable and persuasive without reference to other parts of the application.

The Project Plan

Reviewers expect a project plan within the specified page length or a reasonable page length. If there is no recommended page limit, keep in mind that a project plan of 20 to 25 single-spaced pages is usually more welcome than one that is 50 to 100 pages. If excessive page length results in the funding source returning the application, the investigators' target audience, the reviewers, usually do not see it. However, when reviewers do see an application that has exceeded the page length they might believe that unfair advantage results from accepting the extra pages and return the application to the PI. If they do not return the application to the PI, they may, nevertheless, be influenced negatively by the investigator including more material than is allowed. We believe that the risks associated with exceeding the page-length rules should not be taken.

Primary headings should coincide with those presented in the instructions. Other headings should be included only to enhance reviewer comprehension. Keep in mind that headings are document markers or guideposts, and too many diminish their usefulness.

Double spacing between paragraphs and paragraph indention provides important white space on each page. This makes reading less tiresome and permits the reviewer's attention to focus on the science. Sometimes investigators cannot fit their material into the required number of pages without using every bit of space on every page. If the problem is not wordiness or inappropriate inclusion of material, the white space on a page might be decreased by using the smallest margins allowed, using 1½ spaces between paragraphs, deleting paragraph indentions, and going to a reference system that requires minimum space. The goal is to include the necessary information in a format that enables the reviewer to comprehend it. With no white space, the investigator may have included the information but sacrificed the reviewer's attention and positive mood. In general, readers find their attention wandering when confronted with page after page of solid type.

Produce the final application with the best technology that is generally available. Although some parts of an application require typewriters, most sections of applications are produced with word processing software and laser printers. However, using a typewriter for the entire document is preferred if a letter-quality printer is not available. Do not include low-clarity photographs. Present legible and well-designed graphs and tables. Captions with type size so small that the letters become dots when reproduced can be a source of reviewer frustration. Bind the application according to instructions, or simply but securely if instructions are not provided. A common instruction is to submit each copy held together with a rubber band. Excessive binding and printing efforts are not necessary and may detract from a favorable impression.

Summary

The entire research application must be neat. It must conform to type size and spacing instructions, or it must have type size and spacing that make it easy to read. It should be the length expected by the reviewer, and, if there are no instructions, it should be a reasonable length. Keep in mind that the objective is to create a positive mood in the reviewer and to hold his or her attention so that an accurate evaluation of the project's science is possible.

Excite the Reviewers' Intellect

The two major aspects of a project plan that contribute to intellectual excitement are its organization and its content. The organization of the project plan has a major role in its intellectual impact because it provides a map of the content. Without a good map, the content of a project plan can become like a sentence without spaces between the words. Reviewers will organize the material, whatever the quality of the map. The better the map, therefore, the more likely the reviewer will arrive at the same conclusions as the PI about its content.

Organization

A project plan cannot be intellectually exciting if its organization does not emphasize the arguments leading to the conclusions, the beauty of the methodology used to implement the plan, and the elegance of the analysis. The best template to use in organizing a project proposal is provided by the funding source.

The Specific Aims (Introduction)

Educate the reviewers about the particular topic. State the broad, long-term goals of the project in the particular area of investigation. Along with this statement, include a sentence or two about what the project will lead to or accomplish and the benefits of its findings, including cost savings or diminution in some misfortune. These two kinds of information presented early in the application allow the reviewer to quickly place the project in the context it is designed to be placed.

The specific aims, together with the hypotheses or questions generated, are stated next. The organization can vary here. Sometimes it is difficult to decide which aims should appear first because there is no logical order for them. Whatever the order of the specific aims, the hypotheses and questions should be presented either with the specific aim or following all specific aims, in the same order as the specific aims so that there is no confusion about which hypotheses or questions are associated with which specific aim. The organization is determined by the PI's knowledge of the topic area and the type of project. Think about the order selected. Consider the pros and cons of alternate arrangements. The organization of this first section is important because it is the model for each succeeding section's organization.

Literature Review

This section's organization should follow that of the Specific Aims section and the logic of the project. Be sure that the early discussion of the proposed project's rationale deflects confusion and solidly places the project in the appropriate context.

Discuss the literature for each specific aim as a unit, if that is possible. If the specific aims stem from a common body of literature, then the relationship between the literature and each of the aims must be clearly presented. An effective organization strategy is to use the scientific logic as a guide. This organization leads reviewers through the literature in a manner that enables them to arrive at conclusions similar to those of the PI. This strategy might be used to discuss the literature associated with each aim or across aims. Although a chronological order of published literature in some instances incorporates the logical progression of the scientific development, it is not always the case. Because it is critical that reviewers arrive at conclusions similar to the PI's, an organization strategy that achieves this is a high priority.

Research Design and Methods

The order of this section is determined by discipline convention, investigator's preference, and the project. Be sure not to frustrate a reviewer's expectation by using unconventional arrangements. If there are no conventions, review the order chosen in light of persuasiveness, interest, and logic. The dilemma here is that different scientists have different preferences, but by this stage of application development PIs are probably fairly familiar with the preferences of those working in the topic area. Investigators need to achieve at least an orderly and consistent presentation in this section.

Content

Our advice concerning content is: Do not make assumptions about what reviewers know. Search the project plan for statements that include jargon or are presented with insufficient groundwork. Assuming a well-organized application, the content or lack of content is visible. Be sure to take full advantage of opportunities to communicate the project's excitement. The PI's scientific ability is demonstrated by a succinctly described project, by past activities, and by the care given to the application details. PIs must not give reviewers the impression that they are saying, "Trust me, I am an expert."

Specific Aims (Introduction)

The project context should be described in a compelling manner without exaggerating or overemphasizing the need for the project because this can jeopardize credibility. Statements should be objective and be related to the specific aims because they were developed to represent the funding source's interests. Review the statement about the project's influence on the current state of knowledge, and adjust it as required either for over- or understatement. The specific aims should be succinct statements of the project's expected outcomes, not methods or design. Check that the hypotheses or the questions to be answered by the project are clearly stated. In our experience, stating specific aims is not sufficient because specific aims are not tested.

Literature Review

The review should include relevant literature, recent work, and other relevant material, written by review group members. If the topic is one with alternative investigative directions, do not neglect to summarize these alternative approaches and state the arguments for continuing pursuit along the chosen lines. Be sure that tangential material or asides are eliminated. Reviewers are not interested in everything PIs know. They are interested in how current and past findings are integrated to arrive at the proposed project. Check the presentation to determine that enough material has been included to reveal the integration method and how it leads to the stated conclusions. Be sure not to unwittingly make an unimportant point appear important by using multiple examples.

Research Design and Methods

This is a key section of a project plan because it describes the way data will be collected. Research conclusions are only as good as the data on which they are based. Be sure the design is described, not just named. Reliance on design names alone can introduce ambiguity because across disciplines designs might be the same but have different names, or have the same name and be slightly different. Review, for clarity, the statements about the ability to assess the combined effect of several variables, if this is an important feature of a design. Using variable names to describe the effects is preferable to briefly stating that "the significance of interactions or cross-products will be tested." Check the descriptions of the groups to be studied. Assumptions must not be made about reviewers' knowledge of special subject-group characteristics, whether the group is composed of humans, animals, or cultures. Do not neglect to include information about recruitment and attrition as appropriate.

Instrumentation can be complex and cumbersome to describe. Review the description to determine if a sufficient amount of information has been provided to enable a reviewer to make judgments about the appropriateness, reliability, and validity of the proposed instruments. If they are the "standard" used by investigators in the area of research, less description is required than if they are not commonly used or are cutting edge. Keep in mind that these descriptions need to be presented in ordinary language whenever possible. A full description and complete technical material can be included as an appendix, but this material should be ancillary rather than integral to understanding the data collection procedures.

Procedure sections should include enough information about procedures so a reviewer could replicate them. Search out summary terms such as standard analysis, participant observation, usual arrangement, computer-entered-responses, or usual computer configuration. Provide the series of statements these shorthand descriptions require for replication to be possible. Careful presentation of the details of procedures and their order enables the reviewer to more vividly imagine the project.

Data Collection, Management, and Analysis

Check all the details of data collection, storage, protection, and management descriptions. Statements such as "data were collected" are not sufficient. Detailed information about data collection and its care assures reviewers that data loss is unlikely. Assure reviewers that threats to data during all project phases have been considered. Succinctly describe all data analyses. Frequently, data is collected in a form not amenable to analysis. Explain how data will be modified before analysis, and the reasons for those expected modifications. Because data transformation conventions are variable and discipline specific, PIs need to assure reviewers that they are aware of conventions and requirements and competent data analysts. To communicate how the hypotheses will be tested, describe the statistical tests and their power. A brief discussion of the selected level of power and its calculation is helpful to reviewers.

Personnel, Budget, and Budget Justification

Now that the entire project plan has been reviewed to determine that it coincides with the mission of the funding source, review the personnel to be used, the budget required, and the supporting materials. During the application's development, collaborative needs might change from those originally envisioned and discussed. The most dramatic change occurs when an entire section of a project is changed. Minor modifications in methods and design might also need to be reflected in the budget and budget justification. For example, the percent effort required for investigators might be increased or decreased, or project staff might need to be added. Review the lab work needs, data entry or data collection, and subcontracts such as computer programming or statistical analysis required by the final proposal. It is critical that person-nel, budget, and budget justification match the proposed project needs.

Supporting Materials

The biographical sketches are included as evidence of the group's ability to conduct the proposed project. Review these to be certain that the material is relevant to the final project proposal. The available resources and the environment should also be adequate to complete the project. Do not forget minor project changes that might represent a major change in required resources. An example might be the addition of a lab test that needs to be purchased through a subcontract arrangement rather than internally.

Administrative Approvals

PIs need to revisit their organization's procedure for submitting an application for external funding. These can change frequently and have an important influence on whether an application is mailed on time. Check the forms completed, and the list of steps and signatures required before the application can be mailed to the funding source. Be sure that the materials prepared are correct, so they will move through the system smoothly without time-consuming questions and corrections, and that there is sufficient time for approval signatures. If there is not time for all approval signatures, determine the procedure used to facilitate the application submission on time.

Action Strategies

Ask Someone to Complete the Review Presented in This Chapter

Although a PI can complete the review, we suggest that a colleague be asked. Because the reviewer needs knowledge of what is required by the funding source (available in the instructions) and scientific knowledge, the best person would be an associate who is knowledgeable in the project's scientific area. PIs need to request, specifically, that all perceived problems be noted and that no assumptions be made about meaning or accuracy. Keep in mind that you may need to pay this person.

Request Notification of Receipt

Include a self-addressed stamped postcard with the application, requesting that it be dated and returned when the funding source receives the application. Often the funding source will include the number it assigns the application. This can be useful information should the need arise for communication with the funding source.

PART VI

Other Considerations

CHAPTER **15**

Related Research Issues

T his chapter focuses on selected issues that must be considered when conducting research. For some researchers, these issues may be new, whereas others have watched them evolve over the past several years. The two areas selected for emphasis in this chapter are, first, scientific ethics and the application of ethical principles in the scientific marketplace and, second, the inclusion of women and minority participants in clinical research.

Be Aware of Ethics-Related Issues

Many of us may recall, from our high school or college philosophy courses, that ethics is an area of study concerned with questions related to what is right and wrong as well as what is good and bad. Ethics has been described as part of the glue that holds things together. Generally, ethical principles guide actions and behavior. Ethical statements are consensual principles that provide guidance for research investigators. From an organizational point of view, ethical principles are formally operationalized and codified with laws, rules, guidelines, and regulations. Besides written and formal ethical principles, there are informal working principles or organizational ethics that provide a framework for what is appropriate and acceptable in the research "work environment."

Ethical discussions are fundamentally consensual processes. The scientific community is being forced into open ethical discussions that have targeted waste and abuse. For example, public attention has targeted indirect costs associated with federal grants, particularly National Institutes of Health (NIH) grants. Indirect costs can generally be described as the costs identified by an organization to support a project or study such as rent, electricity, heat, administrative support, and all other institutional support costs deemed necessary by the institution to sustain a project or study. The recent discussion about the need to control indirect costs to universities has focused on placing a cap on the percentage of allowable indirect costs. This discussion has taken place in the U.S. Congress where it has not only related to cost savings and cost controls in the present budget environment but also to the need to control "outrageous expenditures" such as those identified at Stanford University. Indirect costs at Stanford were described by reporters as including flowers for the president's home as well as partial support for the university yacht. Clearly, outrageous expenditures do not occur at most institutions.

Conflict of Interest

Recently, there has also been heightened awareness about conflicts of interest that might influence scientific behavior. The federal government has placed the responsibility for monitoring investigators and the potential for conflict of interest with the awardee organizations. Although the federal government specifically requests that policies be developed by institutions for their awards, many organizations apply the policies to all investigators, regardless of funding source.

The federal government requires that organizations receiving grant and contract funding assure, when applications are submitted, that ownership, participation, or personal financial gain from a contractor or from a grant is not allowable. This assurance usually takes place at the time of submission when the principal investigator (PI) and co-PIs are asked to provide written assurance that they will not receive personal financial gain from a firm either personally or through a family member. In our opinion, there does not appear to be resolution to the ethical discussions and reviews that are currently taking place. But these discussions will continue, largely driven by events and media interest.

Scientific Misconduct

Ethical considerations regarding funded scientific research are now being shaped by media attention and political events. In 1991-1992, Wettstein (1995) reported that 55 institutions received 108 allegations of research misconduct involving research or related activities supported by the U.S. Public Health Service (PHS). The seriousness with which ethical issues are viewed is demonstrated by the publication of the outcomes of misconduct investigations in the *NIH Guide*. The increased interest in ethical behavior has also spawned the development of regulations, procedures, and assurances for "whistleblowers" (Goodman, 1996a).

It should also be noted that one factor that complicates science is differentiating individual and social knowledge because science is inherently a social enterprise (National Academy of Sciences, 1995). In our opinion, many ethical issues relate to misconduct in science, including plagiarism, taking ideas from colleagues, falsifying data, and falsely reporting data and outcomes. These issues are steeped in this scientific tension. Investigators need to be aware that the PHS (1996) defines scientific misconduct as

> fabrication, falsification, plagiarism or other practices that seriously deviate from those that are commonly accepted within the scientific community for proposing, conducting, or reporting research. It does not include honest error or honest differences in interpretations or judgments of data. (42 CFR 50.102)

In 1991 the National Science Foundation adopted a similar definition. Goodman (1996b) reports that the Health and Human Services Committee on Research Integrity, in 1995, proposed the following:

> Research misconduct is significant misbehavior that improperly appropriates the intellectual property or contributions of others, that intentionally impedes the progress of research, or that risks corrupting the scientific record or compromising the integrity of scientific practices. Such behaviors are unethical and unacceptable in proposing, conducting, or reporting research, or in reviewing the proposals or research reports of others. (p. 6)

It appears that scientists need to be mindful of current interests, definitions, and regulations pertaining to misconduct and the thirst for sensationalism in the area of scientific misconduct, which is mostly a gray area.

Human Participants

Ethical considerations related to participants are also receiving increasing attention as protection considerations are enforced by institutional review boards (IRBs). The focus of each IRB is the protection of research participants from unethical, unsafe, and improper procedures. IRBs must ensure that investigators have met research ethical standards as well as federal and state legal research requirements before implementing a study. IRBs have legal authority to obtain modifications to protocols and disapprove studies. Scientific inquiry can be part of the IRB review process because research that is scientifically invalid can do harm to participants.

The core of IRB review is that all human research must include three components to informed consent.

1. Potential respondents must receive adequate information to decide whether to participate in the study described in the consent form. A consent form, which must include specific items, must be readable and understandable for the potential participant. Jargon should be absent.

2. Research respondents must agree to participate in a study voluntarily.

3. Research respondents must be competent; they must have the capacity to consent to the study. This includes each person's ability to clearly make a choice about participating in the study.

It is the responsibility of the investigator to obtain IRB approval before initiating a project. The formal certification of IRB approval must be sent to the funding source. Approval requirements are not standardized. These requirements can range from a few items to an extensive form in the application, which must be completed by the investigator and signed by the institution's authorized official.

Funding sources vary regarding the timing within which they will accept IRB approval notices. Some funding sources will not accept an application without IRB approval. Others will accept an application but must have IRB approval before review. For example, the NIH will not review an application that does not have IRB approval before the review group convenes. Other funding sources do not require IRB approval until the application's funding status has been decided.

Under federal regulations, an IRB can process an investigator's application to conduct a research project involving participants by exemption certification, and expedited review or a full review. The criteria that serve as a guide for a preliminary decision about which type of review would be appropriate can be obtained from the human subjects office. Any questions an investigator has about the conduct of particular research and the IRB criteria should be discussed with the human subjects office.

Women and Minority Participants

The importance of involving women and minority participants in clinical studies was underscored by the Congress with the passage of the NIH Revitalization Act of 1993. The "NIH Guidelines on the Inclusion of Women and

Minorities as Subjects in Clinical Research" was published in the *Federal Register* on March 28, 1994 (and in the *NIH Guide* on March 18, 1994).

NIH *Special Instructions to Applicants Regarding Implementation of NIH Policies Concerning Inclusion of Women and Minorities in Clinical Research Study Populations* (NIH, n.d.) indicate that applications and proposals for NIH grants and cooperative agreements are required to include women and minorities in clinical research unless compelling scientific or other justification for not including either women or minorities is provided. This requirement is to ensure that research findings will be of benefit to all persons at risk for the condition that is being studied. NIH defines clinical research for this policy as involving "human study of etiology, treatment, diagnosis, prevention, or epidemiology of diseases, disorders or conditions including but not limited to clinical trials; and minorities include U.S. racial/ethnic minority populations (specifically: American Indians or Alaskan Natives, Asian/Pacific Islanders, Blacks, and Hispanics).

The special instructions go on to state that there is recognition that it may not be feasible or appropriate in all clinical research to include all U.S. racial/ethnic populations. The NIH will not, however, award grants that do not comply with policies related to the inclusion of women and minority participants. Applicants are urged to include the broadest possible representation. Applicants should include a description of the composition of the proposed population by gender and race/ethnic group. The rationale for the number and kinds of individuals for participation should also be described.

The NIH special instructions continue that applications should incorporate gender and/or minority representation that is appropriate to the scientific objectives in the study design. If the number of participants is not large enough to assess differential effects of procedures or the intervention, the application must explain and justify the reasons. The rationale may be related to research purposes, health of participants, or other reasons including the availability of only a certain population group or distribution of risk factors. If the required information related to women and minorities is not contained in the application, the application will be returned. Peer reviewers are asked to review the research plan for conformity with women and minority policies. If it is judged inadequate it is considered a deficiency.

NIH Outreach Guidelines for Women and Minorities

The NIH developed guidelines for outreach activities, which complement the published guidelines in the *Federal Register* concerning women and minority guidelines. These guidelines are presented as suggestions to assure that women and minority participants are included in NIH clinical research (NIH, 1994a) funded grants and contracts. The guidelines were prepared by a committee of NIH staff to supplement the *NIH Guidelines on the Inclusion of Women and Minorities as Subjects in Clinical Research* (1994) to give clinical researchers a framework for recruiting women and members of minority groups into clinical studies. In addition to providing elements to consider for including women and minority participants, a decision tree provides guidance in determining inclusion of women and minority participants for clinical research and Phase III clinical trials.

The following outreach elements were developed by the NIH committee:

Element 1: Understand the study population. Investigators are encouraged to obtain an understanding of the culture and setting where the study is planned. Medical settings and communities are emphasized. Being sensitive to variability in different settings and participants is important for clinical researchers to consider when studies are planned and implemented. For example, child care can be most important to retain women participants in longitudinal studies. Also stressed is the importance of informed consent so participants can understand their commitment to the study.

Element 2: Establish explicit goals. Goals should be specifically established to recruit and retain study participants. It is recommended that outreach efforts be tailored for a specific population after consulting with institutional leaders from the targeted setting who can provide information about the social and economic needs of participants. Targeting is important to tailor outreach strategies to assure women and minority representation.

Element 3: Achieve agreement on research plans. The outreach guidelines suggest several activities to achieve agreement. The suggestions include discussions with staff and community leaders at every stage of the study, obtaining feedback from recruiting staff, using public meetings to obtain feedback, creating an advisory board to obtain feedback, and providing rewards for staff involvement with the study.

Element 4: Design and conduct evaluations. Creating an evaluation plan is suggested. This evaluation plan should include an assessment of the effectiveness of recruitment and retention strategies. The evaluation results can help provide information to make changes as well as to inform others about outreach strategies that are effective in maintaining women and minorities in clinical research studies.

Element 5: Establish and maintain communication. Opening communication channels is suggested to help researchers obtain a better understanding of the cultural climate from which participants are recruited. Feedback also enhances opportunities for assuring the involvement of women and minorities in clinical research studies.

NIH Review Criteria

The NIH outreach guidelines state that peer reviewers will be instructed to consider the specific following areas in the recruitment and retention of women and minorities for clinical research studies.

- ▦ Evaluate the proposed plan for the inclusion of women and minorities and their subpopulations for appropriate representation to evaluate the proposed justification when representation is limited or absent.

- ▦ Evaluate the proposed exclusion of women and minorities and their subpopulations on the basis that a requirement for inclusion is inappropriate with respect to the health of subjects.

- ▦ Evaluate the proposed exclusion of minorities and women on the basis that a requirement for inclusion is inappropriate with respect to the purpose of the research.

- ▦ Determine whether the design of the clinical trial is adequate to measure potential differences.

- ▦ Evaluate the plans for recruitment, retention, and outreach for study participants. (NIH, 1994a, p. 26)

Action Strategies

Be Aware of Ethical Considerations

We suggest reading *On Being a Scientist: Responsible Conduct in Research*, published in 1995 by the National Academy Press. It can be ordered from them at 2101 Constitution Ave, N.W., Washington, DC 20410 or by calling 1-800-624-6242. This resource provides an overview of ethics that targets graduate students and beginning researchers. In addition to discussing scientific ethics, the booklet includes cases and a bibliography.

For more detailed information related to ethics and teaching ethics, we suggest *Teaching the Responsible Conduct of Research Through a Case Study Approach: A Handbook for Instructors,* which was prepared in 1994 for the Association of American Medical Colleges by S. G. Korenman and A. C. Shipp as a reference. It is available by contacting the Association of American

Medical Colleges, Publication Sales, 2450 N Street, N.W., Washington, DC 20037-1126.

In addition, the American Association for Advancement of Science (AAAS) has produced a series of five videos on scientific research integrity. Each film discusses the different "gray areas" of ethical behavior associated with scientific research. The scenarios presented by the AAAS, like those presented by the Association of American Medical Colleges, will not draw any conclusions. They are meant to be departure points for discussion about the issue presented. For information, contact Alexander Fowler at 202-326-7016, e-mail: afowler@aaas.org ("Research Integrity Videos," 1995). The set of five videos and the *Discussion and Resource Guide* are available for $79.95 plus $6.50 shipping/handling.

A special issue of the *Journal of Mental Health Administration,* titled "Ethics in Mental Health and Substance Abuse Service Delivery," is also available. Ordering information can be obtained from Brian Beauchamp, editorial associate, *JMHA,* 813-974-6407.

Talk About Ethical Considerations During Project Meetings

This may seem naive to some, but open and frank discussions may alleviate future problems. We have learned through our own experiences that it is easy to say that an ounce of prevention is worth a pound of treatment, but hard to put into effect in our own work groups. Individuals new to research may not realize how vulnerable studies are to misleading results and misinterpretations. Project staff need to be aware of the sensitivity of statistical analyses and interpretations to the placement of each data point, so that a cavalier attitude does not develop around data issues. In our opinion, direct communication lines need to be in place between data entry staff and investigators so that if there are any data questions, they can be resolved appropriately.

Assess the Feasibility of Including Women and Minorities in All Clinical Studies

Although investigators might find that including women and minorities in studies requires them to take additional time in planning clinical studies and implementing them, this is important. Clinical studies are currently defined as any study that includes people and are not limited to clinical trials. In our opinion, one of the best ways for PIs to assure themselves and reviewers about the feasibility of including women and minorities in their clinical study is to complete pilot work and to also involve institutional decision makers who have firsthand experience and know the feasibility of involving women and minorities in a specific study.

Become Knowledgeable About Human Participant Concerns

For the new clinical investigator, we suggest contacting the IRB to obtain copies of relevant materials related to protecting participants. Seasoned investigators have learned that interactions with the IRB and remaining current on informed consent requirements and procedures is critical for successful implementation of new and ongoing research studies. Also, PIs need to try to keep abreast of current public policy issues, for example, the current congressional consideration of a bill that is designed to protect families and children by requiring a single, standard parental consent before a federally funded survey or questionnaire can be given to a minor (L.S., 1996).

cHApTER 16

Thinking as the Heart of Science

This chapter discusses spending time with ideas and developing research projects that have roots in theory, the literature, and previous work. We initially examine thinking creatively and present relevant concepts for project development. Although there is no magic formula for developing ideas that can be used for projects and studies, there are situations and contacts that can be established to help the investigator ease this process and make it both exciting and challenging. That challenge and the associated excitement of scientific inquiry and reporting study findings are parts of the enterprise that make seeking project funding worthwhile.

Thinking Creatively

In our experiences, we are all creative, but in different ways. As we prepared this chapter, we talked with investigators who we consider to be scientifically creative and discussed how they are creative and innovative. The responses to our belief that they were creative varied, ranging from "I used to be creative but : . . " to "Thanks for the compliment" to "Yes, thinking is something that I really work on by . . . ."

Further discussion with successfully funded researchers revealed that prosperous scientists can be creative individually as well as creative members of scientific teams and groups. We have worked, and currently interact, with a number of successful research investigators. On the one hand, several of these creative investigators do their best thinking on their own. For example, they may purposefully schedule and take time to develop lines of thought, and to follow this thinking in an organized and disciplined way so that their value can be assessed. On the other hand, other successful researchers are most comfortable with developing ideas in a group setting in which they are able to freely exchange ideas and pyramid ideas, especially within interdisciplinary and multidisciplinary settings and when developing projects. This cross-fertilization and brainstorming are necessary, according to these individuals, to develop, shape, and enhance their thinking. They also find benefits in challenges about logic, validity, feasibility, and usefulness that enable intellectual rigor often not possible without critical feedback.

Which approach is best? Is one of these approaches more successfully used than the other? Frankly, it appears that there are no definitive answers to these questions. The way individuals think and develop ideas may be unique, and it is difficult to make a generalized statement because both individual and group avenues and combinations of these clearly lead to successes. When pressed, many successful investigators are likely to suggest that the science and the project topic should direct creative thinking rather than a predetermined or established strategy. Frequently, both the individual and the group approach are used as they are needed, and many successful investigators do not really think about the process.

Individually directed researchers are more likely to write more articles alone, develop research proposals and projects alone, and do much of their work alone. However, this may not always be the case because many successful individually focused researchers also lead or direct a research team. This research group can include research assistants, postdoctoral fellows, and other scientists who carry out the research, add to the project, and help shape the project. This group is usually more solidly positioned after the study has been developed and after funding is obtained.

Another successful approach is multidisciplinary and interdisciplinary research that involves a team of researchers, each with his or her own scientific interests, theoretical foundations, disciplinary needs, and expertise. An important issue in multidisciplinary research is communication, especially across disciplines. For example, each discipline can use a concept differently, and during discussions there can unknowingly be miscommunication. Thus, it is important to learn to be at ease with asking for clarification of key issues when cross-discipline misunderstandings are likely. It is also important to learn to be comfortable with a wide range of communication styles and personalities. There also may be needs to balance power in the group's interactions. For example, authorship can become a major issue if it is not planned and openly discussed among the research group. In our experiences, individual and group approaches are not mutually exclusive and are often used in combination for developing ideas.

Creativity

Creativity is an important ingredient for developing ideas. Creativity and factors associated with creativity and the related concept of innovation are described in this chapter. Timpe (1987) identified three overall characteristics of creative individuals: flexibility, persistence, and the ability to recombine elements to achieve insights. Timpe goes on to add that the ability to break down large systems into smaller interrelated subsystems and to examine their interrelations are important for creativity. Creativity also involves tolerance and adaptability. Each of these characteristics is suggested to be important. However, flexibility is the characteristic most consistently mentioned in the literature as a factor related to creativity.

Our observations suggest that many promising investigators have stopped their search for external funding because of their own limited flexibility. In our opinion, being flexible and adaptable to change, and being able to capitalize on new and updated information, are core principles for science and for completing a funded study. Persistence is an important component of scientific inquiry. We are reminded of the persistence it takes to develop an application and the time the competitive review process takes, which requires both persistence and flexibility. The ability to persistently recombine elements to achieve insight is one of the foundation blocks of science and reflects the importance of thinking in particular—and thinking with a targeted and systematic approach.

Like Timpe (1987), Himes (1987) describes creative people as being flexible and adds that creative individuals are those who seek solutions in unexplored areas with the following distinct characteristics: *sensitivity to surroundings,* with an ability for making unusual and detailed observations; *flexible, open, curious, and selective,* with a curiosity to look at parts and examine variables; *independent judgment* and the ability to deviate from the past and to view mistakes as situations for developing ideas; *tolerance for ambiguity* and disorder, with limited need to impose premature and simplified structure; and *mental flexibility* to take time to examine data and ideas during an incubation period.

Decker (1985) identified several conditions for innovation. Two of these conditions in our opinion should be considered here. The first is that innovation is work and requires knowledge and usually ingenuity. He goes on to add that innovators rarely work in more than one area and that innovation requires diligence, persistence, and commitment. The second condition is that innovators must build on opportunities that match their abilities and their temperament. Developing ideas is also work. It usually takes a considerable amount of time to shape ideas and to examine possible permutations and combinations of a project's implementation. In our experience, idea development and the related thinking are frequently the most difficult aspects when writing and developing an application. However, after a project is funded, flexibility becomes more important to overcome implementation roadblocks.

Psychological factors have also been linked with creativity. These psychological concepts include brainstorming, motivation, and artistic creativity. Ludwig (1995) examined personal attributes and factors that contributed to creative achievement of historical superstars including composers, artists, and noted scientists. He reported eight characteristics from his comparison of creative superstars with a sample of those less eminent in their creativity. Ludwig summarizes the following eight characteristics of creativity:

1. Early signs of giftedness as a child, which is common to many musical composers

2. Special parenting and mentoring supports in early development from parents who could have their own creative talents

3. Contrariness with frequent disrespect of established beliefs and customs including disrespect for authority

4. Capacity for solitude as well as avoiding groups unless the creative individual is in charge

5. Physical vulnerability with a trend for more physical ailments than the average person

6. A personal seal or professional signature, which is used to mark their works, especially in the arts and sciences

7. A drive for dominance with boundless self-confidence and the drive for supremacy

8. Psychological unease, exemplified by restlessness, impatience, and drive with the need for success, which is not satisfied for long

These creativity factors provide some idea about those characteristics that are important for being creative and for developing ideas. Several of these characteristics may be related to genetic factors and a nurturing childhood environment, whereas others can be learned and practiced. Whichever the case, many of these characteristics are very different from the characteristics we previously mentioned in this book as relevant for project implementation. Those factors include being a small business manager with the ability to interact with a number of staff and other people to manage a well-rounded and viable working group. These creative factors can, in our experiences, hinder the successful completion of funded research in the most effective and efficient manner. There are other factors. For example, the organizational environment can be a critical factor for creativity and innovation. The environment can serve as a stimulant for creativity, or it can dampen creativity with limited time allotted for creativity and creative activities. Motivation is also associated with creativity. This incorporates the need for recognition as well as related rewards—both monetary and acknowledgment.

Ideas

Although this book does not present specific approaches for generating research ideas or questions, there are approaches that can be used and places where ideas can be more readily developed. Timpe (1987), speaking from a business management perspective and within the framework of operating as a member of a team, suggests that successful innovators believe ideas go through four developmental steps: (a) The idea is conceived, (b) additional people become involved as the idea is discussed to achieve general acceptance; (c) the idea is publicized and its potential is investigated; and (d) the innovation is adopted.

Most investigators have an abundance of ideas about potential studies and projects. Experienced investigators learn to be wary of new ideas and subject each idea to an incubation time before committing either material or intellectual resources to it. The time frame for confidence that the idea is both researchable and fundable varies. In our experience, procrastination, rather than difficulties with the idea, usually drives deliberation. Original ideas are often fragile. Their fragility does not arise from their questionable value but from the idea development process. Most of the time, the thought pathways that concluded with an idea are not apparent to the investigator—only the endpoint, the idea, is visible. The idea's assessment can arise from answering the "why" questions about it, but these answers do not provide the underpinning for the idea. This is provided by answers to "what" and "how" questions. What is the theory that provokes the idea? What are the key variables? What are the threats to validity? How does it relate to the literature? What are the threads within this literature that when brought together prompt the idea? How can designs demonstrate the particular phenomenon? How does the idea fit into the broader scientific literature? What is its particular contribution? All of these questions, and more, need to be answered before an idea can be assessed by other scientists. It is during the process of answering these questions that ideas sometimes seem to just keep slipping away. In our experience, this does not necessarily mean that the idea is faulty. It could mean that the most important literature, theory, or design anchor has not been identified. Nevertheless, investigators need to persist when they are strongly attracted to an idea.

In our opinion, the final step in assessing an original idea's value is to describe the thought process and supporting documentation in writing. Investigators are often stunned by how difficult this can be, because often the belief is expressed as "Now all I have to do is write it down." Although writing may not be easy, because we can do much of our thinking without words, it is possible and necessary if the ideas are to be judged by other scientists and to be included in a project application. Thus, preparation and presentation are as important as "selling" the feasibility of the idea and in some instances the utility of the information.

Previous Work and Theory

Scientific investigations extend previous work and are grounded in theory. After the first excitement of an idea has passed, investigators usually note that the scope of the project is too broad, that the procedures required would never be approved by a review group, that the participants or subjects are not available in the numbers required, that additional expertise is required, or that any number of concerns impinging on the project requires adjustments. These are not daunting discoveries, because everyone engaged in developing a project has had some practice in resolving these issues. Early in the project development, these kinds of issues need to be carefully considered along with the impact their resolution has on the choice of coinvestigators. Sometimes the modifications shift the project focus to require including another scientific discipline, a new methodology, or consultants that would not have been a part of the original project. Preliminary developmental work to clarify an idea can include informal conversations as well as conversations at seminars or meetings and hallway conversations. The point we want to make is that it is unwise, in our opinion, to be yoked to a particular colleague as a potential coinvestigator until the topic and methods have been determined. Thus, a project idea usually develops with investigators objectively responding to basic questions regarding its importance, usefulness, and feasibility. This process might suggest a pilot study. Keep in mind, however, that the pilot study must focus on answering pertinent questions. Hypotheses involving a scientific discipline besides the principal investigator's (PI's) or research methodology outside of his or her expertise also need to be scrutinized. PIs either need to gather information themselves or consult with a colleague in the area to be aware of the ramifications of these hypotheses for the entire project.

Literature Review

A careful and complete review of pertinent literature is imperative, in our opinion, because it will foster an understanding of the idea and facilitates writing a comprehensive literature review. A thorough review also helps discipline investigators to cite only the literature directly relevant to the topic.

PIs might already have published articles that include a review of the literature related to the idea that they want to use in the application. If this is the case, it must be updated to include the literature pertaining to the specific procedures, design, or theory incorporated in the project. Failing to update an existing literature review could risk investing time in planning research that has already been completed.

There are advantages to moving through this early phase of idea development slowly. In our opinion, time is needed to scrutinize and reflect on the current literature and to challenge the place of new ideas. We suggest that a PI's productivity during this period not be measured by the number of pages written. Because writing is thinking on paper, writing is often done to improve clarity. However, during this phase, emphasis should be on thinking, not on producing drafts. Problems and research issues occur in layers. More often than not, solving one dilemma or settling on one strategy reveals another layer of issues. Allowing time to consider the implications of tentative solutions can produce a solid rationale and project plan that is more likely to withstand the scrutiny of colleagues and a funding source review group.

Scientific Meetings

After the hypotheses have been shaped, and a solid literature review written, we believe it is time to meet with colleagues and knowledgeable research personnel to critique the idea. For the most part, the investigator's style and the idea under consideration determine whether these meetings are one-on-one or group meetings. Some investigators prefer to meet with those with whom they plan to work. Others choose colleagues who are knowledgeable but who may not be a part of the project or are not associated with the idea. Either strategy can provide the needed information, especially if a carefully thought-out plan is presented.

During these meetings, investigators present the research rationale, procedures, design, and outcome measures. They ask meeting participants to discuss strengths and weaknesses of the plan and to provide suggestions about filling in gaps to improve the project. Keep in mind that the depth of a critique is related to the excellence of the plan. Unfortunately, even though investigators may have been thinking about the idea for several months and believe that every t has been crossed and every i dotted, there is still the possibility that the plan can benefit from additional modification to data collection procedures, participant recruitment procedures, or data collection instruments. These meetings can also help investigators assess the need for and recruitment of coinvestigators.

After idea acceptance and feasibility discussions, coinvestigators and staff can be asked to participate, and additional meetings can further refine the idea and keep everyone informed about the project's development. The purpose of these meetings is to hone the idea and the project procedures. These meetings usually produce additional opinions about the project, greater depth and breadth in the literature review, and assurance of the feasibility of project components under the purview of coinvestigators. However, the PI's task is to integrate and, when appropriate, solicit clarification on suggestions to keep the project properly focused. Sometimes suggestions are made from a slightly different perspective than what the project is taking. PIs must be vigilant that these ideas do not get incorporated because they can place the project at risk for appearing unfocused.

Face-to-face meetings are important during the early phases of the project. However, after the group has become acquainted, telephone calls and electronic mail can be effective means of communication. We suggest that e-mail and fax be used only after the group is fairly well acquainted, to obviate the chance of misunderstandings. An additional factor to consider when using e-mail and fax is confidentiality. Neither of these methods provides the privacy of telephone conversations or regular mail, with e-mail being the most public. In most instances, conversations concerning developing projects require time and thought. From this perspective, e-mail and fax can allow investigators to choose the time for considering the issue. If these methods are not appropriate, investigators might attempt to make a telephone appointment.

Although we continually stress the importance of doing quality work, this does not mean that perfection is a goal. Throughout this process, be prepared to accept limitations in knowledge, resources, or intelligence. In other words, be flexible. Rarely is the ideal research project planned and implemented under ideal circumstances. In view of this, we believe that only after the literature review and the coinvestigator meetings are complete is it useful to discuss the submission deadline. Because considerable intellectual work and negotiation are required to determine whether an idea can be translated into a project application, setting a submission deadline before completion of that process can be frustrating and can produce disenchantment. When the research topic is sufficiently defined, the scope of the project clarified, and the outcomes agreed on, it is then possible to identify a funding source, determine the deadline, and review application information.

Action Strategies

Take Time to Think About Thinking

This may sound too simplistic to be helpful. We believe, nevertheless, that every investigator should spend some time thinking about how they think and the thinking process they use. Thinking about thinking should be useful to better understand personal preferences, taking into account personalities and environmental factors. Investigators who have some notion of how they arrive at valuable ideas will also become aware of the thinking processes of others. When an application is being prepared by a group, the ability to be aware of the thinking process of others can deter impatience and prematurely jettisoning suggestions.

Think About the Development of Ideas

We suggest that investigators be alert so that they become aware of their best thinking time. During our thinking about this subject, we discovered that we think differently and at different times. One of us is most comfortable with ideas and thinking early in the morning, whereas the other is more comfortable late at night. Both of us think when we drive, but we cannot remember developing a viable idea while driving.

The habit of writing ideas down is a good one to develop. One mechanism for this is a notebook that is dedicated to ideas. Notebooks these days take many forms, such as computer files, paper notebooks, or tape recorders. For developing ideas, we believe a paper notebook with unlined pages is best, but the computer file is stiff competition. In this notebook, each idea has its own page—each newborn idea, however fragmented and incomplete. The reason is that these ideas can be reviewed regularly for updating, adding detail, and literature or theoretical support. Eventually, hypotheses might be formed. Sometimes a fragile thought at the top of the page evolves into many pages of notes, literature, research designs, diagrams of organization structure, tables of possible results, and possibly into a grant application. Other outcomes, like throwing the idea away, are also valuable. The process of writing and exploring an idea on a regular basis can reveal its futility, or that there are no prospects for using it in a productive way, and it can be forgotten. We also suggest that the idea not be removed from the notebook, or it might come back as a "new idea."

Writing ideas is a particularly important habit for investigators who have many ideas. A written record not only provides a way to save ideas, but it also frees the investigator for other thoughts. Often when an idea is written we believe it is "safe" and no longer needs protection from other and new ideas. In addition, ideas that are out of active memory are less likely to be undesirable intrusions, as asides, when other ideas are being considered.

Think About How Participation in a Study and/or Working Groups Enhances Thinking

Taking personalities into account, investigators need to find their most effective environment for thinking. Is it in a group process or an individual process? Is it both in tandem? This may be difficult to answer without reflection. We suggest that conclusions not be reached quickly, but that time be taken to collect data and reflect. It would not be surprising if the conclusion depends on the project and the kinds of tasks involved in bringing it to completion. The value of this exercise is that investigators can approach projects with a flexible attitude until the idea is clear and then develop a pattern that is most efficient and effective.

References

American Psychological Association. (1994). *Publication manual of the American Psychological Association* (4th ed.). Washington, DC: Author.

Bill threatens data collection in child survey research [Editorial]. (1995, July 10). *Mental Health News Alert,* pp. 2-3.

Bobbert, L. C. (1992). *Don't talk! communicate!* Kingsport, TN: Printing Concepts.

Brand, S. (1987). *The media lab: Inventing the future at MIT.* London: Viking.

Brenstein, E. (1996). Diversity in work styles. In F. T. L. Leong & J. T. Austin (Eds.), *The psychology research handbook* (pp. 325-341). Thousand Oaks, CA: Sage.

Campbell, J. P., Daft, R. L., & Hulin, C. L. (1982). *What to study: Generating and developing research questions.* Beverly Hills, CA: Sage.

Charrow, R. P. (1993). A primer on research ethics: Learning to cope with federal regulations of research. *Journal of NIH Research, 5,* 76-78.

Cooper, H. M. (1989). *Integrating research: A guide for literature reviews* (2nd ed.). Newbury Park, CA: Sage.

Digiusto, E. (1994). Equity in authorship: A strategy for assigning credit when publishing. *Social Science and Medicine, 38*(1), 55-58.

Decker, P. F. (1985). *Innovation and entrepreneurship: Practical principles.* New York: Harper and Row.

Ezzell, C. (1996). Help us tell your story. *Journal of NIH Research, 8,* 10.

Finn, R. (1996, July 22). New animal care guide leaves details to scientists' discretion. *The Scientist, 10*(15), 1, 4-5.

Fuller, E. O. (1982). The pink sheet syndrome. *Nursing Research, 31*(3), 185-186.

Goodman, B. (1995, June 12). Observers fear funding practices may spell the death of innovative grant proposals. *The Scientist, 9*(12), 1, 8-9.

Goodman, B. (1996a, March 18). Scientific whistleblowers stress that the media are a last resort. *The Scientist, 10*(6), 1, 4.

Goodman, B. (1996b, July 22). HHS panel issues proposals for implementing misconduct report. *The Scientist, 10*(15), 3, 6.

Himes, G. K. (1987). Developing your creative ideas. In A. D. Timpe (Ed.), *Creativity* (pp. 74-82). New York: Facts on File.

Huth, E. J. (1986a). Guidelines on authorship of medical papers. *Annals of Internal Medicine, 104,* 269-274.

Huth, E. J. (1986b). Irresponsible authorship and wasteful publication. *Annals of Internal Medicine, 104,* 257-259.

K.H. (1996, April 5). New York court halts psychiatric research on certain patients deemed "incapable." *Psychiatric News,* pp. 18, 27.

Kerlinger, F. N. (1964). *Foundations of behavioral research.* New York: Holt, Rinehart and Winston.

L.S. (1996, July 9). Bill may be disastrous for studies on nutrition, pregnancy, health care. *Mental Health News Alert,* p. 10.

Ludwig, A. M. (1995). *The price of greatness: Resolving the creativity and madness controversy.* New York: Guilford.

Mandel, H. G. (1995, July 7). Funding of NIH grant applications: Update. *Science, 269,* 13-14.

National Academy of Sciences. (1995). *On being a scientist: Responsible conduct in research.* Washington, DC: National Academy Press.

National Institutes of Health. (1994a, August). *Outreach notebook for the NIH guidelines on inclusion of women and minorities as subjects in clinical research.* Bethesda, MD: Author.

National Institutes of Health. (1994b, December 23). Revision to NIH implementation of expanded authorities. *NIH Guide to Grants and Contracts, 23*(45) [On-line]. Available: wkj@cu.nih.gov

National Institutes of Health. (1995a). NIH reinvention activities status report. *NIH Guide to Grants and Contracts, 24*(14) [On-line]. Available: wkj@cu.nih.gov

National Institutes of Health. (1995b, April 28). Commonly asked questions about equipment under grants. *NIH Guide to Grants and Contracts, 24*(15) [On-line]. Available: wkj@cu.nih.gov

National Institutes of Health. (1995c, July 14). Objectivity in research. *NIH Guide to Grants and Contracts, 24*(25) [On-line]. Available: wkj@cu.nih.gov

National Institutes of Health. (1995d, July 28). Informed consent in clinical mental health research. *NIH Guide to Grants and Contracts, 24*(27) [On-line]. Available: wkj@cu.nih.gov

National Institutes of Health. (1995e, September 22). Health and safety guidelines for grantees and contractors. *NIH Guide to Grants and Contracts, 24*(33) [On-line]. Available: wkj@cu.nih.gov

National Institutes of Health. (1995f, October 6). Investigator-initiated interactive research project grants. *NIH Guide to Grants and Contracts, 24*(35) [On-line]. Available: wkj@cu.nih.gov

National Institutes of Health. (1996a, January 26). American provisions. *NIH Guide to Grants and Contracts, 25*(1) [On-line]. Available: wkj@cu.nih.gov

National Institutes of Health. (1996b, July 5). Peer review rebuttal and appeal processes. *NIH Guide to Grants and Contracts, 25*(22) [On-line]. Available: wkj@cu.nih.gov

National Institutes of Health. (1996c, July 12). NIH reinvention activities: Status report. *NIH Guide to Grants and Contracts, 25*(23) [On-line]. Available: wkj@cu.nih.gov

National Institutes of Health. (1996d, September 20). Exploratory/developmental grants for high/risk/high impact research. *NIH Guide to Grants and Contracts, 25*(31) [On-line]. Available: wkj@cu.nih.gov

National Institutes of Health. (1996e, September 27). Informed consent in research involving human participants. *NIH Guide to Grants and Contracts, 25*(32) [On-line]. Available: wkj@cu.nih.gov

National Institutes of Health, Division of Research Grants. (1995, October). *NIH extramural trends: Fiscal years 1985-1994* (NIH Publication No. 96-3506). Bethesda, MD: Author.

National Research Council. (1992). *Combining information: Statistical issues and opportunities for research.* Washington, DC: National Academy Press.

National Science Foundation. (1995). *Grant proposal guide, NSF 95-27* (Replaces NSF 94-2). Arlington, VA: Author.

NIH guidelines on the inclusion of women and minorities as subjects in clinical research. (1994, March 28). *Federal Register, 59,* 14508-14513.

Ogden, T. E. (1991). *Research proposals: A guide to success.* New York: Raven.

A Pew good scholars. (1995a July 24). *The Scientist, 9*(15), 30.

Pincus, H. A. (Ed.). (1995). *Research funding and resource manual: Mental health and addictive disorders.* Washington, DC: American Psychiatric Association.

Price, J. (1981). *Thirty days to more powerful writing: A step-by-step method for developing a more dynamic writing style.* New York: Fawcett Columbine.

Public Health Service. (1996, July 3). Frequently asked questions concerning the Department of Health and Human Services objectivity in research regulations and the National Science Foundation investigator financial disclosure policy. *Federal Register, 61*(129), 34839 [On-line].

Reif-Lehrer, L. (1995). *Grant application writer's handbook.* Boston: Jones and Bartlett.

Reimold, C. (1984). *Being a boss: An action-oriented step-by-step guide.* New York: Dell.

Relman, A. S. (1990). Publishing biomedical research: Roles and responsibilities. *Hastings Center Report, 20*(3), 23-27.

Research integrity videos. (1995b, June 12). *The Scientist, 19*(13), 30.

Rhein, R. (1996a, January). Dollars & grants: Information about funding for biomedical researchers, targets of opportunity: deciphering NIH grant-award categories. *Journal of NIH Research, 8,* 36-38.

Rhein, R. (1996b, August). Dollars & grants: Information about funding for biomedical researchers, reviewing the peer reviewers: NIH weighs reforms of study section scoring. *Journal of NIH Research, 8,* 51-53.

Ries, J. B., & Leukefeld, C. G. (1995). *Applying for research funding: Getting started and getting funded.* Thousand Oaks, CA: Sage.

Rosenberg, E. (1995, August 21). How federal funding mechanisms stifle basic biomedical research. *The Scientist, 9*(16), 11.

Sankaran, N. (1995, May 29). Grant-makers see pros and cons to giving it all away. *The Scientist, 9*(11), 1, 6-7.

Sapienza, A. M. (1995). *Managing scientists: Leadership strategies in biomedical research and development.* New York: John Wiley.

Special instructions to applicants regarding implementation of NIH policies concerning inclusion of women and minorities in clinical research study populations. (n.d.). Bethesda, MD: National Institutes of Health.

Strunk, W., Jr., & White, E. B. (1979). *The elements of style* (3rd ed.). New York: Macmillan.

Tannen, D. (1994). *Talking from 9 to 5.* New York: William Morrow.

Timpe, A. D. (Ed.). (1987). *Creativity.* New York: Facts on File.

U.S. Department of Health and Human Services. (1995, September 22). Extramural invention reporting—20/20 view. *NIH Guide to Grants and Contracts, 24*(33) [On-line]. Available: wkj@cu.nih.gov

U.S. Department of Health and Human Services, Public Health Service. (1994, April 1). *PHS grants policy statement* (DHHS Publication No. OASH 94-50,000, Ref.). Bethesda, MD: Author.

Watkins, F. C., & Dillingham, W. B. (1992). *Practical English handbook* (9th ed.). Dallas, TX: Houghton Mifflin.

Wettstein, R. M. (1995). Research ethics and human subject issues. In H. A. Pincus (Ed.), *Research funding and resource manual: Mental health and addictive disorders* (pp. 423-437). Washington, DC: American Psychiatric Association.

Zenger, J. H., Musselwhite, E., Hurson, K., & Perrin, C. (1994). *Leading teams: Mastering the new role.* Homewood, IL: Business One Irwin.

Index

About the Authors

Joanne B. Ries is a grant-writing consultant. She received her doctorate of higher education from the University of Kentucky in 1983 and her master's in psychology from the University of Montana. She has been a research facilitator for more than 20 years with concentration on research grant applications for the past 13 years. During this time, she has not only been involved in all phases of the application process but has also been listening carefully to the questions, musings, and concerns of investigators. She has an inside perspective on research activity from brainstorming about research design and statistical approaches to negotiating the administrative maze, and experience with all aspects of the application process from editing for clarity and logic to counting the letters per inch. In 1995, she left her position as Research Facilitator and Departmental Research Director, in the Department of Behavioral Science at the University of Kentucky, to take the position of Grants Facilitator in the Department of Psychiatry at the University of Arizona. While in this position, she played an integral role in developing the externally funded research programs in these departments. In 1996, she launched her career as an independent consultant. She is coauthor of research articles and the 1995 Sage publication *Applying for Research Funding: Getting Started and Getting Funded*; is a consultant for investigators in a variety of disciplines including medicine, nursing, and the behavioral sciences; and has presented grant-writing seminars.

Carl G. Leukefeld is Professor of Psychiatry and Directory of the Drug and Alcohol Research Center at the University of Kentucky. He received his doctorate of social work from the Catholic University of America in 1975 and his master's degree from the University of Michigan. Before going to the University of Kentucky, he was a commissioned officer in the U.S. Public Health Service, and for much of that time he was assigned to the National Institute on Drug Abuse in various clinical, management, and scientific capacities. He has given numerous presentations and has written articles focusing on treatment, criminal justice, prevention, and AIDS. His current research interests include the use of judicial sanctions, drug abuse treatment, the delivery of rural services, and the impact of HIV on the drug abuser. He has coedited and written books, including the 1995 Sage publication *Applying for Research Funding: Getting Started and Getting Funded,* and written peer-reviewed articles. He is also an editor or a consulting editor for four professional journals and has served as a consultant to several international and national organizations including the Council on Europe, World Health Organization, U.S. Customs, U.S. Army, U.S. Navy, Administrative Office of the U.S. Courts, National Institute of Justice, National Institute of Corrections, and American Probation and Parole Association, as well as state and local agencies. He was first chairperson of the National Association of Social Workers, Health and Mental Health Commission. In 1991, he was elected to the National Academy of Practice in Social Work as a distinguished Scholar. He was also selected as Kentucky Colonel in 1991. He is the former chief health service officer of the U.S. Public Health Service and now resides in Lexington, Kentucky.

Printed in the United States
133099LV00002B/235-237/A